Excel® 2010

VISUAL™

Quick Tips

Visual®

by Paul McFedries

WILEY

Wiley Publishing, Inc.

Excel® 2010 Visual™ Quick Tips

Published by
Wiley Publishing, Inc.
10475 Crosspoint Boulevard
Indianapolis, IN 46256
www.wiley.com

Published simultaneously in Canada

Library of Congress Control Number: 2010923565

ISBN: 978-0-470-57776-9

Manufactured in the United States of America

10 9 8 7 6 5 4 3 2 1

Trademarks Acknowledgments

Contact Us

For general information on our other products and services or to obtain technical support, please contact our Customer Care Department within the U.S. at (877) 762-2974, outside the U.S. at (317) 572-3993 or fax (317) 572-4002.

For technical support please visit www.wiley.com/techsupport.

Disclaimer

Wiley Publishing, Inc.

Sales

Contact Wiley
at (877) 762-2974 or
fax (317) 572-4002.

Credits

Executive Editor
Jody Lefevere

Project Editor
Kristin DeMint

Technical Editor
Namir Shammas

Copy Editor
Marylouise Wiack

Editorial Director
Robyn Siesky

Business Manager
Amy Knies

Senior Marketing Manager
Sandy Smith

Vice President and Executive Group Publisher
Richard Swadley

Vice President and Executive Publisher
Barry Pruett

Project Coordinator
Lynsey Stanford

Graphics and Production Specialists
Carrie A. Cesavice

Quality Control Technician
Lauren Mandelbaum

Proofreading and Indexing
Cindy Lee Ballew /
Precisely Write
Johnna VanHoose
Dinse

Screen Artist
Joyce Haughey

About the Author

Paul McFedries is a full-time technical writer. Paul has been authoring computer books since 1991 and he has more than 70 books to his credit. Paul's books have sold more than three million copies worldwide. These books include the Wiley titles *Teach Yourself VISUALLY Excel 2010; Excel PivotTables and PivotCharts Visual Blueprint, Second Edition; Teach Yourself VISUALLY Windows 7;* and *Teach Yourself VISUALLY Office 2008 for Mac.* Paul is also the proprietor of Word Spy (www.wordspy.com and twitter. com/wordspy), a Web site that tracks new words and phrases as they enter the language. Paul invites you to drop by his personal Web site at www.mcfedries.com or to follow him on Twitter at twitter.com/paulmcf.

Author's Acknowledgments

It goes without saying that writers focus on text, and I certainly enjoyed focusing on the text that you'll read in this book. However, this book is more than just the usual collection of words and phrases. A quick thumb-through of the pages will show you that this book is also chock full of images, from sharp screen shots to fun and informative illustrations. Those colorful images sure make for a beautiful book, and that beauty comes from a lot of hard work by Wiley's immensely talented group of designers and layout artists. They are all listed in the Credits section above, and I thank them for creating another gem. Of course, what you read in this book must also be accurate, logically presented, and free of errors. Ensuring all of this was an excellent group of editors that included project editor Kristin DeMint, copy editor Marylouise Wiack, and technical editor Namir Shammas. Thanks to all of you for your exceptional competence and hard work. Thanks, as well, to acquisitions editor Jody Lefevere for asking me to write this book.

How to Use This Book

Who This Book Is For

This book is for readers who know the basics and want to expand their knowledge of this particular technology or software application.

The Conventions in This Book

❶ Steps

This book uses a step-by-step format to guide you easily through each task. Numbered steps are actions you must do; bulleted steps clarify a point, step, or optional feature; and indented steps give you the result.

❷ Notes

Notes give additional information — special conditions that may occur during an operation, a situation that you want to avoid, or a cross reference to a related area of the book.

❸ Icons and Buttons

Icons and buttons show you exactly what you need to click to perform a step.

❹ Tips

Tips offer additional information, including warnings and shortcuts.

❺ Bold

Bold type shows text or numbers you must type.

❻ Italics

Italic type introduces and defines a new term.

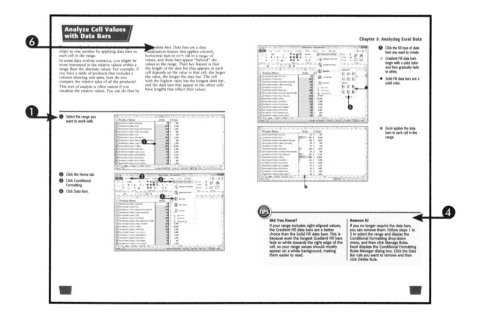

Table of Contents

 Making Excel More Efficient

chapter 2 **Making It Easier to Manage Workbooks**

chapter 3 Customizing Worksheet Presentation

chapter 4 Getting More Out of Formulas

Table of Contents

chapter 5   **Analyzing Excel Data**

chapter 6   **Analyzing Data with PivotTables**

chapter 7 Importing Data into Excel

chapter 8 Querying Data Sources

Table of Contents

chapter 11 **Learning VBA Basics**

Making Excel More Efficient

If you find yourself spending a major part of your day working with Excel, you can make those chores go faster — and so make your overall work life more productive — by making Excel as efficient as possible.

For example, you can launch common commands more quickly by placing them on the Quick Access Toolbar, which requires just a single click to launch a command. Similarly, you can customize the Ribbon with your own tabs and groups to reduce the time it takes to perform certain tasks.

You can also make Excel more efficient by using the mouse wheel to zoom, automatically inserting decimal points, pinning Excel to the Windows 7 taskbar, creating binary workbooks, applying formatting across multiple worksheets, and using dialog box controls to input worksheet data.

In this chapter, you will learn how to perform these and many other tasks that boost your Excel efficiency.

Quick Tips

Customize the Quick Access Toolbar

You can make Excel easier to use by customizing the Quick Access Toolbar to include the Excel commands you use most often. Because you launch Quick Access Toolbar buttons with a single click, adding your favorite commands to the toolbar saves you time.

By default, the Quick Access Toolbar contains three buttons — Save, Undo, and Redo — but you can add any of hundreds of Excel commands.

In a default Excel configuration, the Quick Access Toolbar appears above the Ribbon as

part of the Excel title bar. However, this position only allows you to add a few buttons, as there is only so much space in the title bar. To get much more space to add buttons, you should move the Quick Access Toolbar below the Ribbon.

You can also export your Quick Access Toolbar customizations to a file so that other people can import the same customizations. For more information, see the section, "Export Ribbon Customizations to a File."

---

① Click the Customize Quick Access Toolbar button.

● If you see the command you want, you can click it; Excel adds the button for that command to the Quick Access Toolbar, and you can skip the rest of the steps in this section.

② Click More Commands.

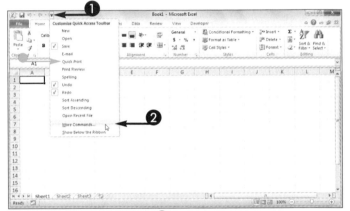

The Excel Options dialog box appears.

● Excel automatically displays the Quick Access Toolbar tab.

③ Click the Choose Commands From drop-down arrow.

④ Click the command category you want to use.

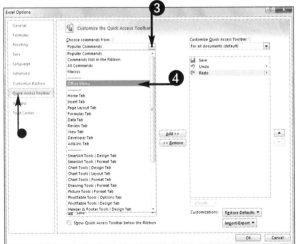

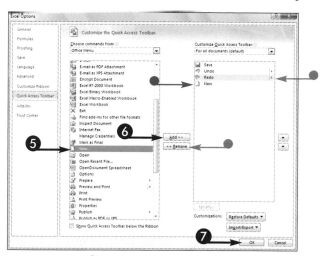

5 Click the command you want to add.

6 Click Add.

● Excel adds the command.

● To remove a command, you can click it and then click Remove.

7 Click OK.

● Excel adds a button for the command to the Quick Access Toolbar.

More Options!

You can increase the space available to the Quick Access Toolbar by moving it below the Ribbon. This gives the toolbar the full width of the Excel window, so you can add many more buttons. Click the Customize Quick Access Toolbar button and then click Show Below the Ribbon.

More Options!

If the command you want to add appears on the Ribbon, you can add a button for the command directly from the Ribbon. Click the Ribbon tab that contains the command, right-click the command, and then click Add to Quick Access Toolbar. Excel inserts a button for the command on the Quick Access Toolbar.

Customize the Ribbon

You can improve your Excel productivity by customizing the Ribbon with extra commands that you use frequently.

Keep in mind that you cannot modify any of the default tabs and groups in Excel, other than hiding tabs you do not use. Instead, you customize the Ribbon by adding a new group to an existing tab, and then adding one or more commands to the new group.

Alternatively, you can add a new tab to the Ribbon, add your own groups to that tab, and then add your commands.

Display the Customize Ribbon Tab

① Right-click any part of the Ribbon.

② Click Customize the Ribbon.

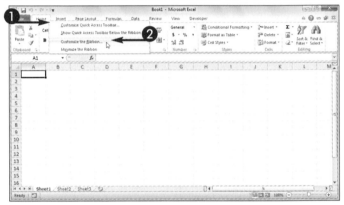

The Excel Options dialog box appears.

● Excel automatically displays the Customize Ribbon tab.

● Use these lists to choose the commands you want to add.

● These lists show the existing tabs and groups.

● To display a tab's groups, you can click the tab's plus sign (+).

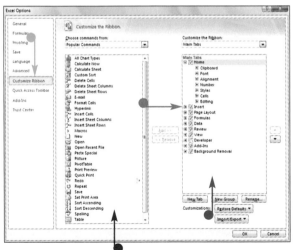

Add a New Group

1 Click the tab you want to customize.

2 Click New Group.

● Excel adds the group.

3 Click Rename.

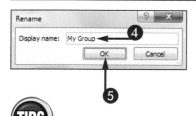

The Rename dialog box appears.

4 Type a name for the group.

5 Click OK.

Excel adds the new group to the tab.

TIPS

More Options!

You can get more space on the Ribbon and reduce clutter by removing any tabs you do not use. For example, if you do not use the Excel reviewing tools, then you might prefer to hide the Review tab to reduce the number of tabs you see on-screen. In the list of tabs that appears below the Customize the Ribbon drop-down list, deselect the check box beside any tab you want to hide.

Try This!

You can change the order in which the tabs appear in the Ribbon. For example, if you use the tools in the Data tab more often than those in the Home tab, then you can move the Data tab to be the first tab in the Ribbon. Use the up and down arrow buttons that appear to the right of the tab list to modify the order. You can also use these buttons to modify the order of the groups within any tab.

7

Although you will mostly prefer to add one or more custom groups to the default Excel tabs, this is not always convenient because it reduces the amount of space available to the other groups in the tab. This can cause the buttons to appear cluttered, making it harder to find the button you need.

In such cases, a better customization method is to create your own tabs and populate them with custom groups and commands.

You can also export your Ribbon customizations to a file so that other people can import the same customizations. For more information, see the section, "Export Ribbon Customizations to a File."

Add a New Tab

① In the Customize Ribbon tab of the Excel Options dialog box, click New Tab.

● Excel adds the tab.

● Excel adds a new group within the tab.

② Click the new tab.

③ Click Rename.

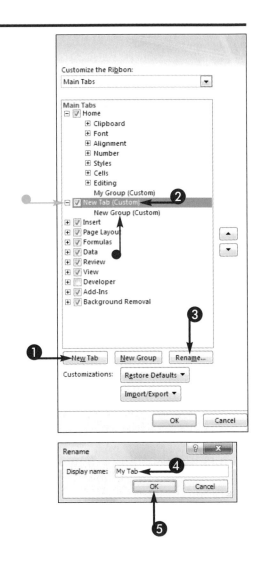

The Rename dialog box appears.

④ Type the name you want to use.

⑤ Click OK.

⑥ Repeat steps 3 to 5 to rename the new group.

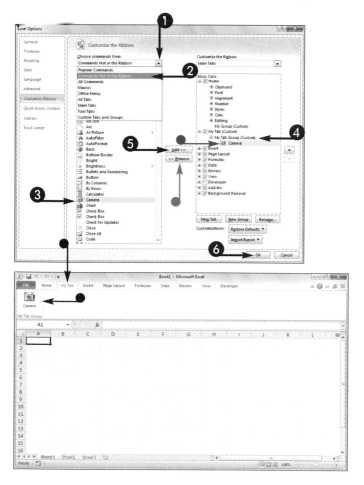

Add a Command

① Click the Choose Commands From drop-down arrow.

② Click the command category you want to use.

③ Click the command you want to add.

④ Click the custom group you want to use.

⑤ Click Add.

● Excel adds the command.

● To remove a custom command, click it and then click Remove.

⑥ Click OK.

● Excel adds the new tab or group, as well as the new command, to the Ribbon.

TIPS

Try This!

You can also customize the tabs that appear only when you select an Excel object. Excel calls these *tool tabs*, and you can add custom groups and commands to any tool tab. Right-click any part of the Ribbon, and then click Customize the Ribbon to display the Excel Options dialog box with the Customize Ribbon tab displayed. Click the Customize the Ribbon list and then click Tool Tabs. Click the tab you want to add, and then follow the steps in this section to customize it.

Remove It!

Right-click any part of the Ribbon, and then click Customize the Ribbon; the Excel Options dialog box appears with the Customize Ribbon tab displayed. To restore a tab, click the tab, click Restore Defaults, and then click Restore Only Selected Ribbon Tab. To remove all customizations, click Restore Defaults and then click Restore All Ribbon Tabs and Quick Access Toolbar Customizations.

Export Ribbon Customizations to a File

You can make it easy to apply Ribbon and Quick Access Toolbar customizations on another computer by exporting your own customizations to a file.

Customizing the Ribbon or the Quick Access Toolbar is not a difficult process, but it can be time-consuming, particularly if you want to make a substantial number of changes. If you use Excel 2010 on another computer, it is likely that you will want to have the same

customizations on the other computer so that you are dealing with a consistent interface no matter where you do your spreadsheet work. Rather than wasting valuable time repeating the same customization steps on the other computer, you can export your customizations to a file. You can then import that file on the other computer, and Excel automatically applies the customizations for you.

① Right-click any part of the Ribbon.

② Click Customize the Ribbon.

The Excel Options dialog box appears.

● Excel automatically displays the Customize Ribbon tab.

③ Click Import/Export.

④ Click Export All Ribbon and Quick Access Toolbar Customizations.

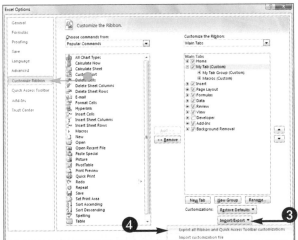

The File Save dialog box appears.

5 Choose a location for the customization file.

6 Type a name for the file.

7 Click Save.

Excel saves the customizations to the file.

8 Click OK.

Apply It!

To apply the Ribbon and Quick Access Toolbar customizations on another computer running Excel 2010, you need to import the customization file that you exported by following the steps in this section. Note, however, that importing a customization file replaces any existing customizations that you have created.

On the computer you are customizing, right-click any part of the Ribbon, and then click Customize the Ribbon to open the Excel Options dialog box with the Customize Ribbon tab displayed. Click the Import/Export drop-down arrow and then click Import Customization File. In the File Open dialog box, locate and then click the customization file, and then click Open. When Excel asks you to confirm that all of your existing customizations will be replaced, click Yes and then click OK. Excel applies the Ribbon and Quick Access Toolbar customizations.

Configure Excel to Use the Mouse Wheel for Zooming

If you frequently zoom in or out of a worksheet, you can save time by configuring Excel to enable you to zoom using the wheel on your mouse.

Zooming a worksheet is a useful technique. For example, you might want to zoom out of a large worksheet to get a sense of the overall structure of the worksheet data. Similarly, zooming in on a section of a worksheet enables you to focus on just that section.

You normally zoom either by using the controls in the View tab's Zoom group, or by using the Zoom slider that appears in the bottom-right corner of the Excel window. These techniques are fine if you only zoom occasionally. However, if you use the zoom feature frequently, it is a good idea to configure Excel to zoom using the mouse wheel.

① Click the File tab button.

② Click Options.

The Excel Options dialog box appears.

③ Click the Advanced tab.

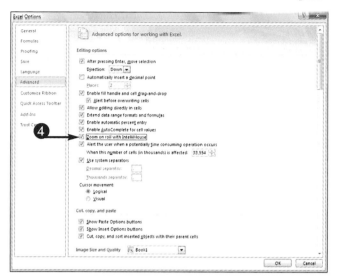

④ Click to select the Zoom on Roll with IntelliMouse option.

Note: *Although the option name specifies the Microsoft IntelliMouse, this option works with any mouse that comes with a standard scroll wheel.*

⑤ Click OK.

You can now zoom in and out of your Excel spreadsheets by turning the mouse wheel.

Try It!

When you activate the Zoom on Roll with IntelliMouse check box, rolling the mouse wheel forward causes Excel to zoom in on the worksheet by 15 percent with each scroll of the wheel; rolling the mouse wheel backward causes Excel to zoom out of the worksheet by 15 percent with each scroll.

Did You Know?

When the Zoom on Roll with IntelliMouse check box is deactivated, rolling the mouse wheel causes Excel to scroll the worksheet: roll the wheel back to scroll down, and roll the wheel forward to scroll up. This is a useful technique, and you can still use it even when the Zoom on Roll with IntelliMouse check box is activated. In that case, hold down the Ctrl key and roll the mouse wheel to scroll the worksheet.

Move in a Different Direction When You Press Enter

In certain cases, you can make your Excel data-entry chores more efficient by changing the direction that Excel moves the selection when you press Enter after you finish editing a cell.

Generally, you enter the data vertically in a column of cells. Excel allows you to do this by automatically moving the selection down to the next cell when you press Enter.

However, in some cases you might need to enter a large amount of data in a row, either from left to right or from right to left, or in a column from top to bottom. Although you can use the arrow keys to force the selection to move in the direction you want, the Enter key is larger than the arrow keys and is thus faster to use and less prone to error. Therefore, you can configure Excel to move the selection in the direction you prefer when you press Enter.

① Click the File tab.

② Click Options.

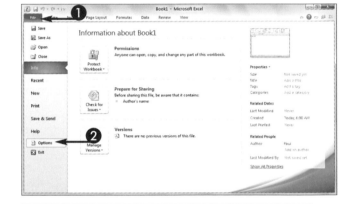

The Excel Options dialog box appears.

③ Click the Advanced tab.

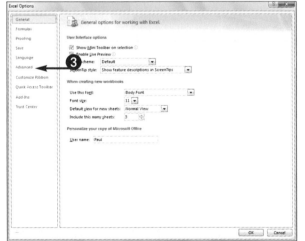

④ Make sure that the After Pressing Enter, Move Selection check box is selected.

⑤ Click the Direction drop-down arrow, and select the direction that you want Excel to move the selection after you press Enter.

⑥ Click OK.

Excel now moves the selection in the direction you specified when you press Enter to confirm a cell entry.

TIP

Did You Know?

If you have only a few data items to enter, you can force Excel to move the selection in the direction of the next cell entry by using the arrow keys. For example, suppose you are entering data in a row from left to right. When you finish editing a cell, press the right arrow key, which moves the selection to the next cell on the right. Similarly, you can press the left arrow key to move the selection to the left, or you can press the up arrow key to move the selection up.

You can make certain Excel data entry tasks more efficient by configuring Excel to automatically insert a decimal point.

Many Excel data entry tasks require you to type a long list of values that use the same number of decimal places. The most common example is a list of currency amounts, which always have two decimal places. When you are entering such values, you type the digits to the left of the decimal point, the decimal point itself, and then the digits to the right of the decimal point. In a long list of values, the extra step required to type the decimal point is a repetitive action that just slows you down.

To speed up this kind of data entry, you can configure Excel to add the decimal point for you automatically. For example, if you tell Excel to automatically add two decimal places, then when you type a number such as 123456, Excel adds the value to the cell as 1234.56.

① Click the File tab.

② Click Options.

The Excel Options dialog box appears.

③ Click the Advanced tab.

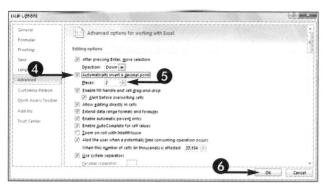

④ Click to select the Automatically Insert a Decimal Point check box.

⑤ Use the Places spin box to specify the number of decimal places you want Excel to add automatically.

⑥ Click OK.

Excel now automatically inserts the number of decimal places you specified when you enter a numeric value into a cell.

● Excel displays Fixed Decimal in the status bar to remind you that it will automatically insert the decimal point.

TIPS

Did You Know?

Even in Fixed Decimal mode, Excel still drops trailing zeroes from your cell entries. For example, if you choose 2 in the Places spin box and you then enter 12340 in a cell, Excel displays the entry as 123.4. If you always want to see two decimal places — that is, 123.40 — then you must format the cells using a two-decimal numeric format, such as Number or Currency.

Try This!

If you choose a number other than 2 in the Places spin box and you always want Excel to display that number of decimal places, you must format the cells with a custom numeric format. In the Home tab, click the dialog box launcher in the Number group. In the Category list, click Custom, and then in the Type text box type **0**, a decimal point (.), and then a **0** for each decimal place that you want displayed. For example, the format 0.000 always displays three decimal places.

Configure When Excel Warns You About Long Operations

To avoid wasting time waiting for a long workbook recalculation to finish, you can configure Excel to warn you when an operation might take an excessively long time.

In a typical worksheet with only a few formulas, the number of operations required to recalculate the worksheet might run into the dozens or hundreds, which Excel can handle instantly. A mid-size worksheet might require a few thousand or even a few tens of thousands of operations to recalculate, but even such larger sheets typically complete recalculation in a second or two.

In a massive worksheet that contains many linked formulas or one or more large data tables, the number of operations required to recalculate the sheet can run into the millions. If that number exceeds 33,554,000 operations, Excel warns you that the recalculation might take some time. You can configure that threshold to a lower or higher number.

If a large data table is causing slow workbook recalculations, you can configure Excel to bypass data tables when it recalculates workbooks. For more information, see Chapter 4.

---

① Click the File tab.

② Click Options.

The Excel Options dialog box appears.

③ Click the Advanced tab.

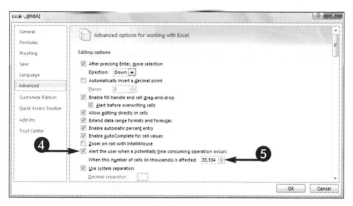

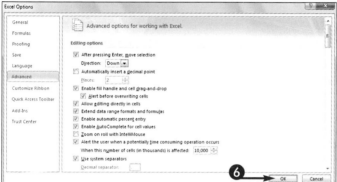

④ Make sure that the Alert the User When a Potentially Time Consuming Operation Occurs check box is selected.

⑤ Use the When This Number of Cells (In Thousands) is Affected spin box to specify the threshold at which Excel displays the long operation warning.

Note: *The number in the spin box is shown in thousands. So, for example, if you enter 1,000 into the spin box, then the threshold is one million cells.*

⑥ Click OK.

Excel now warns you about time-consuming operations when the number of cells affected will be equal to or greater than the number you specified.

Did You Know?
Although you're unlikely to ever come across such an operation, the maximum value that you can specify in the When This Number of Cells (In Thousands) is Affected spin box is 999,999,999. Note, too, that although you can enter a value as small as 1 in the spin box, low values are not recommend because they generate excessive warnings. Unless you have a very slow computer, do not go under ten million operations (10,000 in the spin box).

Remove It!
If you have a fast computer with a lot of memory, then Excel should be able to handle almost all real-world calculations relatively quickly, so you do not need Excel to warn you. In that case, deactivate the warning by following steps 1 to 3 and then clicking to select the Alert the User When a Potentially Time Consuming Operation Occurs check box.

Pin Excel to the Windows 7 Taskbar

You can quickly and easily launch Excel by pinning the Excel icon to the Windows 7 taskbar.

If you use Excel every day, Windows offers some methods for starting the program that are easier than going through the menus. For example, you can pin the Excel icon to the Start menu so that the program is just two mouse clicks away. You do this by right-clicking the Excel icon and then clicking Pin to Start Menu. However, if you use Excel frequently, you might prefer to have it just a single mouse click away. You can achieve this by pinning Excel to the Windows 7 taskbar.

As with previous versions of Windows, the Windows 7 taskbar displays an icon for each running program. However, one of the new features with the revamped Windows 7 taskbar is the capability of storing program icons, much like the Quick Launch Toolbar in previous versions of Windows. Once you have Excel pinned to the taskbar, you can then launch the program by clicking the icon.

You can pin Excel to the taskbar either by running the Pin to Taskbar command, or by clicking and dragging the program icon to the taskbar.

Pin a Program Using a Command

① Click the Start button.

Note: *If you see the Excel icon on the main Start menu, skip to step 4.*

② Click All Programs.

Note: *After you click All Programs, the name changes to Back.*

③ Click Microsoft Office.

④ Right-click Microsoft Excel 2010.

⑤ Click Pin to Taskbar.

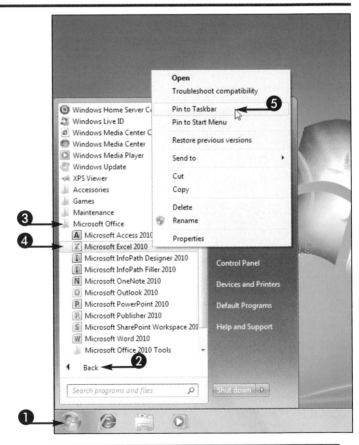

● Windows 7 adds the Excel icon to the taskbar.

Note: *If Excel is already running, you can also right-click the taskbar icon and then click Pin This Program to Taskbar.*

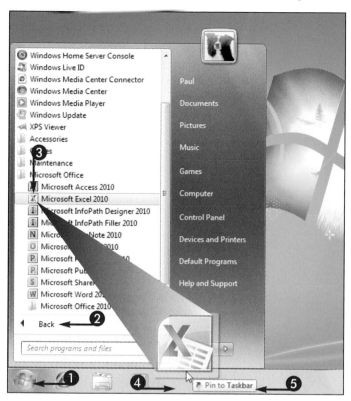

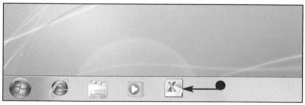

Pin a Program Using Your Mouse

① Click Start.

Note: *If you see the Excel icon on the main Start menu, skip to step 4.*

② Click All Programs.

Note: *After you click All Programs, the name changes to Back.*

③ Click Microsoft Office.

④ Click and drag the Microsoft Excel 2010 icon to any empty section of the taskbar.

⑤ When you see the Pin to Taskbar banner, drop the icon.

● Windows 7 adds the Excel icon to the taskbar.

Change It!

As you drop program icons onto the taskbar, Windows 7 displays the icons from left to right in the order you added them. If you prefer the Excel icon to be in a different place on the taskbar, click and drag the icon to the left or right and then drop it in the new position.

Remove It!

If you decide you no longer require Excel to be pinned to the taskbar, you should remove it to reduce taskbar clutter and provide more space for other taskbar icons. To remove the pinned Excel icon, right-click the icon and then click Unpin this Program from Taskbar.

Make a Workbook Faster by Saving it as Binary

If you have a large or complex Excel workbook, you can make it open and save faster by converting it to the Excel binary file format.

The standard file formats in Excel — Excel Workbook and Excel Macro-Enabled Workbook — are based on the OpenOffice XML Standard, where XML is short for eXtensible Markup Language. XML files are really just complex text files that Excel reads line-by-line when you open the file, and writes line-by-line when you save the file. Excel has been optimized to read and write XML code

extremely quickly, and so the standard Excel file formats are fine for most worksheets.

However, if you have a worksheet that is very large — for example, several thousand rows or more, or several hundred columns or more — or is very complex, then the standard file formats may take a while to open and save. To improve the performance of such files, you can convert them to the Excel Binary Workbook file format. This is identical to the Excel Macro-Enabled Workbook format, except that it uses binary code (which Excel can read and write much faster) instead of XML code.

---

① Open the workbook you want to convert.

② Click the File tab.

③ Click Save As.

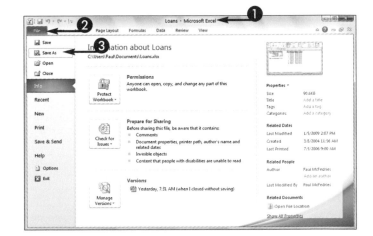

The Save As dialog box appears.

④ Select a location for the new workbook.

⑤ Type a name for the new workbook.

Note: *Because the new workbook will have a different file extension (.xlsb), you do not need to change the filename if you do not want to.*

⑥ Click the Save As Type drop-down arrow.

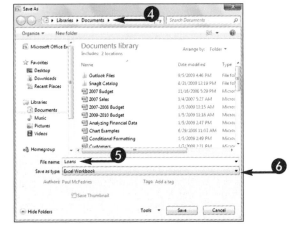

7 Click Excel Binary Workbook.

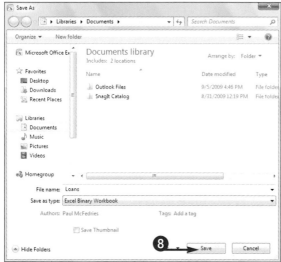

8 Click Save.

Excel saves the new file using the Excel Binary Workbook file format.

Did You Know?

The Excel Binary Workbook file format is compatible with Excel 2010 and Excel 2007. If you want to improve file performance while maintaining compatibility with earlier versions of Excel, save your workbook using the Excel 97-2003 Workbook file format. This is a binary format that is compatible with Excel 97 and all later versions of the program.

Did You Know?

Other than improved performance when opening and saving a file, there is no difference between the Excel Binary Workbook file format and the Excel Macro-Enabled Workbook file format. Both formats support the same features, create files of approximately the same size, and have the same performance once the files are loaded into Excel.

Open a New Window for a Workbook

You can make a large spreadsheet easier to manage by creating a second window for the workbook.

When you are building a spreadsheet, you often have to refer to existing sheet data. For example, when you construct a formula, you may need to refer to specific cells. Similarly, once your spreadsheet is working, you often need to monitor a cell value. For example, if you change the data in one part of the sheet, you might want to see how that change affects the result of a formula elsewhere in the sheet.

This is easy with a small spreadsheet where you can see everything on the screen. However, larger spreadsheets do not fit into a single screen, so the data you need to reference or monitor might not be visible, requiring that you scroll through the sheet to see it.

A better solution is to create a second window for the workbook and then arrange those windows side-by-side (vertically or horizontally). This enables you to display what you are currently working on in one window, and what you need to reference or monitor in the second window.

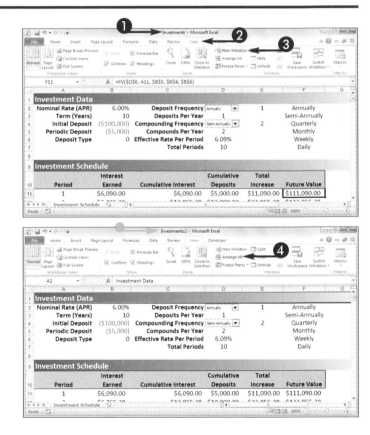

Create a New Workbook Window

① Open the workbook you want to work with.

② Click the View tab.

③ Click New Window.

Arrange the Workbook's WIndows

● Excel creates a second window for the workbook and appends ':2' to the name of the new window.

Note: *Excel also appends ':1' to the name of the original window.*

④ Click Arrange All.

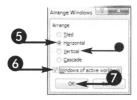

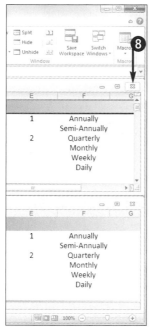

The Arrange Windows dialog box appears.

⑤ Click to select the Horizontal option.

● If your worksheet has just a few columns, you can click to select the Vertical option, instead.

⑥ Click to select the Windows of Active Workbook option.

⑦ Click OK.

Excel arranges the workbook's windows.

⑧ When you are done with the second window, click its Close button to return to using just the original workbook window.

Try This!

If you are using the new window to monitor either the first few rows or columns in the workbook, then you might find it easier to split the worksheet into panes instead of creating a new window. In the View tab, click the Split button and then click and drag the pane borders to define the area you want to monitor. The areas inside each pane scroll independently, so you can keep the data in the other area in view at all times.

Did You Know?

If you are using the new window to monitor a particular cell value in another part of the workbook, Excel offers another method for doing this: the Watch Window. You use this window to monitor the current value of one or more cells. To learn how to use this window, see Chapter 4.

Allow Only Certain Values in a Cell

You can make Excel data entry more efficient by setting up data entry cells to accept only certain values.

When you build a spreadsheet, you may find that some cells can only take a particular range of values. For example, an interest rate cell should take a decimal value between 0 and 1 (or a whole number between 0 and 100 if you have formatted the cell with the Percent number format). Similarly, a cell designed to hold a mortgage amortization term should probably take whole number values between 15 and 35.

To ensure that the proper values are entered, you can set up a cell with data validation criteria that specify the allowed value or values. You can work with numbers, dates, times, or even text length, and you can set up criteria that are between two values, equal to a specific value, greater than a value, and so on. Excel also lets you tell the user what to enter by adding an input message that appears when the user selects the cell.

---

① Click the cell you want to restrict.

② Click the Data tab.

③ Click Data Validation.

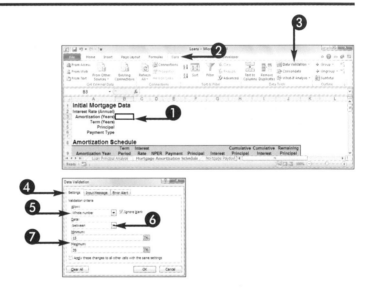

The Data Validation dialog box appears.

④ Click the Settings tab.

⑤ In the Allow drop-down list, click the type of data you want to allow in the cell.

⑥ In the Data drop-down list, click the operator you want to use to define the allowable data.

⑦ Specify the validation criteria, such as the Maximum and Minimum allowable values as shown here.

Note: *The criteria boxes you see depend on the operator you chose in step 6.*

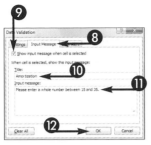

8 Click the Input Message tab.

9 Make sure the Show Input Message When Cell Is Selected check box is activated ( ).

10 Type a message title.

11 Type the message you want to display.

12 Click OK.

● When the cell is selected, the input message appears.

TIPS

More Options!
It is often a good idea to also configure an error message that displays when the user tries to enter data outside of the range you have specified. Follow steps 1 to 3 to open the Data Validation dialog box, and then click the Error Alert tab. Make sure the Show Error Alert After Invalid Data is Entered check box is selected ( ), and then specify the Style, Title, and Error Message.

Remove It!
If you no longer need to use data validation on a cell, you should clear the settings. Follow steps 1 to 3 to display the Data Validation dialog box and then click the Clear All button. Excel removes all the validation criteria, as well as the input message and the error alert. Click OK.

Apply Text or Formatting to Multiple Worksheets

You can speed up the creation of spreadsheet models by applying text and formatting to multiple worksheets at once.

In most workbooks, the worksheets are related in some way, but they generally have significantly different structures. However, in certain cases each worksheet uses an identical structure. For example, each worksheet might have the same overall title. Similarly, in a budget workbook each worksheet might have not only the same title, but also the same headings (Income, Expenses, and so on).

If you just have a small number of worksheets, you can also complete one worksheet's structure, copy the range, and then paste it into the other sheets. For a large number of sheets, however, Excel offers a much faster method. You can collect all the worksheets into a *group* where Excel treats the collection of sheets as a single worksheet. This means that any data you enter into one sheet is automatically entered on the same spot in every other sheet in the group; similarly, any formatting applied to one sheet is also applied to the entire group.

---

① Click the tab of the first worksheet you want to include in the group.

② Press and hold Ctrl.

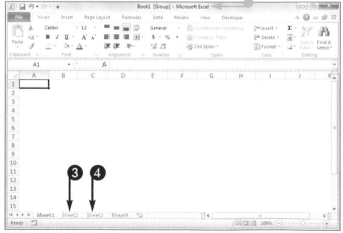

③ Click the tab of the next worksheet you want to include in the group.

● Excel displays [Group] in the title bar to remind you that your worksheets are currently grouped.

Note: *If you select a tab accidentally, click the tab again to remove the worksheet from the group.*

④ Repeat step 3 for each worksheet you want to include in the group.

⑤ Release the Ctrl key.

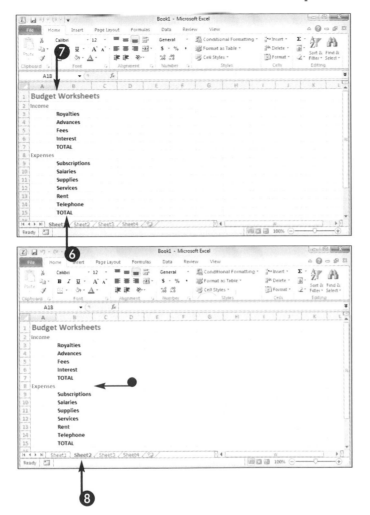

6 Add the text and other data you want to display on the grouped worksheets.

7 Apply the formatting that you want to use on the grouped worksheets.

8 Click the tab of a worksheet in the group.

● The data and formatting you added to the original worksheet also appear in the other worksheets in the group.

More Options!

If you have a workbook with a large number of worksheets and you want to include most or all of those sheets in your group, do not click each worksheet tab individually. To group every sheet, right-click any tab and then click Select All Sheets; alternatively, click the first tab you want to include in the group, hold down Shift, and then click the last tab you want to include.

Remove It!

To exclude a worksheet from the group, hold down Ctrl and click the worksheet's tab. To collapse the entire group, either click any tab that is not part of the group, or right-click a grouped tab and then click Ungroup Sheets.

You can make the Office Clipboard easier to use and more efficient by configuring Office to display the Clipboard quickly.

A *clipboard* is a memory location that is used to store data temporarily. Windows comes with a clipboard that stores data that you either cut or copy, and you can then paste the data to a document.

The Windows Clipboard can only store one item at a time, which is not always convenient or useful. However, Office 2010 comes with its own memory storage area — called the Office Clipboard — that can store up to 24 cut

or copied items. You can paste the most recently cut or copied item using the Paste command, but to paste an older item, you must display the Office Clipboard, and then double-click the item you want to paste.

Unfortunately, displaying the Office Clipboard takes a few steps, so if you use this tool frequently, you might prefer a faster method. You can configure Office to display the Office Clipboard automatically either as soon as it contains at least two items, or whenever you press Ctrl+C twice in succession.

Display the Office Clipboard Automatically

1 Click the Home tab.

2 In the Clipboard group, click the dialog box launcher icon.

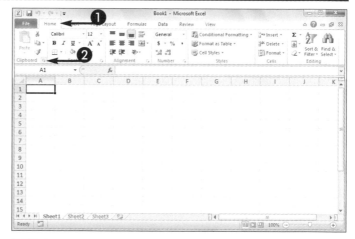

The Office Clipboard task pane appears.

3 Click Options.

4 Click Show Office Clipboard Automatically.

Excel now displays the Office Clipboard automatically whenever it contains two or more items.

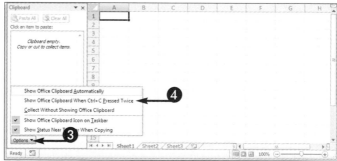

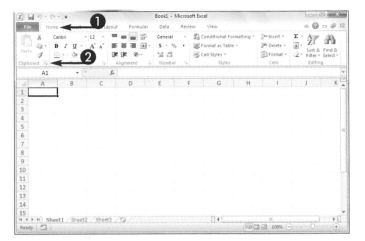

Display the Office Clipboard Using the Keyboard

1 Click the Home tab.

2 In the Clipboard group, click the dialog box launcher icon.

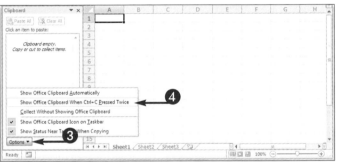

The Office Clipboard task pane appears.

3 Click Options.

4 Click Show Office Clipboard When Ctrl+C Pressed Twice.

Excel now displays the Office Clipboard automatically whenever you press Ctrl+C twice in a row.

More Options!

By default, the Office Clipboard icon appears in the notification area of the Windows taskbar. When you have the Office Clipboard displayed and you cut or copy an item in any Office application, the icon displays a notification that says "X of 24 - Clipboard," where X is the number of items on the clipboard.

If you find these notifications distracting and not very useful, you can turn them off. Click the Home tab, and then click the Clipboard group's dialog box launcher icon to open the Office Clipboard. Click the Options button and then click to deactivate the Show Status Near Taskbar When Copying command. To disable the actual icon, click to deactivate the Show Office Clipboard Icon on Taskbar command.

Use Dialog Box Controls to Input Data

You can make worksheet data entry easier and more accurate by using dialog box controls such as check boxes, option buttons, lists, and spin boxes.

If you are building a worksheet for data entry, your main concerns should be speed and accuracy. That is, you want users to be able to input data as quickly as possible, while still making the entered data as accurate as possible. The easiest way to achieve both goals in Excel is to add dialog box controls — also called form controls — to your worksheet. These are controls such as check boxes and lists that you are familiar with from dialog boxes.

The benefit to using form controls is that they reduce the amount of typing required by the user entering data. For example, rather than having the person type Yes or No in a cell, they can activate or deactivate a check box, instead. Similarly, rather than having the user memorize a cell's possible inputs, you can provide a list of the allowable values.

To use worksheet form controls, you must first customize the Ribbon to display the Developer tab, as described in the first Tip.

Add a Control to a Worksheet

1 Click the Developer tab.

2 Click Insert.

3 Click the control you want to add.

● In this case, you need to click a control from the Form Controls section of the Insert Controls gallery.

4 Click and drag on the worksheet at the spot where you want the control to appear.

● As you drag, Excel displays the border of the control.

5 When the control is the size and shape you want, release the mouse.

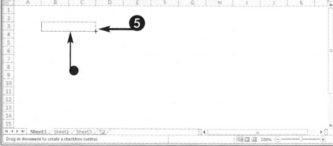

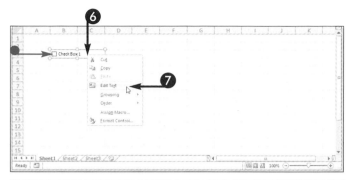

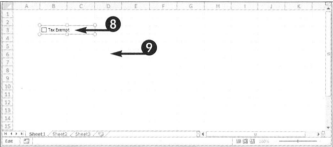

- Excel adds the control to the worksheet.

⑥ If the control comes with a text label, right-click the control.

⑦ Click Edit Text.

Note: *You can also double-click the text.*

Excel opens the label text for editing.

⑧ Type the name you want to use for the control.

⑨ Click outside the control.

Excel removes the selection handles from the control.

Note: *To select the control later on, hold down Ctrl and click the control.*

TIPS

Important!
To use the worksheet form controls, you must customize the Excel Ribbon to display the Developer tab. Right-click any part of the Ribbon and then click Customize the Ribbon. The Excel Options dialog box appears with the Customize Ribbon tab displayed. In the Customize the Ribbon list box, click to select the Developer option, and then click OK.

Did You Know?
When you are dragging the control on the worksheet, you can make the control's border snap to the worksheet's cells by holding down the Alt key as you drag. If you want the control to be a perfect square, hold down Shift as you drag. If you want the control to be centered on the spot where you start dragging, hold down Ctrl as you drag.

continued

Adding a form control to a worksheet does not do very much by itself. To make the control useful, you must link it to a worksheet cell. That way, when the user changes the state or value of the control, the resulting change is reflected in the linked cell.

The value you see in the linked worksheet cell depends on the type of control. A check box inserts the value TRUE when it is checked, and FALSE when it is unchecked. Option buttons return a number based on the selected option: the first option returns 1, the second option returns 2, and so on. Scroll bars and spin boxes return a value from a range of values that you specify. List boxes and combo boxes get their items from a worksheet range, and they return the position of the selected item in the list, where the first item in the list returns 1, the second item returns 2, and so on. To get the actual list value, you must use the INDEX() worksheet function, as described in the second Tip.

Link a Control to a Worksheet Cell

① Right-click the control.

② Click Format Control.

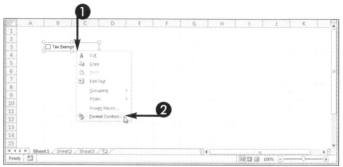

The Format Control dialog box appears with the Control tab displayed.

③ Click inside the Cell Link box.

④ Click the cell you want to use to store the control's value.

● Excel inserts the cell address in the Cell Link box.

⑤ Click OK.

When the user changes the value of the control, the new value appears in the linked cell.

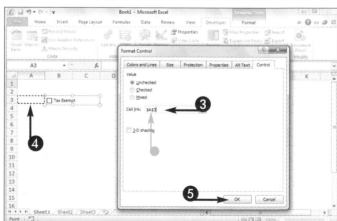

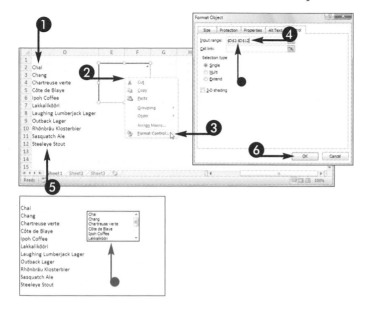

Populate a List Control with Values

1 Add the list items in a vertical or horizontal range on the worksheet.

2 Right-click the list box or combo box control.

3 Click Format Control.

The Format Object dialog box appears with the Control tab displayed.

4 Click inside the Input Range box.

5 Select the range that includes the list values.

● Excel inserts the range address in the Input Range box.

6 Click OK.

● The values from the worksheet range appear as items in the list control.

TIP

More Options!

If you add a scroll bar or spin box control to the worksheet, you must configure the control to return a value from a specified range. Right-click the control and then click Format Control. In the Control tab of the Format Control dialog box, use the Minimum Value and Maximum Value spin boxes to specify the range. Use the Incremental Change spin box to specify how much the control value changes when the user clicks a scroll or spin arrow. Click OK.

Important! When you click an item in a list control, the item's position in the list appears in the linked worksheet cell. To get the actual item, you need to add the following formula to a cell:

= INDEX(input_range, cell_link)

Replace *input_range* with the address of the range that holds the list values, and replace *cell_link* with the address of the control's linked cell.

Check for Accessibility Problems

If you have a workbook that will be used by people with disabilities, you should check that workbook for accessibility problems that could make it harder for the disabled to read and navigate the document.

Spreadsheets that seem ordinary to most people can pose special challenges to people with disabilities. For example, a person with a visual impairment might have trouble seeing images, charts, form controls, and other non-text elements. Similarly, a person with physical disabilities might have trouble navigating a worksheet.

Fortunately, such problems are often easily fixed. For example, adding a text description — called *alt text* — to a chart or other non-text element helps the visually impaired understand what the element does; avoiding non-standard worksheet structures such as merged cells helps the physically disabled navigate a worksheet.

You can use the Accessibility Checker task pane to look for these and other accessibility problems, and learn how to fix them.

---

① Open the workbook you want to check.

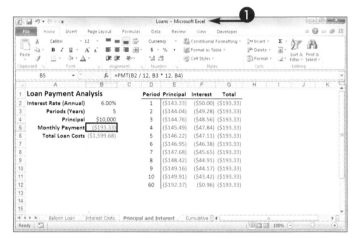

② Click the File tab.

③ Click Info.

④ Click Check for Issues.

⑤ Click Check Accessibility.

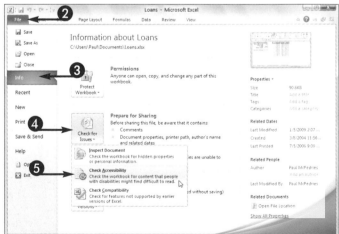

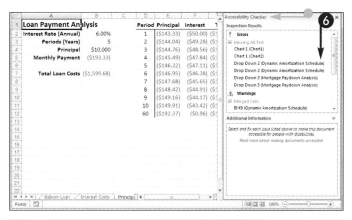

- Excel displays the Accessibility Checker task pane.

6 Click an item in the Inspection Results section.

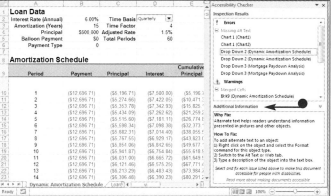

- Excel uses the Additional Information section to tell you why you should fix the problem and the steps required to fix it.

Important!

If you know your worksheet will be used by people with disabilities, you should build a new sheet with accessibility as your goal. Here are a few pointers for making a worksheet more accessible:

- Make extensive use of text headings to annotate the worksheet and make it easier to understand the structure of the sheet. In particular, every row and column should have a unique heading.

- Do not overuse white space such as blank rows and columns. White space usually helps make a worksheet look less cluttered, but a sheet that has little or no white space is much easier for the disabled to navigate. Use Excel formatting such as row heights and column widths to create space within the worksheet.

- Use named ranges whenever possible, as named ranges are relatively easy to navigate using the Go To command in Excel. (To name a range, select it, click the Formulas tab, and then click Define Name.)

Making It Easier to Manage Workbooks

To get the most out of Excel, you need to manage your workbook files, and this chapter will show you the best ways to do this. For example, you will learn how to increase the number of recent workbooks that Excel displays, open one or more workbooks automatically at startup, and create a workspace of workbooks that you can open all at once.

You will also learn a few useful techniques for changing workbook defaults to suit the way you work, including the default file

location, the default font and font size, and the default number of worksheets.

You will also learn practical workbook techniques such as repairing a corrupt file, converting a workbook to PDF format, creating a custom workbook template, creating a new workbook from an existing one, comparing two workbooks side by side, and checking for workbook features that are not supported by earlier versions of Excel.

Quick Tips

You can make it easier to find the workbooks you use most often by increasing the number of files that Excel displays on its Recent list.

When you click the File tab and then click Recent, Excel displays a list of the workbooks that you have used most recently, and clicking an item in the list opens that workbook. The Recent list is therefore a quick way to open a file, but only if the workbook you want appears in that list.

To improve the chances that a workbook appears in the Recent list, you can increase the number of files that Excel displays. The default is 22, but you can specify a number as high as 50.

If you run your PC at a relatively low resolution, such as 1024 x 768, Excel only has space to display the first few recent documents, and it adds a scroll bar to the list so you can navigate the rest. However, having to scroll to a recent document just slows you down, so you can reduce the number of recent documents to about 15, or whatever number prevents the scroll bar from appearing.

1 Click the File tab.

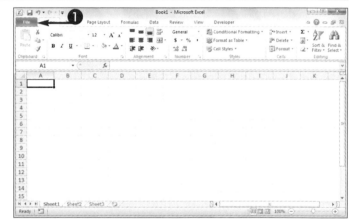

2 Click Options.

The Excel Options dialog box appears.

③ Click Advanced.

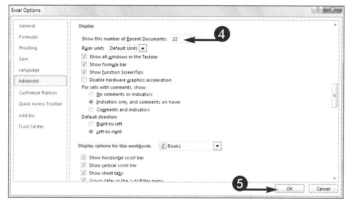

④ Use the Show This Number of Recent Documents spin box to specify the number of recent workbooks you want to display.

⑤ Click OK.

The next time you click the File tab and then click Recent, you see the number of recent workbooks that you specified.

More Options!

Excel 2010 gives you a few options for manipulating the list of recent documents. For example, if a workbook that you use only rarely appears on the list, you should remove it to make space for a file that you use often. Right-click the workbook and then click Remove From List. If you want a particular workbook to always appear on the list, click the pin icon to the right of the file.

Did You Know?

If you are running Excel 2010 on Windows 7, you can take advantage of jump lists to open recent Excel workbooks. Pin the Excel icon to the taskbar as described in Chapter 1. You can then right-click the icon to access the recent workbooks. You can also pin items to this list by clicking the pin icon or by dragging and dropping a workbook onto the Excel icon.

If you have one or more workbooks that you always open each time you start Excel, you can save time by having Excel open the workbooks for you automatically.

You may often open the same few workbooks each time you start Excel. For example, if you are doing the customer billing for your business, you might always open the accounts-receivable workbooks. Similarly, you might have some workbooks that you use throughout the day, so you always open them as soon as Excel starts.

The Recent list can help you open these workbooks quickly, but an even easier method is to configure Excel to open the workbooks automatically at startup. You do this by moving the workbooks to a folder that contains no other workbooks, and then configuring Excel to automatically open every workbook in that folder at startup.

This task assumes that you have created such a folder and have moved into that folder the workbook files that you want to open automatically.

① **Click the File tab.**

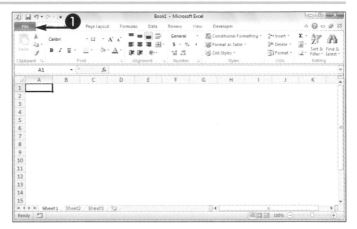

② **Click Options.**

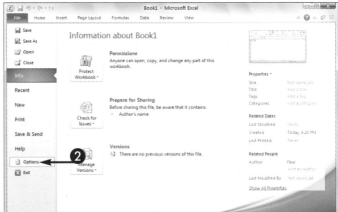

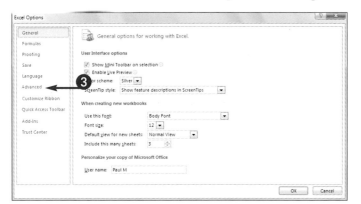

The Excel Options dialog box appears.

③ Click Advanced.

④ Use the At Startup, Open All Files In text box to type the location of the folder that contains the workbooks you want Excel to open.

⑤ Click OK.

The next time you launch Excel, it automatically opens all the workbooks in the folder you specified.

Desktop Trick!

If you are not sure about the exact location of the folder you want to use, open Windows Explorer and navigate to the folder. In Windows 7 or Windows Vista, right-click the Address box and then click Copy Address; in Windows XP, select the Address box text and then press Ctrl+C. You can then follow steps 1 to 3, click in the At Startup, Open All Files In text box, and paste the address by pressing Ctrl+V.

Remove It!

If you no longer want Excel to open workbooks automatically at startup, there are two ways you can disable this feature. The first method is to follow steps 1 to 3, delete the path from the At Startup, Open All Files In text box, and then click OK. Alternatively, open the folder that you specified in step 4 and then move all the workbooks to a different location.

Create a Workspace of Workbooks

If you have multiple workbooks that you always open as a group, you can save time by creating a workspace for those files and then opening the workspace when you need them.

If you are a regular Excel user, you may have several workbooks open in Excel all or most of the time. Similarly, if you are working on a project, you may require several project-related workbooks to be open at the same time.

Whether the workbooks are ones you use regularly or are project-related, having the files

open gives you easy access to the data you require; however, opening all those files each time you need them can be inconvenient. To make this task easier, you can define a workspace that includes those files. A *workspace* is a special file that acts as a pointer to a collection of workbooks. When you open the workspace file, Excel automatically opens all the files contained in the workspace.

Create a Workspace

① Open all the workbooks that you want to include in the workspace.

② Close any workbooks that you do not want to include in the workspace.

③ Click the View tab.

④ Click Save Workspace.

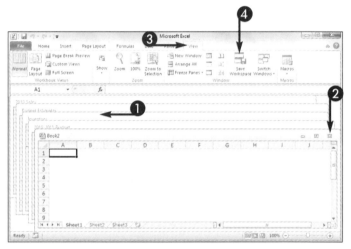

The Save Workspace dialog box appears.

⑤ Choose a location for the workspace file.

⑥ Use the File Name text box to type a name for the workspace file.

⑦ Click Save.

Note: *If any of your open workbooks have unsaved changes, Excel prompts you to save those changes. In each case, click Save.*

Excel saves the workspace file.

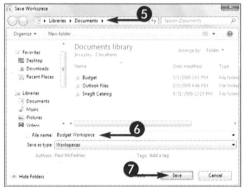

Open a Workspace

1 Click the File tab.

2 Click Open.

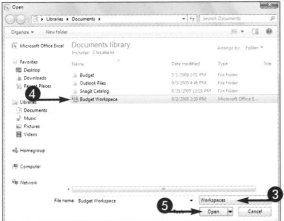

The Open dialog box appears.

3 Click here and select Workspaces.

4 Click the workspace file you want to open.

5 Click Open.

Excel opens each workbook that is part of the workspace.

Did You Know?

You do not need to restrict yourself to a single workspace file. For example, you could create a separate workspace file for each project you are currently working on. This enables you to quickly switch from one set of workbooks to another, or even open multiple workspaces at the same time.

Customize It!

When you open a workspace or switch from one workspace to another, you usually want to close all the open workbooks to avoid cluttering the Excel window. Rather than close each workbook manually, customize the Quick Access Toolbar or the Ribbon with the Close All command, which closes all open files. See Chapter 1 to learn how to customize these Excel features.

If you store your Excel workbooks in a special folder, you can save time and effort opening and saving these workbooks by making that folder the default file location.

By default, when you save a new workbook, Excel displays your user profile's Documents folder (or My Documents in Windows XP) in the Save As dialog box. Similarly, when you run the Open command, Excel automatically displays your Documents (or My Documents) folder in the Open dialog box.

The folder that Excel displays automatically in the Save As and Open dialog boxes is called the default file location. If you store your Excel workbooks elsewhere, it is inconvenient to always navigate to that folder before you can save or open a workbook. To make saving and opening more efficient, you can change the default file location to the folder you use to store your Excel workbooks.

① Click the File tab.

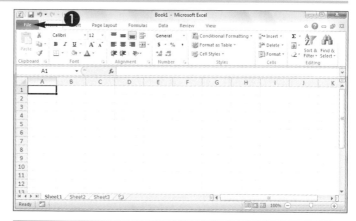

② Click Options.

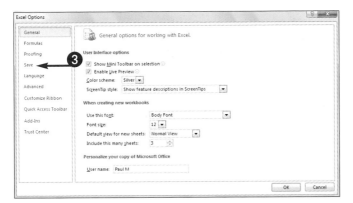

The Excel Options dialog box appears.

③ Click Save.

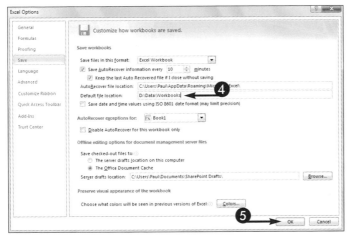

④ Use the Default File Location text box to type the path to the folder you want to use as the default.

⑤ Click OK.

Excel now displays your folder automatically in the Save As and Open dialog boxes.

Did You Know?

Unfortunately, Excel does not offer a Browse button or similar feature to help you choose the folder you want to use as the default file location. If you are unsure of the exact path to enter, you can use Windows Explorer to copy the correct path. To learn how, see the first Tip in the section, "Open Workbooks Automatically at Startup," earlier in this chapter.

Try This!

Excel can also accept a network location as the default file location. This must be a shared network folder, and you must have sufficient permissions to save files to the folder and make changes to the files in the folder. In the Default File Location text box, enter a network address in the form \\SERVER\Share, where SERVER is the name of the network computer, and Share is the name of the shared folder.

Set the Default Font and Font Size for New Workbooks

You can configure Excel to suit your font preferences by setting the default font and default font size that Excel uses for new workbooks.

When you create a workbook, Excel automatically applies certain formatting options, such as the font and the font size. The default font is Body Font, which refers to the font used for regular worksheet text in whatever theme is applied to the workbook. (Each theme also defines a Headings Font, which Excel uses for cells formatted with a heading or title style.)

Using Body Font as the default means that the worksheet font changes when you change the workbook theme. (See Chapter 3 to learn more about workbook themes.) This may be the font behavior you prefer, but if you would rather have the same font regardless of the theme, then you need to configure that font as the default.

You can also configure Excel with a default font size. The standard size is 11 points, but you can specify a larger or smaller size if you prefer.

① Click the File tab.

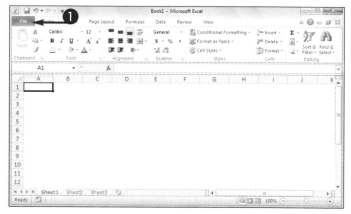

② Click Options.

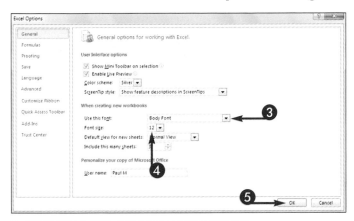

The Excel Options dialog box appears.

③ On the General tab, click here and select the default font you want to use.

④ Click here and select the default size you want to use.

⑤ Click OK.

Excel warns you that the change will not go into effect until you restart the program.

⑥ Click OK.

⑦ Close and restart Excel.

All new workbooks that you create now use the font and font size that you specified.

TIPS

More Options!

Rather than configure a default font for Excel, you might prefer to apply a particular font only for certain workbooks. Press Ctrl+A to select the entire worksheet and then, in the Home tab, use the Font drop-down list to set the font for the sheet. If you prefer different fonts for headings and body text, then you can create a custom theme font, as described in Chapter 3.

Remove It!

If you no longer want to use your specified font and font size as the default, you can return to the original Excel configuration. Follow steps 1 and 2 to display the General tab of the Excel Options dialog box. In the Use This Font drop-down list, click Body Font. Then, in the Font Size drop-down list, click 11. Click OK to apply your changes.

Set the Default Number of Worksheets for New Workbooks

If you normally either delete existing sheets from or add worksheets to a new workbook, you can save time by configuring Excel to always include your preferred number of worksheets in each new file.

By default, Excel includes three blank worksheets in each new workbook that you create. However, if you never use more than a single worksheet in most of your workbooks, you really do not need the extra two worksheets and may waste time deleting them.

Conversely, you might find that you always use four, five, or more worksheets in most of your workbooks. In this scenario, you would have to waste time adding the new sheets to the workbook.

In both cases, you can save time by telling Excel the number of worksheets you prefer to have in your new workbooks.

① Click the File tab.

② Click Options.

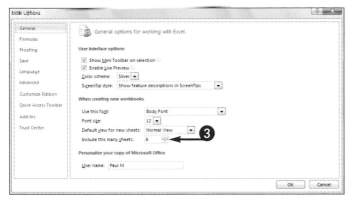

The Excel Options dialog box appears.

③ On the General tab, click this spin box to specify the number of worksheets you want in each new workbook.

④ Click OK.

Each time you create a new workbook, Excel now includes the number of worksheets that you specified.

Try This!

What if you want to determine the number of sheets in each new workbook as you create your workbooks, rather than as a general rule? For example, a simple loan amortization model might require just a single worksheet, whereas a company budget workbook might require a dozen worksheets.

The following macro solves this problem by enabling you to specify the number of sheets you want in each new workbook.

```
Sub NewWorkbookWithCustomSheets()
    Dim currentSheets As Integer
    With Application
        currentSheets = .SheetsInNewWorkbook
        .SheetsInNewWorkbook = InputBox( _
            "How many sheets do you want" & _
            "in the new workbook?", , 3)
        Workbooks.Add
        .SheetsInNewWorkbook = currentSheets
    End With
End Sub
```

For more information about adding a macro to Excel, see Chapter 11.

Repair a Corrupted Workbook File

If you have an Excel workbook that you can no longer open because the file has become corrupted, Excel offers a repair option that should enable you to fix the file.

Excel workbooks rarely have problems and they generally open successfully. However, a hard disk error or memory error could create a problem that corrupts the file. When that happens and you try to open the workbook,

Excel displays an error message telling you either that it does not recognize the file format or that the file is corrupted.

Whatever the cause, it is important that you do not lose any data, so Excel offers an Open and Repair command that first attempts to repair the file, and then to open the repaired workbook in Excel.

① Click the File tab.

② Click Open.

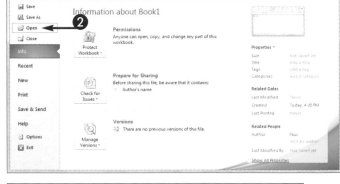

The Open dialog box appears.

③ Click the workbook you want to repair.

④ Click the Open drop-down list.

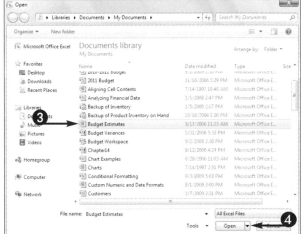

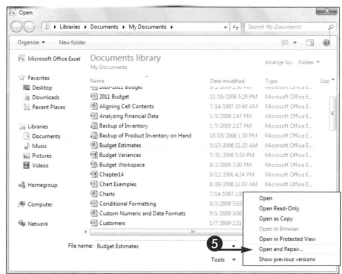

⑤ Click Open and Repair.

⑥ In the dialog box that appears, click Repair.

Excel repairs and then opens the file.

TIPS

More Options!

If Excel cannot repair the workbook, you may still be able to save the workbook's data. Follow steps 1 to 5 to select the Open and Repair command. In the dialog box that appears, click Extract Data. In the dialog box that appears, click Recover Formulas if you want Excel to try and recover the workbook's formulas. If that does not work, repeat Steps 1 to 5, click Extract Data, and then click Convert to Values, instead; this tells Excel to convert all the formulas to their results. After Excel repairs the file, click Close.

More Options!

Another option you have to recover some or all of your work is to open a previous version of the workbook, if one exists. Follow steps 1 to 4 to display the Open drop-down list, and then click Show Previous Versions. Excel displays a list of the available versions of the workbook. Click the version you want to use — usually the most recent version that you believe is not corrupted — and then click Open.

Convert a Workbook to a PDF File

If you want to share an Excel workbook with another person who does not have Excel, you can save that workbook as a Portable Document Format (PDF) file.

Microsoft Office is by far the most popular productivity suite, and Microsoft Excel is by far the most popular spreadsheet program. However, although this means that many people have Excel, it does not mean that everyone does. So if you want a non-Excel user to see your Excel data and results, you must

find some way of sharing your workbook with that person.

One easy way to do this is by using a PDF file, which uses a near-universal file format that displays documents exactly as they appear in the original application, but can be configured to prevent people from making changes to the document. Most people have the Adobe Acrobat PDF reader on their system, and a free version is easily obtained online from adobe.com.

---

1 Open the workbook you want to convert to a PDF.

2 Click the File tab.

3 Click Save & Send.

4 Click Create PDF/XPS Document.

5 Click Create PDF/XPS.

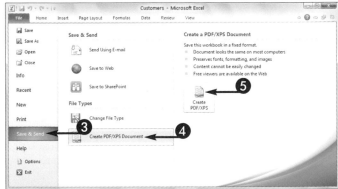

The Publish as PDF or XPS dialog box appears.

6 Choose a location for the file.

7 Type a name for the file.

8 Make sure the Save as Type drop-down list shows PDF.

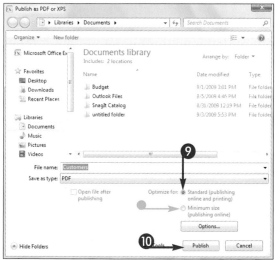

9 Click to select the Standard option.

● If you will be sharing the PDF file online, you can create a smaller file by clicking to select the Minimum Size option, instead.

10 Click Publish.

Excel publishes the file as a PDF.

More Options!

By default, Excel publishes only the current worksheet to the PDF. If you want to publish the entire workbook, instead, follow steps 1 to 9 to open the Publish as PDF or XPS dialog box and set up the file. Click the Options button to open the Options dialog box, click to select the Entire Workbook option, and then click OK.

Did You Know?

One problem with PDF is that it is a proprietary standard (it is owned by Adobe Systems) and you may prefer to use a format based on open standards. That is the idea behind the XML Paper Specification, or XPS. XPS uses XML (eXtensible Markup Language) for the document syntax and the ZIP format for the document container file, so it is based on open and available technologies. In the Publish as PDF or XPS dialog box, click the Save as Type drop-down list and then click XPS Document.

Create a Workbook Template

You can save yourself and other people a great deal of time by converting an existing workbook to an Excel template that you can then use as the basis for new workbooks.

After you have spent some time constructing a workbook — adding tabs, inserting labels, data, and formulas, and formatting everything just so — you may find that you need a similar workbook for another purpose. Rather than starting from scratch, you can either use the Save As command or the New from Existing command (discussed in the section, "Create a New Workbook from an Existing File") to create a new workbook based on the existing workbook.

However, if you or someone else needs to use the existing workbook as the basis for many other workbooks, it is much easier to convert the workbook to a template file. You can then easily create new workbooks based on that template.

① Open the workbook that you want to save as a template.

② Click the File tab.

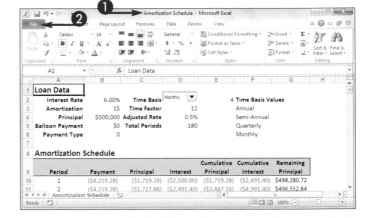

③ Click Save As.

The Save As dialog box appears.

4 Use the File Name text box to type a name for the template file.

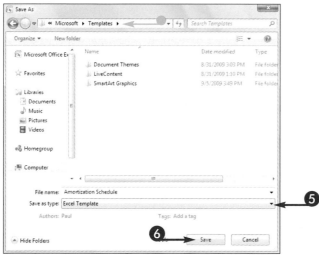

5 Click here and select Excel Template.

● Excel automatically chooses the Templates folder as the save location.

6 Click Save.

Excel saves the workbook as a template file.

TIPS

Apply It!

To use your new template, first make sure you have closed the new template file. Click the File tab, click New, and then click My Templates. Excel opens the New dialog box, which includes the Personal Templates tab that lists the templates you have saved to the Templates folder. Click the template you want to use, and then click OK.

Did You Know?

In the Save As dialog box, the Save as Type list offers three different types of templates. The Excel Template file type creates a template file that is compatible with Excel 2010 and Excel 2007. If your workbook includes macros and you also want those macros in your template, choose the Excel Macro-Enabled Template file type. If you require a template file that is compatible with earlier versions of Excel, choose the Excel 97-2003 Template file type.

Create a New Workbook from an Existing File

You can save time and effort by creating a new workbook from an existing workbook file.

One of the secrets of Excel productivity is to minimize the number of times you have to "reinvent the wheel." That is, you should not create a new workbook from scratch if you already have an existing workbook that contains some or all of the data, formulas, or formatting that you require in the new file.

One way to do this is to open the original file and then use the Save As command to create a copy of the workbook either under a different name or in a different location.

However, Excel 2010 offers a different method that is a bit more efficient because it does not require you to first open the existing file.

---

① Click the File tab.

② Click New.

③ Click New from Existing.

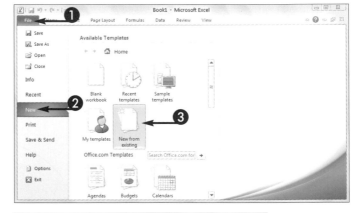

Excel displays the New from Existing Workbook dialog box.

④ Click the workbook you want to use as the basis for the new file.

⑤ Click Create New.

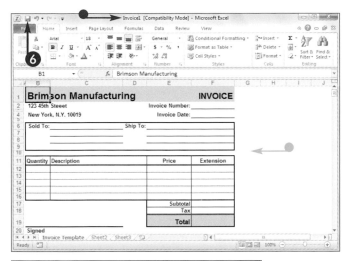

- Excel creates a new workbook based on the existing file.

- Excel appends '1' to the name of the original file.

6 Click the Save icon.

The Save As dialog box appears.

7 Choose a location for the new file.

8 Use the File Name text box to name the new file.

9 Click Save.

Excel saves the new workbook.

Caution!

When you use the Save As command to create a copy of an open workbook, the copy is protected because you saved it to the hard disk. This is not the case for a workbook that you create using the New from Existing command, because that file is in an unsaved state. Therefore, be sure to run the Save command as soon as possible to preserve the file on your hard disk.

Did You Know?

When you run the New from Existing command, Excel treats the existing file as a temporary template that it uses to create the new file. This is useful because it also means that Excel adds the existing file to its Recent Templates list. This means you can create another workbook from the same existing file by clicking the File tab, clicking New, clicking Recent Templates, and then double-clicking the file.

Compare Two Workbooks Side by Side

You can easily compare two Excel workbooks by using the View Side by Side command.

It is often useful to compare the contents of two different workbooks. For example, you might want to compare two workbooks that contain the same type of data for two different divisions, departments, or other entities. Similarly, you might have sent a copy of a workbook to a colleague for editing, and you now want to compare the original and the copy to see what changes your colleague made.

You could compare the two workbooks by switching back and forth between them, but Excel offers a much easier method. With the View Side by Side command, Excel tiles your two workbooks within the Excel window, and as you scroll through one, Excel automatically scrolls through the other by the same amount.

Note that, despite the name, the View Side by Side command tiles the workbooks vertically, not horizontally as you might expect.

① Open the two workbooks that you want to compare.

Note: *It does not matter if you also have other workbooks open at the same time.*

② Switch to one of the workbooks that you want to compare.

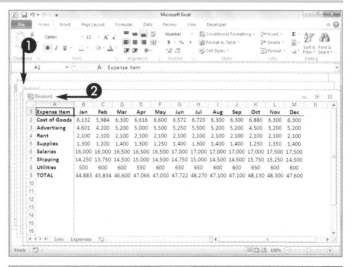

③ Click the View tab.

④ Click the View Side by Side icon.

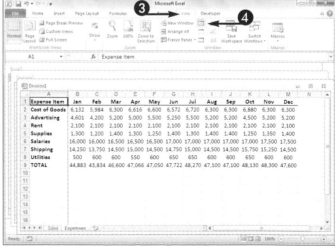

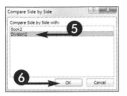

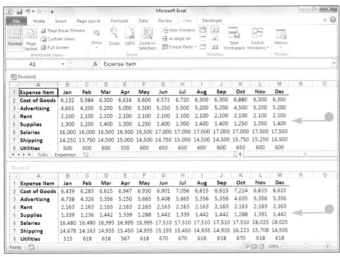

The Compare Side by Side dialog box appears.

⑤ Click the other workbook that you want to use in the comparison.

⑥ Click OK.

● Excel arranges the windows of the two workbooks so that you can compare them.

Did You Know?

If you resize, maximize, minimize, or restore the Excel window, Excel recon-figures the window to display all your open workbooks in a tiled view. To restore the View Side by Side view, click the View tab and then click Reset Windows Position (⊞). You can also click this command to restore the view if you resize any of the workbook windows.

More Options!

By default, Excel configures the View Side by Side feature with *synchronous scrolling:* when you scroll vertically or horizontally in one window, Excel automatically scrolls the other window by the same amount in the same direction. If you prefer to keep one window in the same position while you scroll the other, click the View tab and then click to turn off the Synchronous Scrolling (⊞) button.

Check for Features Not Supported by Earlier Excel Versions

You can ensure that other people can view and work with your Excel files by checking your workbooks for features that are not compatible with earlier versions of Excel.

Each new version of Excel includes many new features, and some of these features introduce functionality that is incompatible with earlier versions of Excel. Examples of features new to Excel 2010 that are incompatible with all previous versions of Excel are sparklines, slicers, and the new names that Excel 2010 uses for many existing statistical functions.

Other recent Excel features that are not compatible with versions of Excel prior to 2007 are table styles, some cell styles, and SmartArt graphics.

At best, these incompatible features can cause your workbook to appear different to other people; at worst, they can cause errors. If you will be distributing a workbook to users of earlier versions of Excel, use the Compatibility Checker to look for incompatible features in the workbook.

---

① Open the workbook you want to check.

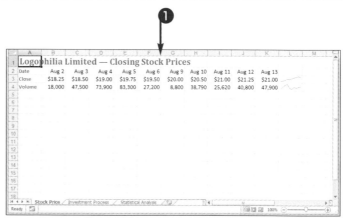

② Click the File tab.

③ Click Info.

④ Click Check for Issues.

⑤ Click Check Compatibility.

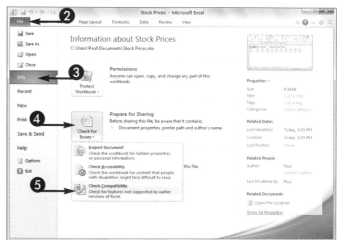

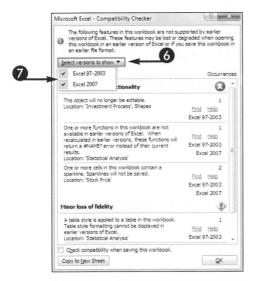

The Compatibility Checker appears.

⑥ Click the Select Versions to Show drop-down arrow.

⑦ Click an Excel version if you do not want to see compatibility issues for that version.

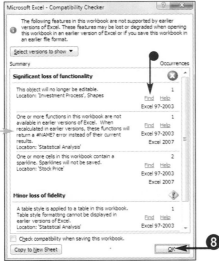

● Excel displays the workbook's compatibility issues.

● To see the specific cell, range, or object that has the problem, you can click the Find link.

⑧ Click OK.

TIP

More Options!

If you have other changes to make to the workbook before distributing the file, you may prefer to check compatibility as you go along. Rather than running the steps in this section every time, follow steps 1 to 5 to open the Compatibility Checker, and then click to select the Check Compatibility When Saving this Workbook check box.

Excel then checks for incompatible features automatically each time you save the workbook. If it finds incompatible items, Excel displays the Compatibility Checker to let you know. Note the problematic items and click Continue to save the document.

Chapter

3

Customizing Worksheet Presentation

The best Excel worksheets offer accurate data as well as useful analysis through the use of formulas, scenarios, and other tools. However, a successful Excel spreadsheet also presents its data and results in an attractive, easy-to-read, and easy-to-understand format. So although formatting your worksheet may seem like the last thing you want to do, it is worth taking a bit of extra time to do it well and present your work in its best light.

This chapter shows you several techniques that enable you to take control of Excel formatting through customization. You will learn how to build custom numeric formats; data and time formats; fill lists; cell styles; table styles; workbook colors, fonts, and themes; headers and footers; and more.

Quick Tips

You are not limited to predefined numeric formats in Excel; you can create a custom cell format that displays information just how you want it.

The predefined numeric formats give you a lot of control over how your numbers are displayed, but they have their limitations. For example, no built-in format enables you to display a number such as 0.5 without the leading zero, or to display temperatures using, say, the degree symbol. To overcome these and other limitations, you need to create your own custom numeric formats.

You can create custom numeric formats either by editing an existing format or by creating your own format. The formatting syntax and symbols are explained in the Tip.

Every Excel numeric format, whether built-in or customized, has the following syntax:

positive;negative;zero;text

The four parts, separated by semicolons, determine how various numbers are presented. The first part defines how a positive number is displayed, the second part defines how a negative number is displayed, the third part defines how zero is displayed, and the fourth part defines how text is displayed.

① Select the range you want to format.

② Click the Home tab.

③ In the Number group, click the dialog box launcher icon.

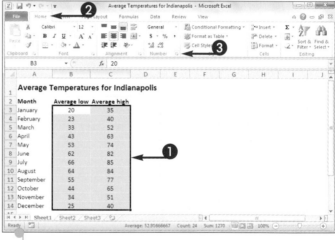

The Format Cells dialog box appears with the Number tab selected.

● If you want to base your custom format on an existing format, you can click the category and then click the format.

④ Click Custom.

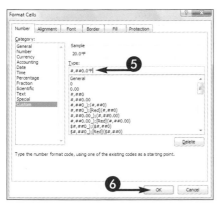

5 Type the symbols and text that define your custom format.

6 Click OK.

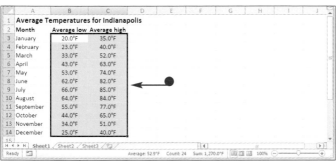

● Excel applies the custom format.

Customize It!

Use the symbols listed in the following table to build your custom numeric formats.

Symbols for Custom Numeric Formats	
Symbol	**Description**
#	Holds a place for a digit and displays the digit exactly as typed. Excel displays nothing if no number is entered.
0	Holds a place for a digit and displays the digit exactly as typed. Excel displays 0 if no number is entered.
?	Holds a place for a digit and displays the digit exactly as typed. Excel displays a space if no number is entered.
. (period)	Sets the location of the decimal point.
, (comma)	Sets the location of the thousands separator. Excel marks only the location of the first thousand.
/ (forward slash)	Sets the location of the fraction separator.
%	Multiplies the number by 100 (for display only) and adds the percent (%) character.

You can enhance your worksheet display of dates and times by creating your own custom date and time formatting.

Date and time formats determine how Excel displays data values and time values in a range. For a date, the date format determines whether Excel displays the value with the year, month, date, or all three, and whether you see short values such as Fri or long values such as Friday. For a time, the time format determines whether Excel displays the value with the hour, minute, second, or all three.

Although the built-in date and time formats are fine for most applications, you might need to create your own custom formats. For example, you might want to display just the day of the week (for example, Friday). To do this, you can create custom date and time formats. You can do so either by editing an existing format or by creating your own format. The formatting syntax and symbols are explained in the Tip.

① Select the range you want to format.

② Click the Home tab.

③ In the Number group, click the dialog box launcher icon.

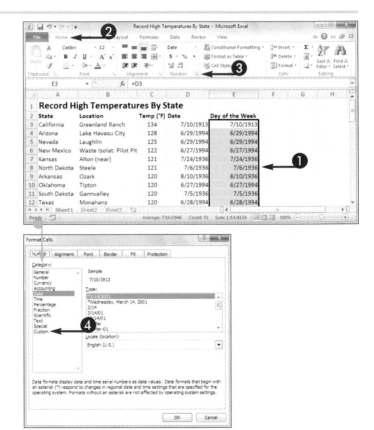

The Format Cells dialog box appears with the Number tab selected.

● If you want to base your custom format on an existing format, click either the Date or Time category and then click the format.

④ Click Custom.

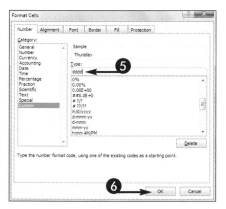

⑤ Type the symbols and text that define your custom format.

⑥ Click OK.

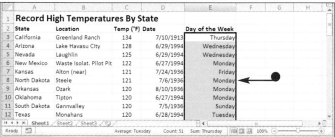

● Excel applies the custom format.

Customize It!
Use the symbols in the following table to build your custom date and time formats.

Symbol	Description
d	Displays a day number without a leading zero (1–31).
dd	Displays a day number with a leading zero (01–31).
ddd	Displays a three-letter day abbreviation (Mon).
dddd	Displays a full day name (Monday).
m	Displays a month number without a leading zero (1–12).
mm	Displays a month number with a leading zero (01–12).
mmm	Displays a three-letter month abbreviation (Aug).
mmmm	Displays a full month name (August).
yy	Displays a two-digit year (00–99).
yyyy	Displays a full year (1900–2078).
h	Displays an hour without a leading zero (0–24).
hh	Displays an hour with a leading zero (00–24).
m	Displays a minute without a leading zero (0–59).
mm	Displays a minute with a leading zero (00–59).
s	Displays a second without a leading zero (0–59).
ss	Displays a second with a leading zero (00–59).

If you regularly widen or narrow your Excel columns, you can configure Excel with a new default width that matches your preferred size.

The default column width in new Excel workbooks is 8.38 characters (72 pixels). If you require a different width, Excel gives you a couple of ways to proceed. The easiest method is to double-click the right edge of the column's header, which causes Excel to adjust the column width to fit the widest item in the

column. Alternatively, you can click and drag the right edge of the column header to the width you prefer.

These techniques are not time consuming for a column or two, but if you find yourself constantly inserting new columns and adjusting the width each time, then you should configure Excel to use your preferred column width as the default for the workbook.

① Click the Home tab.

② Click Format.

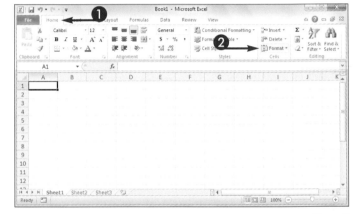

③ Click Default Width.

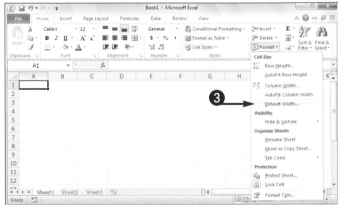

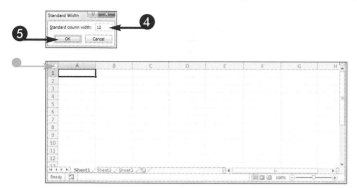

The Standard Width dialog box appears.

④ Type the column width you want to use.

⑤ Click OK.

● Excel formats all the columns with the new width.

Note: *Each time you insert a new column, Excel formats it with the new default width.*

More Options!

Rather than configuring a new default width, you might prefer to leave the default as is and change the width of all the columns at once. Press Ctrl+A to select the entire worksheet. Click the Home tab, click the Format drop-down arrow, and then click Column Width. Use the Column Width text box to type the width you want to use, and then click OK.

Did You Know?

If you modify the width of a column before you set the default column width, Excel does not change the width of the modified column when you apply the new default. If you want all your columns to use the new default, follow the technique in the previous Tip to reset all the column widths to 8.43 characters.

If you do not need to see or work with a column or row temporarily, you can make your worksheet easier to read and navigate by hiding the column or row.

If your entire spreadsheet model fits within your screen, then viewing and navigating the data is not a problem. However, it is common for worksheet data to extend beyond the screen by having more columns than can fit horizontally, by having more rows than can fit

vertically, or both. Rather than scrolling horizontally or vertically to see your data, you can temporarily hide columns or rows you do not need to see at the moment.

Hiding a column or row is also useful if you are showing someone a worksheet that contains private or sensitive data that you do not want the person to see. For other ways to enhance Excel privacy and security, see Chapter 10.

Hide a Row

① Click in any cell in the row you want to hide.

② Click the Home tab.

③ Click Format.

④ Click Hide & Unhide.

⑤ Click Hide Rows.

Note: You can also hide a row by pressing Ctrl+9.

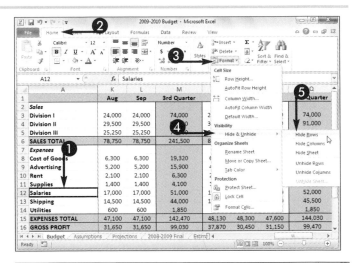

● Excel removes the row from the worksheet display.

● Excel displays a slightly thicker header border between the surrounding rows to indicate that a hidden row lies between them.

Another way to hide a row is to move the mouse pointer over the bottom edge of the row header and then click and drag the edge up until the height displays 0.

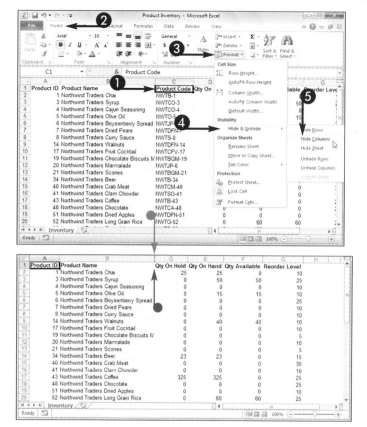

Hide a Column

① Click in any cell in the column you want to hide.

② Click the Home tab.

③ Click Format.

④ Click Hide & Unhide.

⑤ Click Hide Columns.

Note: *You can also hide a column by pressing Ctrl+0.*

● Excel removes the column from the worksheet display.

● Excel displays a slightly thicker header border between the surrounding columns to indicate that a hidden column lies between them.

Another way to hide a column is to move the mouse pointer over the right edge of the column header and then click and drag the edge to the left. Excel displays a banner that shows the current width; when that banner displays the width as 0, release the mouse button.

Reverse It!

To display a hidden row, select the row above and the row below the hidden row, click the Home tab, click the Format drop-down arrow, click Hide & Unhide, and then click Unhide Rows. Alternatively, move the mouse pointer between the headers of the selected rows and then double-click. To unhide row 1, right-click the top edge of the row 2 header and then click Unhide.

To display a hidden column, select the column to the left and the column to the right of the hidden column, click the Home tab, click the Format drop-down arrow, click Hide & Unhide, and then click Unhide Columns. Alternatively, move the mouse pointer between the headers of the selected rows and then double-click. To unhide column A, right-click the left edge of the column B header and then click Unhide.

You can make it easier to enter a common series of text values by setting up those values as a custom fill list.

In Excel, the *fill handle* is the small, black square in the bottom-right corner of the active cell or range. This versatile little tool can do many useful things. For example, if you click and drag the fill handle of a single cell, Excel copies the cell value to the cells you select. If you enter a couple of values, selecting the two cells and then dragging the range's fill handle usually creates a series of values based on the two values.

Using the fill handle to create a series is useful and efficient because it means you do not have to enter all the series values manually. However, Excel can only create these automatic series from certain types of cell values: numbers, dates, times, or alphanumeric values that end with numbers. For other series that you use regularly, you can create a custom fill list.

① Click the File tab.

② Click Options.

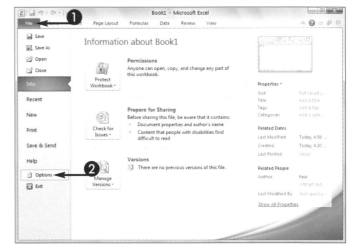

The Excel Options dialog box appears.

③ Click Advanced.

④ In the General section, click Edit Custom Lists.

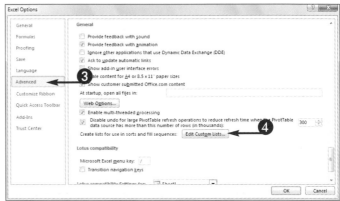

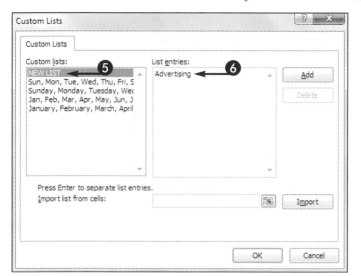

The Custom Lists dialog box appears.

⑤ Click NEW LIST.

⑥ Type an entry for the custom list.

⑦ Press Enter.

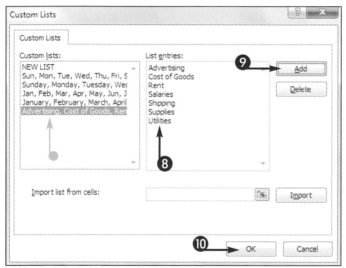

⑧ Repeat steps 6 and 7 to define all the list entries.

⑨ Click Add.

● Excel adds the list.

⑩ Click OK.

TIPS

Did You Know?

You can save time by entering the custom fill list values in advance on a worksheet. Once you have done that, select the range that contains the custom list entries, and then follow steps 1 to 4 to open the Custom Lists dialog box. Click the Import button to add the list, and then click OK.

Delete It!

If you no longer want to use a custom fill list, you should delete it. Follow steps 1 to 4 to open the Custom Lists dialog box. Click the list you no longer need, click the Delete button, and then click OK when Excel asks you to confirm the deletion. Click OK in the Custom Lists dialog box when you are done.

You can give yourself more space to work within the Excel window by turning off window elements that you do not need to use.

As your worksheet model grows beyond what can fit on a single screen, it can become frustrating if you have to constantly scroll vertically or horizontally to see other parts of the worksheet model.

If maximizing the Excel window and the workbook does not solve the problem, then you can get more space to display the worksheet by turning off certain elements of the Excel window. Specifically, you can turn off the formula bar, the horizontal and vertical scroll bars, and the row and column headers. To return to the regular view, you press Esc.

---

① Click the File tab.

② Click Options.

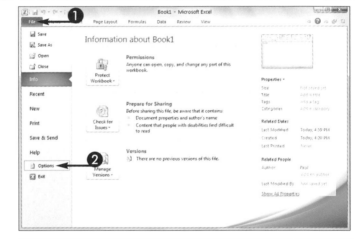

The Excel Options dialog box appears.

③ Click Advanced.

④ In the Display section, click to select the Show Formula Bar option.

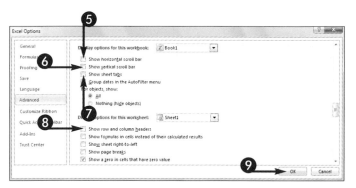

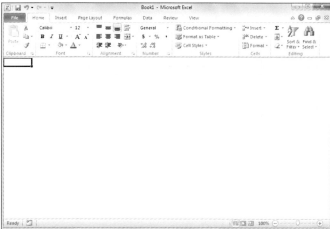

5 Click to select the Show Horizontal Scroll Bar option.

6 Click to select the Show Vertical Scroll Bar option.

7 Click to select the Show Sheet Tabs option.

8 Click to select the Show Row and Column Headers option.

9 Click OK.

Excel hides the window elements.

More Options!

Excel offers a faster way to hide the formula bar and the row and column headings. Click the View tab, and then click the Show button. In the menu that appears, click to select both the Formula Bar and Headings options. You can also hide everything except the title bar by clicking the Full Screen button in the View tab.

More Options!

Excel 2010 does not offer an option for toggling the status bar off and on. However, you can do this through the Visual Basic Editor window, which you display by pressing Alt+F11. In the Microsoft Visual Basic window, click the View menu and then click Immediate Window. (Alternately, you can press Ctrl+G.) In the Immediate window, type **Application. DisplayStatusBar=False** and press Enter.

You can make it easier to format cells the way you want by creating a custom cell style.

A cell style is a combination of up to six formatting options: the numeric format; the horizontal and vertical alignment; the font, including the typeface, style, size, color, and text effects; the border; the background color and fill effects; and cell protection.

Excel comes with several dozen predefined cell styles, many of which vary with the document theme. However, Excel also has many cell styles that are independent of the current theme, including styles for sheet titles and headings, and styles that identify totals, calculations, and output cells.

If none of the predefined cell styles is right for your needs, you can use the Format Cells dialog box to apply your own formatting. If you want to reuse this formatting in other workbooks, you should save the formatting options as a custom cell style.

---

1. Click the Home tab.
2. Click Cell Styles.
   - The Cell Styles gallery appears.
3. Click New Cell Style.

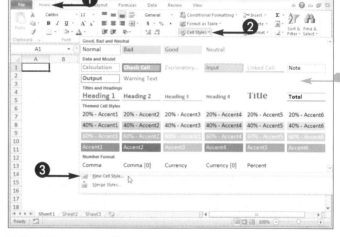

The Style dialog box appears.

4. Type a name for the style.
5. Click Format.

The Format Cells dialog box appears.

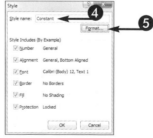

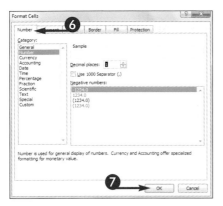

6 Use the tabs to select the formatting options you want in your cell style.

7 Click OK.

8 Click OK in the Style dialog box (not shown).

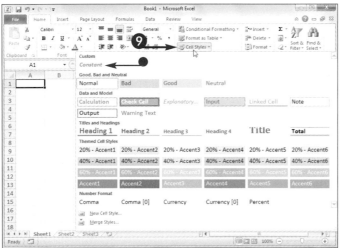

9 Click Cell Styles.

● Your cell styles appear in the Custom section of the Cell Styles gallery.

Try This!

If you already have a cell that is formatted using the options you want to use in your custom cell style, you can use that cell to make it much easier to create your custom style. Select the cell, follow steps 1 to 3 to open the Style dialog box, and then name the new cell style. Click to deselect the check box for each type of formatting you do not want to include, and then click OK.

Remove It!

If you no longer need a custom cell style, you should delete it to reduce clutter in the Cell Styles gallery. Click the Home tab and then click Cell Styles to open the Cell Styles gallery. Right-click the custom cell style and then click Delete. Excel removes the custom cell style and clears the style's formatting from any cell to which you applied the style.

You can make it easier to format tables the way you prefer by creating a custom table style.

A table style is a combination of formatting options that Excel applies to thirteen different table elements, including the first and last column, the header row, the total row, and the entire table. For each element, Excel applies one or more of the following formatting options: the font, including the typeface, style, size, color, and text effects; the border; and the background color and fill effects.

Excel comes with dozens of predefined table styles, all of which vary with the document theme. If none of the predefined table styles is right for your needs, you can use the Format Cells dialog box to apply your own formatting to the various table elements. If you want to reuse this formatting in other workbooks, you should save the formatting options as a custom table style.

---

① Click the Home tab.

② Click Format as Table.

● The Table Styles gallery appears.

③ Click New Table Style.

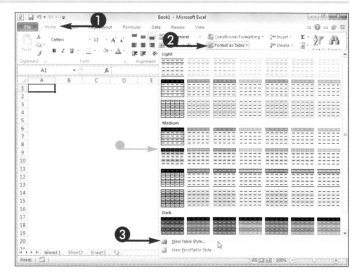

The New Table Quick Style dialog box appears.

④ Type a name for the style.

⑤ Click the table element you want to format.

⑥ Click Format.

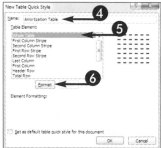

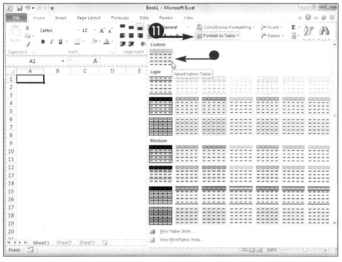

The Format Cells dialog box appears.

7 Use the tabs to select the formatting options you want in your cell style.

Note: *Depending on the table element you are working with, some of the formatting options may be disabled.*

8 Click OK.

9 Repeat steps 5 to 8 to set the formatting for the other table elements, as needed.

10 Click OK in the New Table Quick Style dialog box (not shown).

11 Click Format as Table.

● Your table styles appear in the Custom section of the Table Styles gallery.

More Options!

If you want to use your custom table style for all or most of the tables you create, you should set the custom style as the default. When you are creating a new custom table style, follow steps 1 to 9 and then click to select the Set as Default Table Quick Style for This Document option. For an existing custom table style, click the Home tab, click Format as Table, right-click the custom style, and then click Set As Default.

Remove It!

If you no longer need a custom table style, you should delete it to reduce clutter in the Table Styles gallery. Click the Home tab and then click Format as Table to open the Table Styles gallery. Right-click the custom table style, click Delete, and then click OK. Excel deletes the custom table style. Tables formatted with the style revert to the default table style.

Create a Custom Color Scheme

You can gain more control over the look of your workbooks by creating your own custom color scheme.

Each Excel theme comes with more than 20 built-in color schemes that make it easy to apply colors to your worksheets. However, if no scheme offers the exact colors you want, you can create your own scheme. Each scheme consists of twelve color elements, including the following:

Text/Background 1 - Dark: The dark text color that Excel applies when you choose a light background color.

Text/Background 2 - Light: The light text color that Excel applies when you choose a dark background color.

Text/Background 3 - Dark: The dark background color that Excel applies when you choose a light text color.

Text/Background 4 - Light: The light background color that Excel applies when you choose a dark text color.

There are also six elements — named Accent 1 through Accent 6 — that Excel uses as colors for chart data markers, as well as two colors for hyperlinks (followed and unfollowed).

---

① Click the Page Layout tab.

② Click Colors.

③ Click Create New Theme Colors.

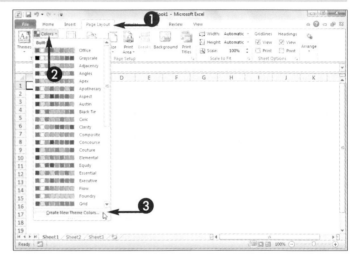

The Create New Theme Colors dialog box appears.

④ Use the drop-down list for each theme color to choose the color you want for that element.

● The Sample area shows what your custom color scheme looks like.

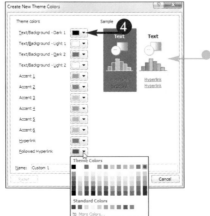

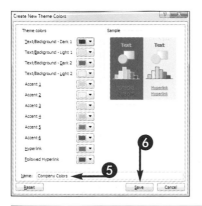

5 Type a name for your custom color scheme.

6 Click Save.

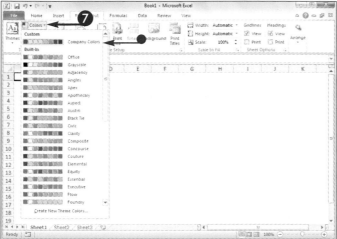

7 Click Colors.

● Your custom color scheme appears in the Custom section of the Colors gallery.

Try This!

If an existing color scheme is close to what you want, you can save some time and effort by using that color scheme as your starting point. In the Page Layout tab, click the Themes button and then click the theme you want to use. Click the Colors button and then click the color scheme. Click Colors again and then click Create New Theme Colors. The color scheme you selected appears in the Create New Theme Colors dialog box.

Remove It!

If you no longer use a custom color scheme, you should delete it to reduce clutter in the Colors gallery and to make it easier to navigate your custom schemes. Click the Page Layout tab and then click the Colors button. Right-click the custom color scheme you no longer need, click Delete, and then click Yes when Excel asks you to confirm the deletion.

Create a Custom Font Scheme

You can gain more control over the look of your workbook text by creating your own custom font scheme.

Each Excel theme comes with more than two dozen built-in font schemes that make it easy to apply fonts to your worksheets. Each font scheme defines two fonts: a larger font, called the *heading font,* for title and heading text; and

a smaller font, called the *body font,* for regular worksheet text. The typeface is often the same for both types of text, but some schemes use two different typefaces, such as Cambria for titles and headings and Calibri for body text. However, if no font scheme offers the exact typefaces you want, you can create your own scheme.

1 Click the Page Layout tab.

2 Click Fonts.

3 Click Create New Theme Fonts.

The Create New Theme Fonts dialog box appears.

4 Use the Heading Font drop-down list to choose the typeface you want to use for titles and headings.

5 Use the Body Font drop-down list to choose the typeface you want to use for regular text.

● The Sample area shows what your custom font scheme looks like.

6 Type a name for your custom font scheme.

7 Click Save.

8 Click Fonts.

● Your custom font scheme appears in the Custom section of the Fonts gallery.

Try This!

If an existing font scheme is close to what you want, you can save some time by using that font scheme as your starting point. In the Page Layout tab, click the Fonts button and then click the font scheme you want to use. Click the Fonts button again and then click Create New Theme Fonts. The font scheme you selected appears in the Create New Theme Fonts dialog box.

Remove It!

If you no longer use a custom font scheme, you should delete it to reduce clutter in the Fonts gallery and to make it easier to navigate your custom schemes. Click the Page Layout tab and then click the Fonts button. Right-click the custom font scheme you no longer need, click Delete, and then click Yes when Excel asks you to confirm the deletion.

You can save time and gain more control over formatting your Excel workbooks by creating and saving a custom workbook theme, which customizes workbook colors, fonts, and effects. You can then apply this theme to future workbooks.

In Excel, a workbook theme is a predefined collection of formatting options that you can apply all at once just by selecting a different theme. Each theme comes with preset formatting in three categories: color scheme, font scheme, and effect scheme (which includes formatting such as drop shadows and 3-D effects).

If none of the predefined themes offer the exact formatting you require, you can modify

any theme by selecting a different color scheme, font scheme, or effects scheme. You can even create your own custom color and font schemes, as described in the sections, "Create a Custom Color Scheme" and "Create a Custom Font Scheme."

However, if you go to all this trouble to get your workbook formatting just right, it is time-consuming to have to repeat the same steps for other workbooks you open or create. To avoid this problem, you can save your theme customizations as a new workbook theme. This enables you to apply the custom formatting to any workbook just by selecting the custom theme.

① Click the Page Layout tab.

② Click Colors and then either click an existing color scheme or create a new color scheme.

Note: *For more information, see the section, "Create a Custom Color Scheme."*

③ Click Fonts and then either click an existing font scheme or create a new font scheme.

Note: *For more information, see the section, "Create a Custom Font Scheme."*

④ Click Effects and then click the effect scheme you want to use.

⑤ Click Themes.

⑥ Click Save Current Theme.

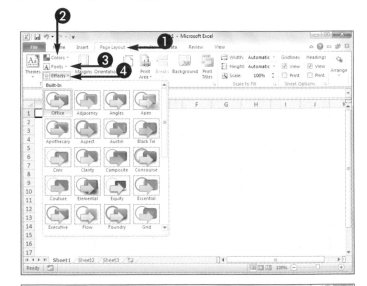

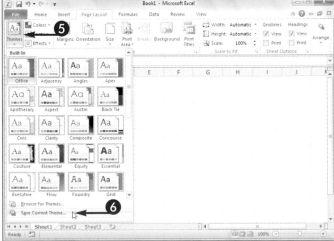

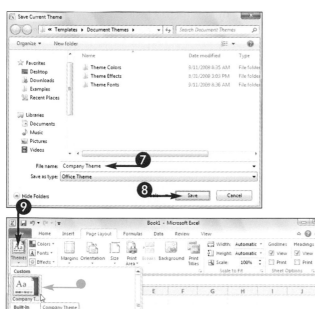

The Save Current Theme dialog box appears.

⑦ Type a name for your custom theme file.

⑧ Click Save.

⑨ Click Themes.

● Your custom theme appears in the Custom section of the Themes gallery.

Try This!

If an existing document theme is close to what you want, you can save some time by using that theme as your starting point. In the Page Layout tab, click the Themes button and then click the theme you want to use. Follow steps 2 to 7 to modify the theme and then save the custom theme file.

Remove It!

If you no longer use a custom workbook theme, you should delete it to reduce clutter in the Themes gallery and to make it easier to navigate your custom themes. Click the Page Layout tab and then click the Themes button. Right-click the custom theme you no longer need, click Delete, and then click Yes when Excel asks you to confirm the deletion.

If you will be printing a workbook, you can enhance the printout by building a custom header and footer that includes information such as the page number, date, filename, and even a picture.

If you will be distributing hard copies of a workbook, it is a good idea to include text that helps the reader understand and read the printout. This text could include the document title, the filename, the page numbers, the current date and time, explanatory text, and so on.

You could add at least some of this text to the actual worksheets, but Excel gives you a more convenient method: the workbook header and footer. The *header* is an area between the top of the page text and the top margin, while the *footer* is an area between the bottom of the page text and the bottom margin. Excel offers a number of tools that make it easy to build a custom header and footer.

Display the Header and Footer Tools

① Click the View tab.

② Click Page Layout.

Excel switches to Page Layout view.

● You can also click the Page Layout button.

③ Click the Click to Add Header text.

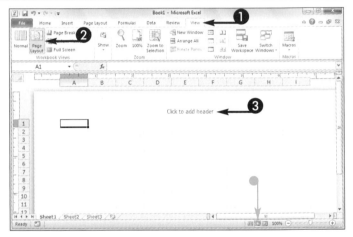

● Excel opens the header area for editing.

● Excel adds the Header & Footer Tools tab.

④ Click the Design tab.

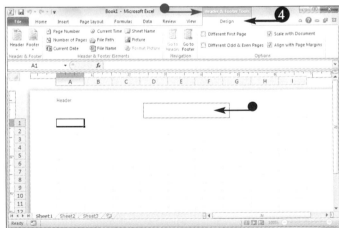

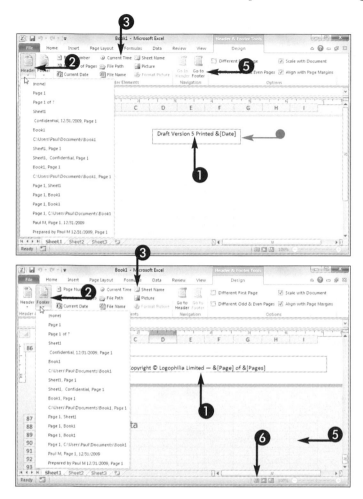

Build a Custom Header

1. Type any text you want in the header.

2. If you want to include a predefined header item, click Header and then click the item.

3. Click a button in the Header & Footer Elements group to add that element to the header.

● Excel inserts a code into the header, such as &[Date] for the Current Date element as shown here.

4. Repeat steps 1 to 3 to build the header.

5. Click Go to Footer.

Build a Custom Footer

1. Type any text you want to display in the footer.

2. If you want to include a predefined footer item, click Footer and then click the item.

3. Click a button in the Header & Footer Elements group to add that element to the footer.

4. Repeat steps 1 to 3 to build the footer.

5. Click outside the footer.

6. Click the Normal icon to exit Page Layout view.

More Options!

You can have a different header and footer on the first page, which is useful if you want to add a title or explanatory text to the first page. In the Design tab, click to select the Different First Page option. You can also have different headers and footers on the even and odd pages of the printout, such as showing the filename on the even pages and the page numbers on the odd pages. In the Design tab, click to select the Different Odd & Even Pages option.

Did You Know?

Before you print the workbook, you might want to get the big picture and see the header, footer, and sheet text all at once. To do this, click File and then click Print. In the Print tab that Excel displays, the right side of the tab shows you a preview of the workbook printout. Click the arrows to scroll through the pages.

Customize the Excel Status Bar

You can make the status bar more useful and easier to read by customizing it to show the information you most want to see.

The Excel status bar offers a great deal of useful information, such as the current cell mode (for example, Enter or Edit), the current zoom percentage, and the sum, average, and count of any numeric cells you have selected.

However, the status bar may not be set up optimally for you. For example, although the status bar includes a Scroll Lock indicator to

tell you when Scroll Lock is on, it does not display the Caps Lock and Num Lock indicators by default, which are arguably more important.

Similarly, you might prefer to see different numeric calculations, such as maximum and minimum values in the selection, or you might prefer to hide the Zoom slider if you never use it.

You can perform all of the customizations and more by using the Customize Status Bar menu.

---

① **Right-click the status bar.**

● Excel displays the Customize Status Bar menu.

● A check mark indicates that the status bar currently displays the item.

● The values shown in the right side of the menu tell you the current value of each item.

② **Click a displayed item to hide it.**

③ **Click a hidden item to display it.**

● Excel removes the item you want to hide from the status bar.

● Excel adds the item that you want to see on the status bar.

④ **Repeat steps 2 and 3 to continue customizing the status bar.**

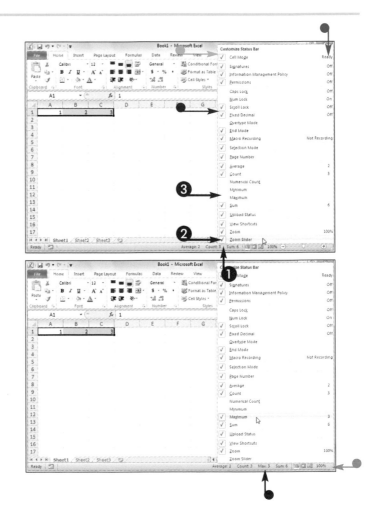

You can create a simpler Excel layout that also gives you more space to work by minimizing the Ribbon.

The Ribbon is an innovative and useful tool, and it is much faster to use than the old pull-down menus once you get used to it. However, the Ribbon is quite large, and so it takes up a lot of precious space in the Excel window that could otherwise be used to display worksheet data. Also, the Ribbon changes as you select different elements within

a worksheet, such as an image, a table, or a chart. This is part of the usefulness of the Ribbon, but these changes can be distracting.

To get more space to work and to simplify the Excel interface, you can minimize the Ribbon so that it shows just the tabs. You can still work with the Ribbon by clicking the tabs, but once you have selected a command or option, Excel minimizes the Ribbon once again.

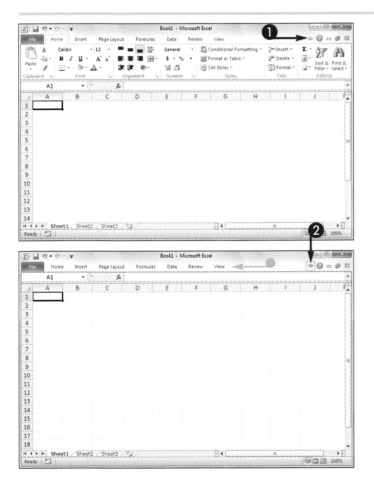

❶ Click the Minimize the Ribbon button.

● Excel displays only the Ribbon tabs.

❷ To restore the Ribbon, click the Minimize the Ribbon button again.

Note: *You can toggle the Ribbon between minimized and displayed by pressing Ctrl+F1 or by right-clicking the Ribbon and then clicking Minimize the Ribbon.*

Chapter

4

Getting More Out of Formulas

Although Excel works well as both a simple database and a data visualization tool, for most people, Excel is all about calculations in general, and formulas in particular. Almost all spreadsheets include at least a few formulas, and many models have dozens of formulas.

Regardless of the size of your spreadsheet, if it contains formulas, then there are tools

and techniques you need to know about to help you get more out of those formulas. These include toggling between displaying formulas and results; monitoring a formula result with a Watch Window; creating array formulas and links to other worksheets; and troubleshooting formula errors.

Quick Tips

Paste a Formula's Result

You can control the output that a copied formula displays by pasting the formula's result rather than the actual formula.

After you copy a formula that uses relative cell references, when you paste the formula, Excel automatically adjusts the cell references. For example, if the destination cell is one row down from the original cell, Excel adds 1 to the value of each row reference in the formula. This is usually welcome behavior because it

helps you to repeat similar formulas without having to retype them.

However, this automatic adjustment of cell references means that you always end up with a different formula after you paste the original. One way to avoid this is to use absolute cell references (see the section, "Use Absolute Cell References in a Formula"). Alternatively, if you are only interested in the formula result, you can paste the copied formula as a value.

---

① **Select the cell containing the formula you want to copy.**

Note: *This task uses a single cell, but the technique also works for a range of cells.*

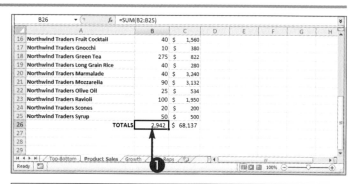

② **Click the Home tab.**

③ **Click the Copy icon.**

Note: *You can also copy the selected cell by pressing Ctrl+C.*

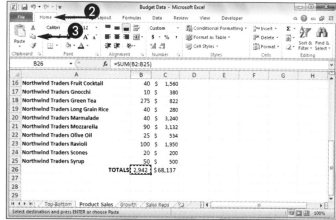

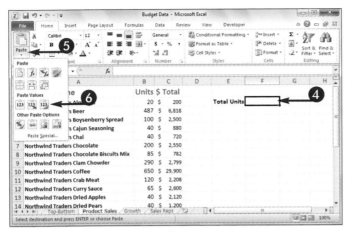

④ Click the cell where you want to paste the formula value.

⑤ Click the Paste drop-down arrow.

⑥ Click a Paste Values option.

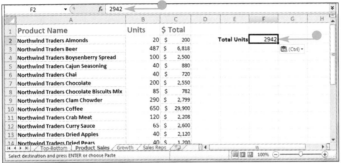

● Excel pastes just the value of the formula, not the actual formula.

More Options!

If the copied cell has a number format applied, or any other cell formatting, when you paste the result using the Paste Values command, Excel does not copy the formatting to the destination cell. To include the original number format in the pasted cell, click the Paste drop-down arrow and click Values & Number Formatting, instead; to transfer all of the original cell formatting, click Values & Source Formatting.

Try This!

If you are interested in displaying a formula result in a particular cell, you can paste just the value of that formula, but that pasted value will be incorrect if the inputs to the formula change in the future. To ensure that a particular cell always displays the current formula result, select the destination cell, press the equals key (=), click the original cell, and then press Enter. This simple formula tells Excel to always display the value of the original cell's formula.

Show Formulas Instead of Results

You can more easily review and troubleshoot a worksheet by changing its display to show the formulas in each cell instead of those formulas' results.

If you want to check the formula for a particular cell, you cannot examine the formula just by looking at the cell because Excel displays the result of the formula instead of the formula. You must click the cell so that Excel displays the formula in the Formula bar.

That is fine for a single cell, but what if you need to check all the formulas in a particular worksheet? You could simply click each cell that contains a formula, but that is impractical in a sheet with dozens of formulas, and it does not enable you to easily compare one formula with another to look for errors or anomalies. Instead, you can change the worksheet view to display the formulas in each cell rather than the formula results.

---

① Switch to the worksheet that contains the formulas you want to display.

② Click the File tab.

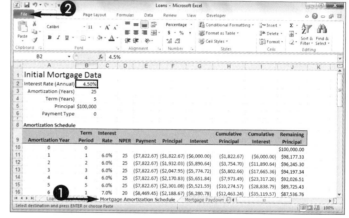

③ Click Options.

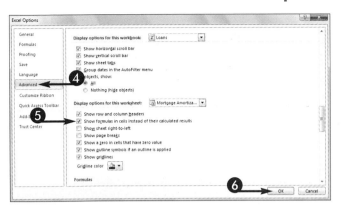

The Excel Options dialog box appears.

④ Click Advanced.

⑤ Click to select the Show Formulas In Cells Instead of Their Calculated Results option.

⑥ Click OK.

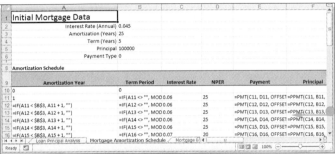

● Excel displays the formulas instead of their results.

Note: You can also toggle the display between formulas and results by pressing Ctrl+`.

Try This!

The technique you learned in this section applies only to the current worksheet. If you want to view the formulas in every sheet in a workbook, run the following VBA macro:

```
Sub ToggleFormulasAndResults()
    Dim win As Window
    Dim wv As WorksheetView
    For Each win In ActiveWorkbook.Windows
        For Each wv In win.SheetViews
            wv.DisplayFormulas = Not wv.DisplayFormulas
        Next 'wv
    Next 'win
End Sub
```

See Chapter 11 to learn how to add and run a VBA macro in Excel.

Use a Watch Window to Monitor a Cell Value

You can make it easier to keep tabs on the value of a particular cell by adding that cell to the Excel Watch Window.

When you build a spreadsheet model, it is often useful to monitor the value of a cell, particularly if that cell contains a formula. For example, if a cell calculates the average of a range of values, you might want to monitor the average as the data changes to see if it reaches a particular value.

Monitoring a cell value is easy if you can see the cell, but that will not always be the case. For example, the data referenced by the cell's formula might reside in a different worksheet or off-screen in the current worksheet. Rather than constantly navigating back and forth to check the cell value, you can use the Excel Watch Window to monitor the value. The Watch Window stays onscreen at all times, so no matter where you are within Excel, you can see the value of the cell.

① Select the value you want to watch.

② Click the Formulas tab.

③ Click Watch Window.

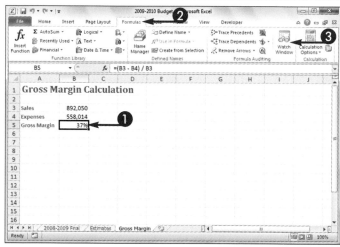

The Watch Window appears.

④ Click Add Watch.

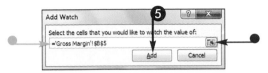

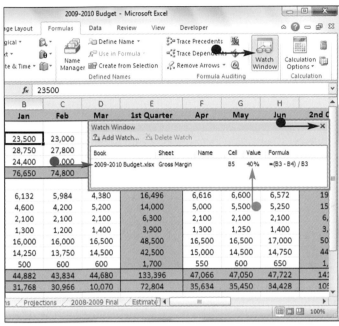

The Add Watch dialog box appears.

● The selected cell appears in the reference box.

● If the cell is incorrect, you can click here and then click the cell you want to monitor.

❺ Click Add.

● Excel adds the cell to the Watch Window.

● The value of the cell appears here.

As you work with Excel, the Watch Window stays on top of the other windows so you can monitor the cell value.

● If the Watch Window gets in the way, you can hide it by either clicking the Close button (X) or by clicking Watch Window in the Formula tab.

Did You Know?

You are not restricted to monitoring just a single cell in the Watch Window. You can add as many watch items as you need. Note, too, that although you can use the Watch Window as a handy way to monitor a cell value, you can also use it to navigate. That is, if you double-click a watch item, Excel automatically selects the corresponding cell.

Remove It!

If you no longer need to monitor a particular cell value, you should delete the cell's watch item to reduce clutter in the Watch Window. Click the Formulas tab and then click Watch Window to open the Watch Window. Click the watch you no longer need, and then click Delete Watch. Excel removes the watch.

Use Absolute Cell References in a Formula

You can improve the accuracy of your formulas and make them easier to copy by using absolute cell references.

When you use a cell reference in a formula, Excel looks at the cell address relative to the location of the formula. For example, suppose that you have the formula =A1*2 in cell A3. To Excel, this formula says, "Multiply the contents of the cell two rows above this one by 2." This is called the *relative reference format,* and it is the default format for Excel. This means that if you copy this formula to cell A4, the relative

reference is still "Multiply the contents of the cell two rows above this one by 2," but the formula changes to =A2*2 because A2 is two rows above A4.

When you refer to a cell in a formula using the *absolute reference format* — such as A1 instead of A1 — Excel uses the physical address of the cell. For example, Excel interprets the formula =A1*2 as "Multiply the contents of cell A1 by 2." No matter where you copy this formula, the cell reference does not change.

---

① Select the cell that contains the formula you want to edit.

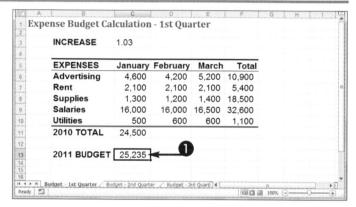

② Press F2.

● Excel opens the cell for editing.

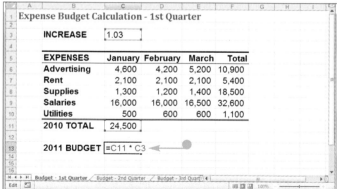

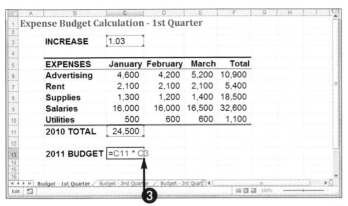

③ Place the cursor inside the cell reference you want to work with.

④ Press F4.

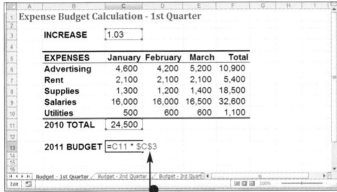

● Excel converts the reference to absolute format by adding a dollar sign ($) before the column letter and before the row number.

Note: *You can also convert a relative reference to absolute format by inserting the dollar signs manually.*

⑤ Press Enter.

Did You Know?

Excel also supports the *mixed referenced format*, which combines relative and absolute references. For example, a reference such as $A1 uses an absolute reference for column A, but a relative reference for row 1. Similarly, A$1 uses a relative reference for column A, but an absolute reference for row 1. Use mixed references when you want to copy a cell but keep either the column or row the same in the copied cells.

Remove It!

If you no longer need to use an absolute reference to a particular cell, you can edit the formula to use a relative reference. Select the cell, press F2, and then place the cursor within the absolute reference. Either press F4 until you get a relative reference (that is, all the dollar signs are removed), or delete the dollar signs manually.

You can use an array formula to enter a formula into multiple cells using just a single operation. This can save you a lot of time when you have to enter the same formula into many different cells.

When you work with a range of cells, it might appear as though you are working with a single thing. In reality, however, Excel treats the range as a number of discrete units.

This is in contrast to an *array*, which is a group of cells or values that Excel treats as a

unit. In a range configured as an array, for example, Excel no longer treats the cells individually. Instead, it works with all the cells at once, which enables you to do things such as apply a formula to every cell in the range using just a single operation.

One way to create an array is to use an *array formula*, which is a single formula that enters its results in multiple cells.

① Select the range you want to use for the array formula.

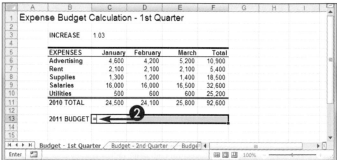

② Type = to start your formula.

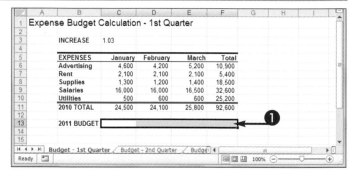

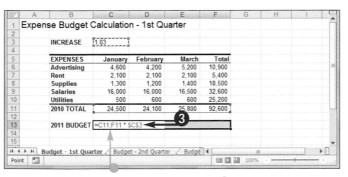

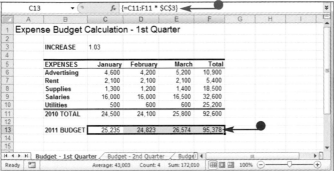

③ Type your formula.

● In the places where you would normally enter a cell reference, you can type a range reference that includes the cells you want to use.

④ When the formula is complete, press Ctrl+Shift+Enter.

● Excel enters the array formula into all the selected cells.

● The formula is surrounded by braces ({ and }). This identifies the formula as an array formula.

Note: *When you enter array formulas, you never need to enter these braces yourself; Excel adds them automatically.*

Did You Know?

In an array formula, Excel sets up a correspondence between the array cells and the cells of the range used in the formula. In this section's example, the array consists of cells C13 through F13, and the range used in the formula consists of cells C11 through F11. Excel sets up a correspondence between array cell C13 and input cell C11, between D13 and D11, and so on. To calculate the value of cell C13, for example, Excel takes the value from cell C11 and substitutes that in the formula.

Change It!

Excel treats arrays as a unit, so you cannot move or delete part of an array. If you need to work with an array, you must select the entire range. Note that you can select an array quickly by selecting one of its cells and pressing Ctrl+/. If you want to reduce the size of an array, select it, click inside the formula bar, and then press Ctrl+Enter to change the entry to a normal formula. You can then select the smaller range and re-enter the array formula.

Apply Range Names to Formulas

You can save a great deal of time and effort by getting Excel to replace range references in your formulas with the corresponding range name.

If you have been using range references in your formulas and you name those ranges later, Excel will not automatically apply the new names to the formulas. Fortunately, you can get Excel to automatically replace range addresses with the corresponding range names.

By default, Excel also renames all cell references that can be described as the intersection of a named row and a named column. For example, if you have a tabular range with a row named January and a column named Rent, Excel applies the name January Rent to the cell that is the intersection of these two ranges.

---

① Select the range in which you want to apply the names.

Note: *Select a single cell if you want to apply the names to the entire worksheet.*

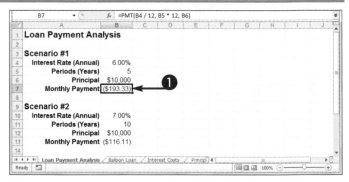

② Click the Formulas tab.

③ Click the Define Name drop-down arrow.

④ Click Apply Names.

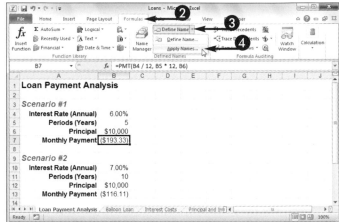

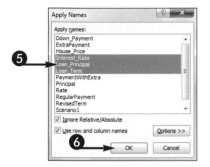

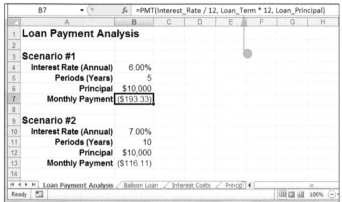

The Apply Names dialog box appears.

⑤ Click each name that you want to apply.

⑥ Click OK.

● Excel replaces range references with the corresponding range names.

More Options!
In the Apply Names dialog box, if you select the Ignore Relative/ Absolute option, Excel replaces relative range references only with names that refer to relative references, and it replaces absolute range references only with names that refer to absolute references.

More Options!
When Excel uses the names of rows and columns to rename cell references, it automatically omits the column name if all the references in a formula refer to the same column. To change this, in the Apply Names dialog box, click Options and then select the Omit Column Name If Same Column option. You can also tell Excel not to omit row names by selecting the Omit Row Name If Same Row option.

Create a Link to Another Worksheet

You can save time and add flexibility to your formulas by creating links to cells that reside in other worksheets. This enables you to take advantage of work you have done in other worksheets, so that you do not have to waste time repeating your work on the current worksheet.

You will often need to use a previously calculated result as part of a new formula. For example, if profit is up this year, but you want to know by how much, you must create a formula that subtracts last year's profits from this year's profits. Assuming your current worksheet contains a calculation for this year's profits, how do you include last year's profits in your formula? One way would be to look up the number and then just copy it to your formula, but that is problematic because you might copy the number incorrectly or the number might change.

The better solution is to create a link in your formula that references the cell that holds the profits result from last year.

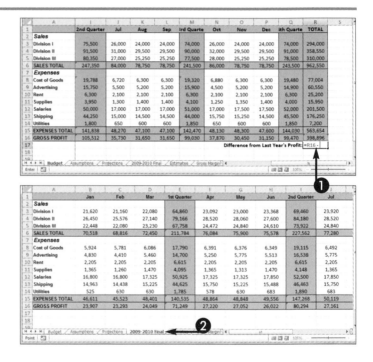

① Click in the cell in which you want to build the formula, type =, and then type any operands and operators you need before adding the range reference.

② Press Ctrl+Page Down until the worksheet you want to use appears.

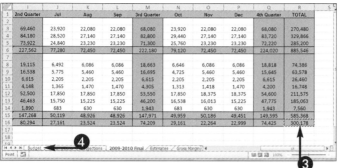

	Jul	Aug	Sep	rd Quarte	Oct	Nov	Dec	th Quarte	TOTAL
Sales									
Division I	26,000	24,000	24,000	74,000	26,000	24,000	24,000	74,000	294,000
Division II	31,000	29,500	29,500	90,000	32,000	29,500	29,500	91,000	358,550
Division III	27,000	25,250	25,250	77,500	28,000	25,250	25,250	78,500	310,000
SALES TOTAL	84,000	78,750	78,750	241,500	86,000	78,750	78,750	243,500	962,550
Expenses									
Cost of Goods	6,720	6,300	6,300	19,320	6,880	6,300	6,300	19,480	77,004
Advertising	5,500	5,200	5,200	15,900	4,500	5,200	5,200	14,900	60,550
Rent	2,100	2,100	2,100	6,300	2,100	2,100	2,100	6,300	25,200
Supplies	1,300	1,400	1,400	4,100	1,250	1,350	1,400	4,000	15,950
Salaries	17,000	17,000	17,000	51,000	17,000	17,500	17,500	52,000	201,500
Shipping	15,000	14,500	14,500	44,000	15,750	15,250	14,500	45,500	176,250
Utilities	650	600	600	1,850	650	600	600	1,850	7,200
EXPENSES TOTAL	48,270	47,100	47,100	142,470	48,130	48,300	47,600	144,030	563,654
GROSS PROFIT	35,730	31,650	31,650	99,030	37,870	30,450	31,150	99,470	398,896

Difference from Last Year's Profit: =R16 - '2009-2010 Final'!R16

③ Select the range you want to use.

④ Press Ctrl+Page Up until you return to the original worksheet.

● A reference to the range on the other worksheet appears in your formula.

⑤ Type any operands and operators you need to complete your formula.

⑥ Press Enter.

Excel calculates the formula result.

TIPS

Did You Know?

Rather than selecting the other worksheet range with your mouse, you can type the range reference directly into your formula. Type the worksheet name, surrounded by single quotation marks (') if the name contains a space; then type an exclamation mark (!); finally, type the cell or range address. An example would be 'Expenses 2010'!B2:B10.

Did You Know?

You can also create a link to a cell in another workbook. First, make sure that the workbook you want to reference is open. When you reach the point in your formula where you want to add the reference, click the Excel icon ([XI]) in the Windows taskbar, and then, in the list of open workbooks that appears, click the other workbook to switch to it. Click the worksheet tab that has the range you want to reference, and then select the range. Click the Excel icon and then click the original workbook to switch back to it. Excel adds the other workbook range reference to your formula.

Combine Two Ranges Arithmetically

You can manipulate one range's data in a separate range by using the Excel Paste Special command to combine this range with another range using a mathematical operation such as addition or multiplication.

When you are building a spreadsheet, you may sometimes find that the data you are using is not correct, or is not producing the answers you seek. For example, a particular range of numbers might need to be doubled, or a range's data may work better if every value is increased by 10.

One way to approach this situation would be to create a new range that includes formulas that produce the data you want. For example,

if you want a range's data doubled, you can create a new range where each cell references one of the original cells and multiplies it by 2. Unfortunately, you cannot then delete the original cells because doing so would produce errors in the new formulas.

You can avoid this problem by creating a new range that has the factor you want to use to modify the original range, and then combining the two ranges using the appropriate arithmetic operation. Note that the new range does not have to consist only of constant values, as in the examples here; the new range can use whatever values you require.

---

① Create a range that includes the factor by which you want to modify the original range.

Note: *The new range must be the same size and shape as the original range.*

② Select the original range.

③ Click the Home tab.

④ Click the Copy icon.

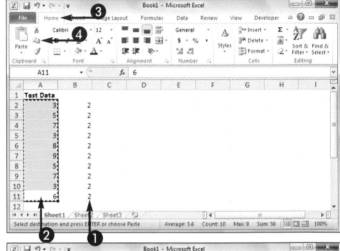

⑤ Select the range that contains the factors.

⑥ Click the Paste drop-down arrow.

⑦ Click Paste Special.

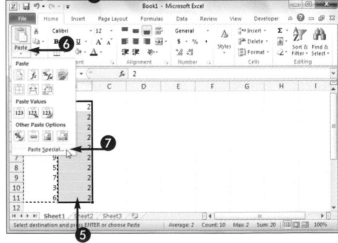

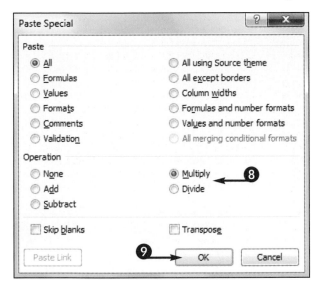

The Paste Special dialog box appears.

⑧ Click to select the arithmetic operation you want to use.

⑨ Click OK.

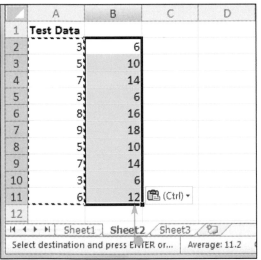

● Excel combines the two ranges using the arithmetic operation you selected.

More Options!

If your original data is in a column but your range of factors is in a row, you can still combine the two ranges arithmetically. (This is also true if your original range is a row and your factor range is a column.) Follow steps 1 to 7 to open the Paste Special dialog box and select the arithmetic operation you want to use. Click to select the Transpose option near the bottom of the Paste Special dialog box, and then click OK.

Troubleshoot a Formula by Stepping Through Each Part

If you have a formula that is returning an inaccurate or erroneous result, you can troubleshoot the problem by stepping through each part of the formula.

Simple formulas that add or multiply a few numbers or use a straightforward function such as SUM are usually easy to troubleshoot because they contain only a few operators and operands.

However, many Excel formulas can be quite complex, with functions nested inside other functions, multiple sets of parentheses, several different operators, multiple range references, and so on. These more involved formulas are much harder to troubleshoot because it is often not obvious what part of the formula is causing the trouble.

You can use the Evaluate Formula command to help troubleshoot such formulas. This command enables you to step through the various parts of the formula to see the preliminary results returned by each part. By examining these interim results, you can often see where your formula goes awry.

If you still have trouble pinpointing the error, see the section "Audit a Formula to Locate Errors," later in this chapter.

---

① Select the cell that contains the formula you want to troubleshoot.

② Click the Formulas tab.

③ Click Evaluate Formula.

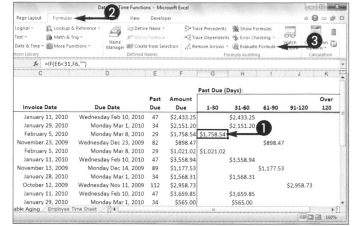

The Evaluate Formula dialog box appears.

● Excel underlines the first expression that it will evaluate.

④ Click Evaluate.

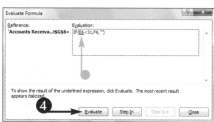

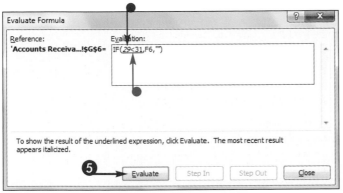

● Excel evaluates the underlined term and then displays the result in italics.

● Excel underlines the next expression that it will evaluate.

⑤ Click Evaluate.

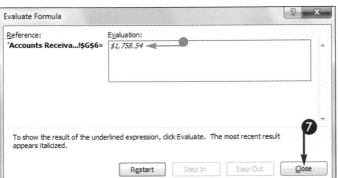

⑥ Repeat step 5 to continue evaluating the formula's expressions.

Note: Continue evaluating the formula until you find the error or want to stop the evaluation.

● If you evaluate all the terms in the formula, Excel displays the final result.

⑦ Click Close.

More Options!

If you do not see where your formula is going wrong, it is possible that the error exists in one of the cells referenced by the formula. To check this, when Excel underlines the cell reference, click the Step In button at the bottom of the Evaluate Formula dialog box. This tells Excel to display that cell's formula in the Evaluate Formula dialog box, so you can then evaluate this secondary formula to look for problems. To return to the main formula, click the Step Out button.

Try This!

If you suspect that a particular expression is causing the problem, you may not want to step through the rest of the formula to test this one expression. To avoid this, open the formula cell for editing, and then select the expression that you want to evaluate. Either click the Formulas tab and then click Calculate Now (▥) in the Calculation group, or press F9. Excel evaluates the selected expression. Press Esc when you are done.

Skip Data Tables When Calculating Workbooks

You can reduce the time it takes for Excel to calculate a workbook if you configure Excel to bypass data tables when it is recalculating the workbook.

When you are analyzing data with Excel, if you are interested in studying the effect a range of values has on the formula, it is often useful to set up a data table. You learn how to do this in Chapter 5.

Because a data table is an array, Excel treats it as a unit, so a worksheet recalculation means

that the entire data table is always recalculated. This is not a big problem for a small data table that has a few dozen formulas. However, it is not uncommon to have data tables with hundreds or even thousands of formulas, and these larger data tables can really slow down worksheet recalculation. To avoid this problem, you can configure Excel to skip data tables when it calculates worksheets.

① Click the File tab.

② Click Options.

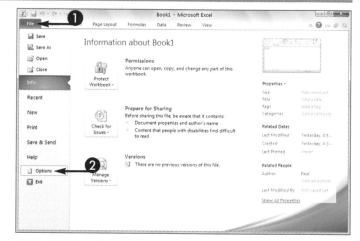

The Excel Options dialog box appears.

③ Click Formulas.

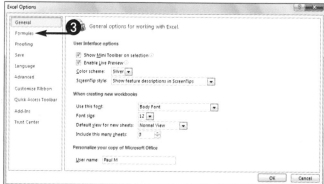

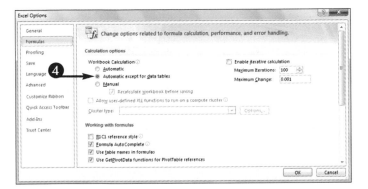

④ Click to select the Automatic Except for Data Tables option.

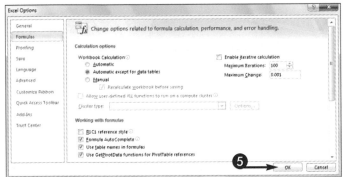

⑤ Click OK.

The next time you calculate a workbook, Excel bypasses the data tables.

Try This!

When you want to recalculate a data table, you can follow steps 1 to 3, click to deselect the Automatic Except for Data Tables option, click OK, and then recalculate the workbook. On the other hand, you might prefer to leave the Automatic Except for Data Tables option selected. In that case, to recalculate the data table you select any cell inside the data table and press F9.

More Options!

If you often turn the Automatic Except for Data Tables option on and off, Excel offers a faster method for toggling this setting. Click the Formulas tab, click Calculation Options in the Calculation group, and then select the Automatic Except for Data Tables option. Alternatively, from the keyboard, press Alt+M, press X, and then press E.

You can perform certain types of Excel calculations by using the iterative calculation feature.

In some Excel calculations, you cannot derive the answer directly. Instead, you need to perform a preliminary calculation, feed that answer into the formula to get a new result, feed the new result into the formula, and so on. The idea is that each new result gets closer to — *converges* on — the actual answer. The process of plugging the preliminary results back into the formula is called *iteration*.

As an example, consider a formula that calculates net profit by subtracting the amount paid out in profit sharing from the gross profit. This is not a simple subtraction because the profit sharing amount is calculated as a percentage of the net profit. To solve this problem, you set up your formula and then let Excel iterate the result.

---

① Build a formula that requires an iterative calculation to solve.

● Circular reference arrows are displayed in the table.

● In the Formulas tab, you can click Remove Arrows to hide the circular reference arrows.

② Click the File tab.

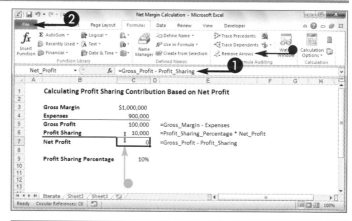

③ Click Options.

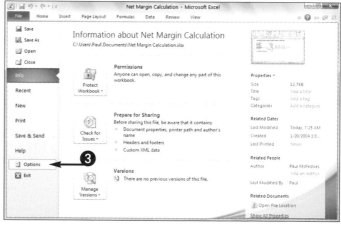

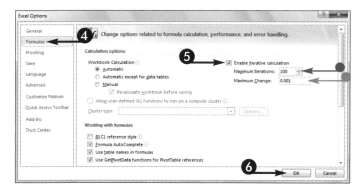

The Excel Options dialog box appears.

④ Click Formulas.

⑤ Click to select the Enable Iterative Calculation option.

● If Excel fails to converge on the solution, you can try typing a higher value in the Maximum Iterations text box.

● If you want a more accurate solution, you can try typing a smaller value in the Maximum Change text box.

Note: *The Maximum Change value tells Excel how accurate you want your results to be. The smaller the number, the more accurate the calculation, but the iteration takes longer.*

⑥ Click OK.

Excel performs the iteration.

● The iterated result appears in the formula cell.

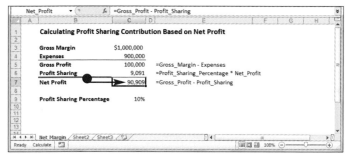

Important!

You see in this task that after you build your formula, Excel displays circular reference arrows. These arrows usually indicate an error, but not in this case. When you set up an iterative calculation, you are by definition setting up a circular reference formula because there are terms on the left and right sides of the equals sign that depend on each other. In this section's example, the formula in C7 references the Profit_Sharing cell, which is C6. However, the Profit_Sharing cell references the Net_Profit cell, which is C7, so the references are circular.

Try This!

It can sometimes be useful to watch the progress of the iteration one step at a time. To set this up, follow steps 1 to 4 to open the Excel Options dialog box and display the Formulas tab. Select the Manual option, and type **1** in the Maximum Iterations text box. Click OK to return to your worksheet. Now, each time you press F9, Excel performs a single pass of the iteration.

Display Text Rather than Error Values

You can avoid unsightly and unhelpful error values in your worksheets by using the IFERROR function to display a text string rather than an error.

If Excel encounters an error when calculating a formula, it often displays an error value as the result. For example, if your formula divides by zero, Excel indicates the error by displaying the value #DIV/0 in the cell.

This is often useful because it lets you know that a formula did not calculate properly, so you can investigate the problem. However,

there may be times when you know the error is temporary or is otherwise unimportant. For example, if your worksheet is missing some data, then a blank cell might be causing the #DIV/0 error.

Rather than displaying an error value, you can use the IFERROR function to test for an error and display a more useful result in the cell:

IFERROR(*expression*, *error_result*)

Here, *expression* is the formula you are using, and *error_result* is the text you want Excel to display if the formula produces an error.

① Select the range that contains the formulas you want to edit.

② Press F2.

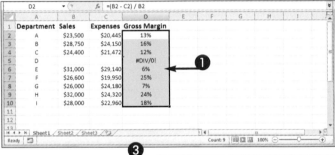

● Excel opens the first cell for editing.

③ After the formula's equals sign (=), type **iferror(**.

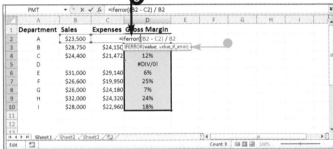

116

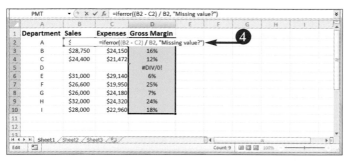

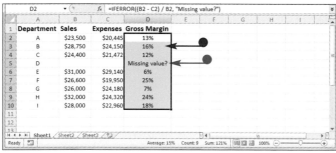

④ After the formula, type a comma followed by the text, in quotation marks, that you want Excel to display in place of any error, followed by a closing parenthesis.

⑤ Press Ctrl+Enter.

● Excel displays the formula result in cells where there is no error.

● Excel displays the text message in cells that generate an error.

TIP

Did You Know?
Excel has a number of error values that it can generate. The following six are the most common:

Excel's Most Common Error Values	
Error	**Description**
#DIV/0	Your formula is dividing by zero. Check the divisor input cells for values that are either zero or blank.
#N/A	Your formula could not return a legitimate result. Check that your function arguments are appropriate for each function.
#NAME?	Your formula uses a range name or function name that Excel does not recognize. Check your range names and function names.
#NUM!	Your formula uses a number inappropriately. For example, you entered a negative number as the argument for the SQRT(). Check the arguments for your mathematical functions to make sure they use the correct types of numbers.
#REF#	Your formula contains an invalid cell reference. This usually occurs when you delete a cell referenced by a formula. Restore the deleted cell or adjust the formula to use a different cell.
#VALUE!	Your formula uses an inappropriate value in a function argument. For example, you might have used a string value instead of a numeric value. Check your function arguments to make sure they use the correct data type.

Check for Formula Errors in a Worksheet

You can take advantage of the background error checking in Excel to look for formula errors in a worksheet.

If you use Microsoft Word, you are probably familiar with the wavy green lines that appear under words and phrases that the grammar checker has flagged as being incorrect. The grammar checker operates by using a set of rules that determine correct grammar and syntax. As you type, the grammar checker operates in the background and constantly monitors your writing. If something you write goes against one of the grammar checker's

rules, the wavy line appears to let you know there is a problem.

Excel has a similar feature: the formula error checker. It is similar to the grammar checker, in that it uses a set of rules to determine correctness, and it operates in the background to monitor your formulas. If it detects that something is amiss, it displays an *error indicator* — a green triangle — in the upper-left corner of the cell containing the formula. You can then use the associated smart tag to see a description of the error and to either fix or ignore the error.

1 Examine your worksheet for a cell that displays the error indicator.

2 Click the cell.

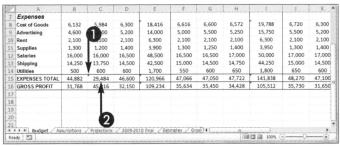

- The error smart tag appears.

3 Move the mouse pointer over the smart tag.

- Excel displays a description of the error.

4 Click the smart tag.

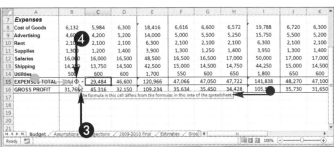

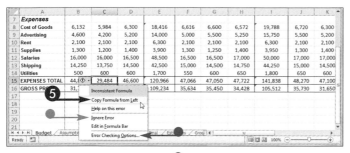

- Excel displays the smart tag options.

⑤ Click the command that fixes the formula.

Note: The name of the command depends on the error. You only see this command if Excel can fix the error.

- If the formula is not an error, you can click Ignore Error, instead.

- Excel adjusts the formula.

- Excel removes the error indicator from the cell.

⑥ Repeat steps 1 to 5 until you have checked all your worksheet formula errors.

TIPS

Customize It!

To pick and choose which error-checking rules you want Excel to enforce, click the File icon, click Options to display the Excel Options dialog box, and then click the Formulas tab. (Alternatively, click an error smart tab and then click Error Checking Options in the drop-down list that appears.) In the Error Checking Rules section, click to deselect the check box of any rule you do not want Excel to enforce. Click OK.

Customize It!

If your workbook uses green colors for text or cell backgrounds, or if you have clip art, SmartArt, or other graphics that use a great deal of green, then you might not notice the error indicators. To use a different color, click the File icon, click Options to display the Excel Options dialog box, and then click the Formulas tab. In the Error Checking section, use the Indicate Errors Using This Color list to click the color you prefer, and then click OK.

Audit a Formula to Locate Errors

If you know or suspect that a formula error is caused by an error in another cell, you can audit the formula to locate the cell that is causing the error.

If a formula error is the result of referencing other cells that contain errors or inappropriate values, you must determine which cell is causing the error. This is straightforward if the formula references only a single cell, but it becomes progressively more difficult as the number of references increases.

To determine which cell is causing the error in your formula, you can use the auditing features

in Excel to visualize and trace a formula's input values and error sources. Auditing operates by creating *tracers* — arrows that literally point out the cells involved in a formula. You can use tracers to find three kinds of cells: *precedents*, which are cells that are directly or indirectly referenced in a formula; *dependents*, which are cells that are directly or indirectly referenced by a formula in another cell; and *errors*, which are cells that contain an error value and are directly or indirectly referenced in a formula.

Trace Precedents

1 Click the cell containing the formula whose precedents you want to trace.

2 Click the Formulas tab.

3 Click Trace Precedents.

● Excel adds a tracer arrow to each direct precedent.

4 Repeat step 3 until you have added tracer arrows for all the formula's indirect precedents.

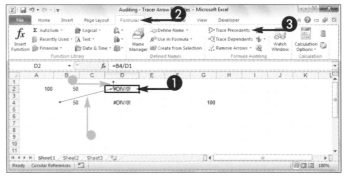

Trace Dependents

1 Click the cell containing the formula whose dependents you want to trace.

2 Click the Formulas tab.

3 Click Trace Dependents.

● Excel adds a tracer arrow to each direct dependent.

4 Repeat step 3 until you have added tracer arrows for all the formula's indirect dependents.

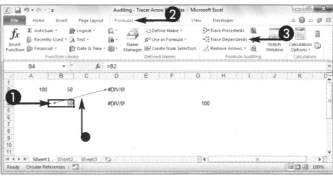

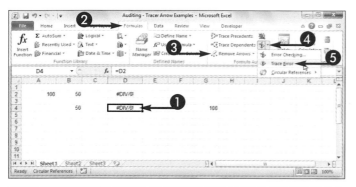

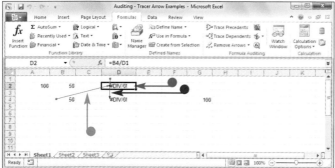

Trace Errors

1 Click the cell containing the error you want to trace.

2 Click the Formulas tab.

3 Click Remove Arrows.

Note: You must first remove any existing arrows before you can trace an error.

4 Click here to display the Error Checking drop-down list.

5 Click Trace Error.

● Excel selects the cells that contain the original error.

● Excel displays tracer arrows showing the selected cells' precedents and dependents.

● A red tracer arrow indicates an error.

More Options!

If you have a large spreadsheet, you can use the Error Checking feature to look for and trace errors. Click the Formulas tab, and then click Error Checking (🔲) in the Formula Auditing group. Excel displays the Error Checking dialog box, which displays the first error, if any. You have the following choices:

● Trace Error: You see this button if the error is caused by an error in another cell. Click this button to display tracer arrows for the formula's precedents and dependents.

● Show Calculation Steps: You see this button if the error is caused by the cell's formula. Click this button to launch the Evaluate Formula feature, as described in the section, "Troubleshoot a Formula by Stepping Through Each Part."

● Ignore Error: Click this button to bypass the error.

Use the Previous and Next buttons to navigate the worksheet errors.

Analyzing Excel Data

Excel is an excellent tool for storing data and for building formulas that manipulate that data in some way to produce a result. However, you will often need to examine your Excel data to look for patterns, view a range of solutions to a problem, or perform complex calculations that go beyond a single formula. These more advanced uses of Excel comprise *data analysis*, which is the subject of this chapter.

Here you will learn a number of useful data analysis techniques, including highlighting

cells that meet some criteria; visualizing data with data bars, color scales, and icon sets; and creating your own rules for applying conditional formats to cells.

In this chapter you will also learn about several of the most useful and powerful features in Excel, including data tables, scenarios, Goal Seek, worksheet consolidation, filtering, outlines, and the Analysis ToolPak add-in.

Quick Tips

Highlight Cells That Meet Some Criteria

You can make a worksheet easier to analyze by applying a conditional format to a range so those cells stand out.

A conditional format is formatting that Excel applies only to cells that meet the criteria you specify. For example, you can tell Excel to only apply the formatting if a cell's value is greater or less than some specified amount, between two specified values, or equal to some value.

You can also look for cells that contain specified text, cells with dates that occur during a specified timeframe, and more.

When you set up your conditional format, you can specify the font, border, and background pattern, which helps to ensure that the cells that meet your criteria stand out from the other cells in the range.

① Select the range you want to work with.

② Click the Home tab.

③ Click Conditional Formatting.

④ Click Highlight Cells Rules.

⑤ Click the operator you want to use for the condition.

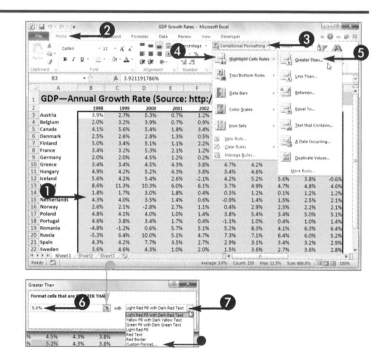

A dialog box appears, whose name depends on the operator you clicked in step 5.

⑥ Type the value you want to use for the condition.

● You can also click here and then click in a worksheet cell.

Depending on the operator, you may need to specify two values.

⑦ Click here and then click the formatting you want to use.

● To create your own format, click Custom Format.

Greater Than

Format cells that are GREATER THAN:

| 5.0% | | with | Light Red Fill with Dark Red Text ▾ |

8

OK   Cancel

8 Click OK.

● Excel applies the formatting to cells that meet the condition you specified.

GDP Growth Rates - Microsoft Excel

A1   *fx* GDP—Annual Growth Rate (Source: http://swivel.com/)

GDP—Annual Growth Rate (Source: http://swivel.com/)

	A	1998	1999	2000	2001	2002	2003	2004	2005	2006	2007
3	Austria	3.9%	2.7%	5.3%	0.7%	1.2%	0.8%	2.2%	1.9%	2.6%	2.1%
4	Belgium	2.0%	3.2%	3.9%	0.7%	0.9%	1.3%	2.9%	1.5%	2.1%	1.8%
5	Canada	4.1%	5.6%	5.4%	1.8%	3.4%	2.0%	2.9%	4.6%	3.2%	2.8%
6	Denmark	2.5%	2.6%	2.8%	1.3%	0.5%	0.7%	2.4%	3.4%	2.5%	2.1%
7	Finland	5.0%	3.4%	5.1%	1.1%	2.2%	2.4%	3.7%	3.3%	3.7%	2.8%
8	France	3.4%	3.2%	5.3%	1.2%	0.2%	0.0%	1.6%	1.2%	1.9%	2.0%
9	Germany	2.0%	2.0%	4.5%	1.2%	0.2%	0.0%	1.6%	1.2%	1.9%	1.1%
10	Greece	3.4%	3.4%	4.5%	4.3%	3.8%	4.7%	4.2%	3.7%	3.5%	3.2%
11	Hungary	4.9%	4.2%	5.2%	4.3%	3.8%	3.4%	4.6%	4.1%	3.5%	3.6%
12	Iceland	5.6%	4.2%	5.4%	2.6%	-2.1%	4.2%	5.2%	5.6%	3.8%	-0.6%
13	Ireland	8.6%	11.3%	10.3%	6.0%	6.1%	3.7%	4.9%	4.7%	4.8%	4.6%
14	Italy	1.8%	1.7%	3.0%	1.8%	0.4%	0.3%	1.2%	0.1%	1.2%	1.2%
15	Netherlands	4.3%	4.0%	3.5%	1.4%	0.6%	-0.9%	1.4%	1.5%	2.5%	2.1%
16	Norway	2.6%	2.1%	-2.8%	2.7%	1.1%	0.4%	2.9%	2.5%	2.2%	2.1%
17	Poland	4.8%	4.1%	4.0%	1.0%	1.4%	3.8%	5.4%	3.4%	5.0%	5.1%
18	Portugal	4.6%	3.8%	3.4%	1.7%	0.4%	-1.1%	1.0%	0.4%	1.0%	1.4%
19	Romania	-4.8%	-1.2%	0.6%	5.7%	5.1%	5.2%	8.3%	4.1%	6.3%	6.4%
20	Russia	-5.3%	6.4%	10.0%	5.1%	4.7%	7.3%	7.1%	6.4%	6.0%	5.2%
21	Spain	4.3%	4.2%	7.7%	3.5%	2.7%	2.9%	3.1%	3.4%	3.2%	2.9%
22	Sweden	3.6%	4.6%	4.3%	1.0%	2.0%	1.5%	3.6%	2.7%	3.6%	2.8%

Sheet1 / Sheet2 / Sheet3

Ready   100%

TIPS

More Options!

Excel enables you to specify multiple conditional formats. For example, you could set up one condition for cells that are greater than some value, and a separate condition for cells that are less than some other value. You can apply unique formats to each condition. Follow steps 1 to 8 to configure the new condition.

Remove It!

If you no longer require a conditional format, you can delete it. Follow steps 1 to 3 to select the range and display the Conditional Formatting drop-down menu, and then click Manage Rules. Excel displays the Conditional Formatting Rules Manager dialog box. Click the conditional format you want to remove and then click Delete Rule.

Highlight the Top or Bottom Values in a Range

To quickly and easily view the extreme values in a range, you can apply a conditional format to the top or bottom values of that range.

When you are analyzing worksheet data, it is often useful to look for items that stand out from the norm. For example, you might want to know which sales reps sold the most last year, or which departments had the lowest gross margins.

Excel enables you to perform these kinds of analyses by setting up *top/bottom rules,* where

Excel applies a conditional format to those items in a range that are at the top or bottom of that range of values.

For the top or bottom values, you can specify a number, such as the top 5 or 10, or a percentage, such as the bottom 20 percent.

When you set up your top/bottom rule, you can specify the font, border, and background pattern, which helps to ensure that the cells that meet your criteria stand out from the other cells in the range.

1 Select the range you want to work with.

2 Click the Home tab.

3 Click Conditional Formatting.

4 Click Top/Bottom Rules.

5 Click the type of rule you want to create.

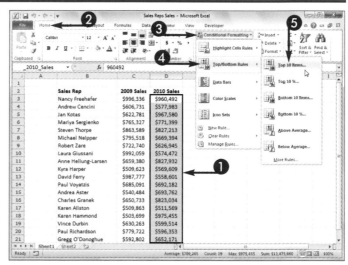

A dialog box appears, whose name depends on the type of rule you clicked in step 5.

6 Type the value you want to use for the condition.

7 Click here and then click the formatting you want to use.

● To create your own format, click Custom Format.

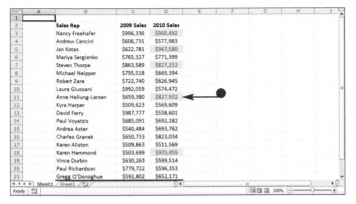

⑧ Click OK.

● Excel applies the formatting to cells that meet the condition you specified.

More Options!

Excel also enables you to create top/bottom rules based on the average value in the range. First, follow steps 1 to 4 to select the range and display the Top/Bottom Rules menu. Then click either Above Average to format those values that exceed the range average, or Below Average to format those values that are less than the range average.

Remove It!

If you no longer require a top/bottom rule, you can delete it. Follow steps 1 to 3 to select the range and display the Conditional Formatting drop-down menu. Click Clear Rules, and then click Clear Rules from Selected Cells. Excel removes the rule from the range.

Analyze Cell Values with Data Bars

You can analyze how the values in a range relate to one another by applying data bars to each cell in the range.

In some data analysis scenarios, you might be more interested in the relative values within a range than the absolute values. For example, if you have a table of products that includes a column showing unit sales, how do you compare the relative sales of all the products?

This sort of analysis is often easiest if you visualize the relative values. You can do that by

using *data bars*. Data bars are a data visualization feature that applies colored, horizontal bars to each cell in a range of values, and these bars appear "behind" the values in the range. Their key feature is that the length of the data bar that appears in each cell depends on the value in that cell: the larger the value, the longer the data bar. The cell with the highest value has the longest data bar, and the data bars that appear in the other cells have lengths that reflect their values.

① Select the range you want to work with.

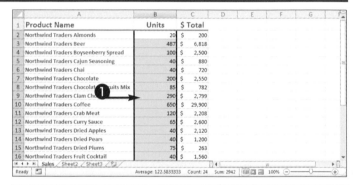

② Click the Home tab.

③ Click Conditional Formatting.

④ Click Data Bars.

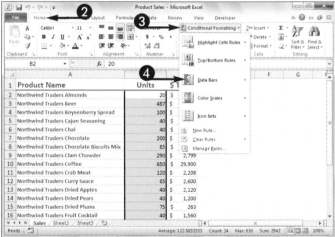

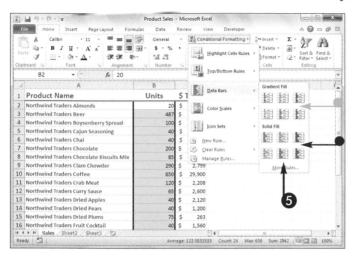

⑤ Click the fill type of data bars you want to create.

● Gradient Fill data bars begin with a solid color and then gradually fade to white.

● Solid Fill data bars are a solid color.

● Excel applies the data bars to each cell in the range.

TIPS

Did You Know?

If your range includes right-aligned values, the Gradient Fill data bars are a better choice than the Solid Fill data bars. This is because even the longest Gradient Fill bars fade to white towards the right edge of the cell, so your range values should mostly appear on a white background, making them easier to read.

Remove It!

If you no longer require the data bars, you can remove them. Follow steps 1 to 3 to select the range and display the Conditional Formatting drop-down menu, and then click Manage Rules. Excel displays the Conditional Formatting Rules Manager dialog box. Click the Data Bar rule you want to remove and then click Delete Rule.

Analyze Cell Values with Color Scales

You can analyze the distribution of values in a range, you can pick out anomalous values, and you can make value judgments about the data by applying color scales to each cell in the range.

When analyzing worksheet data, it is often useful to get some idea about the overall distribution of the values. For example, it might be useful to know whether a range has a lot of low values and just a few high values.

Similarly, you might want to know if the range includes any *outliers,* values that are much higher or lower than all or most of the other values.

Finally, you may also want to make value judgments about your data. For example, high sales and low numbers of product defects are "good," whereas low margins and high employee turnover rates are "bad."

You can analyze your worksheet data by using *color scales.* A color scale compares the relative values of cells in a range by applying shading to each cell, where the shading color is a reflection of the cell's value.

---

① **Select the range you want to work with.**

② **Click the Home tab.**

③ **Click Conditional Formatting.**

④ **Click Color Scales.**

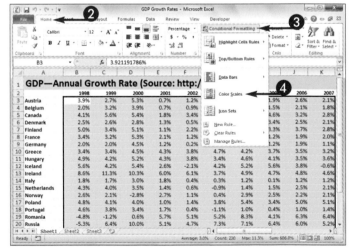

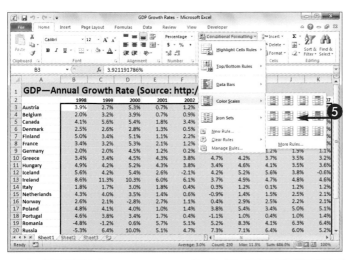

⑤ Click the color scale that has the color scheme you want to apply.

● Excel applies the color scales to each cell in the range.

Did You Know?

Excel color scales come in two varieties: 3-color scales and 2-color scales. If your goal is to look for outliers or to make value judgments about your data, go with a 3-color scale because outliers stand out more, and you can assign your own values to the colors (such as positive, neutral, and negative). Use a 2-color scale when you want to look for patterns in the data, as a 2-color scale offers less contrast.

Remove It!

If you no longer require the color scales, you can remove them. Follow steps 1 to 3 to select the range and display the Conditional Formatting drop-down menu, and then click Manage Rules. Excel displays the Conditional Formatting Rules Manager dialog box. Click the Color Scale rule you want to remove and then click Delete Rule.

Analyze Cell Values with Icon Sets

You can help analyze large sets of data by applying to each cell an icon that has a symbolic association. The symbol gives you a visual clue about the cell's relative value compared with the overall distribution of values in the range.

When you are trying to make sense of a large data set, symbols that have common or well-known associations are often useful for clarifying the data. For example, for most people a check mark means something is good or finished or acceptable, whereas an X means something is bad or unfinished or unacceptable;

a green circle is positive, whereas a red circle is negative (think traffic lights).

Excel puts these and many other symbolic associations to good use with the *icon sets* feature. You use icon sets to visualize the relative values of cells in a range. In this case, Excel adds a particular icon to each cell in the range, and that icon tells you something about the cell's value relative to the rest of the range. For example, the highest values might be assigned an upward-pointing arrow, the lowest values a downward-pointing arrow, and the values in between a horizontal arrow.

---

① Select the range you want to work with.

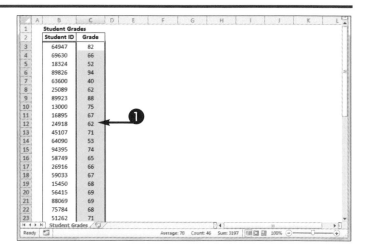

② Click the Home tab.

③ Click Conditional Formatting.

④ Click Icon Sets.

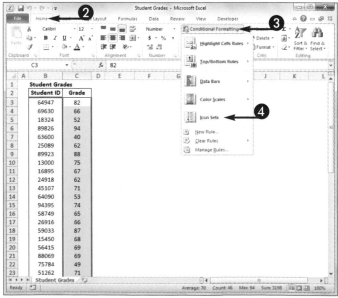

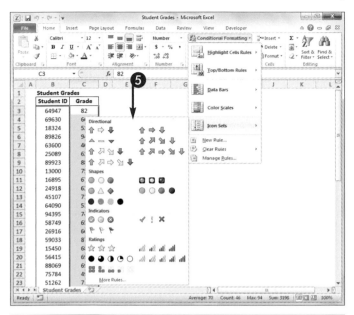

⑤ Click the type of icon set you want to apply.

The categories include Directional, Shapes, Indicators, and Ratings.

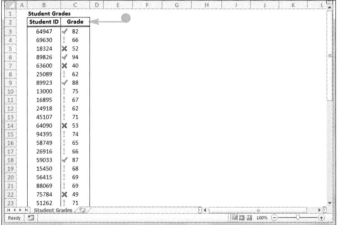

● Excel applies the icons to each cell in the range.

TIPS

Did You Know?

The Excel icon sets come in four categories: Directional, Shapes, Indicators, and Ratings. Use Directional icon sets for indicating trends and data movement; use Shapes icon sets for pointing out the high (green) and low (red) values; Use Indicators to add value judgments; and use Ratings to show where each cell resides in the overall range of data values.

Remove It!

If you no longer require an icon set, you can remove it. Follow steps 1 to 3 to select the range and display the Conditional Formatting drop-down menu, and then click Manage Rules. Excel displays the Conditional Formatting Rules Manager dialog box. Click the Icon Set rule you want to remove and then click Delete Rule.

Create a Custom Conditional Formatting Rule

You can tailor your format-based data analysis by creating a custom conditional formatting rule that suits how you want to analyze and present the data.

The predefined conditional formatting rules in Excel — highlight cells rules, top/bottom rules, data bars, color scales, and icon sets — give you an easy way to analyze worksheet values through data visualization.

However, you might find that these predefined rules do not suit particular types of data or data analysis. For example, the icon sets assume

that higher values are more positive than lower values, but that is not always true; in a database of product defects, lower values are better than higher ones. Similarly, data bars are based on the relative numeric values in a range, but you might prefer to base them on the relative percentages or on percentile rankings.

To get the type of data analysis you prefer, and to create your own formats, you can create a custom conditional formatting rule and apply it to your range.

---

1 Select the range you want to work with.

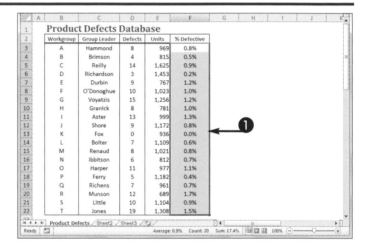

2 Click the Home tab.

3 Click Conditional Formatting.

4 Click New Rule.

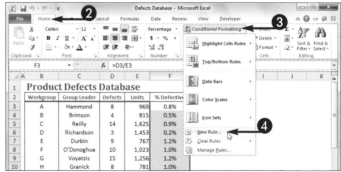

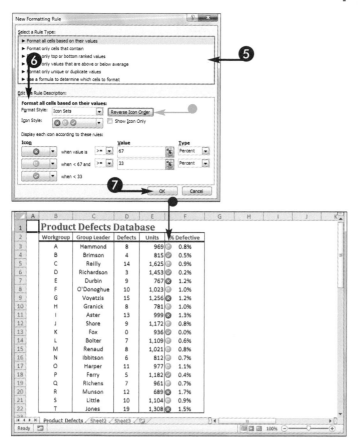

The New Formatting Rule dialog box appears.

5 Click the type of rule you want to create.

6 Edit the rule's style and formatting.

The controls you see depend on the rule type you selected.

● With Icon Sets, click Reverse Icon Order if you want to reverse the normal icon assignments, as shown here.

7 Click OK.

● Excel applies the conditional formatting to each cell in the range.

Modify It!

If you need to make changes to your custom conditional formatting rule, follow steps 1 to 3 to select the range and display the Conditional Formatting drop-down menu, and then click Manage Rules. Excel displays the Conditional Formatting Rules Manager dialog box. Click the rule you want to modify and then click Edit Rule.

Remove It!

If you want to delete a custom rule for a worksheet, click the Home tab, click the Conditional Formatting drop-down arrow, and then click Manage Rules to open the Conditional Formatting Rules Manager dialog box. In the Show Formatting Rules For list, click This Worksheet. Click the rule you want to remove and then click Delete Rule. If you have multiple custom rules defined for a worksheet and you no longer require them, you can remove all of them. Click the Home tab, click the Conditional Formatting drop-down arrow, click Clear Rules, and then click Clear Rules from Entire Sheet.

Calculate Multiple Solutions to a Formula

You can enhance your Excel data analysis by setting up a worksheet model that automatically calculates multiple solutions to a formula.

Perhaps the most basic method for analyzing worksheet data is a technique called *what-if analysis*. With what-if analysis, you first calculate a formula D, based on the input from variables A, B, and C. You then say, "What if I change variable A? Or B or C? What happens to the result?"

One way to do this is to set up the worksheet model and then manually change the formula's input cells. For example, if you are calculating a loan payment, you can enter different interest rate values to see how this affects the payment.

The problem with this method is that you see only a single result at one time. If you are interested in studying the effect a range of values has on the formula, you need to set up a *data table*. This is a table that consists of the formula you are using, and multiple input values for that formula. Excel automatically creates a solution to the formula for each different input value.

① Type the input values you want.

To enter the values in a column, you can start the column one cell down and one cell to the left of the cell containing the formula, as shown here.

To enter the values in a row, you can start the row one cell up and one cell to the right of the formula.

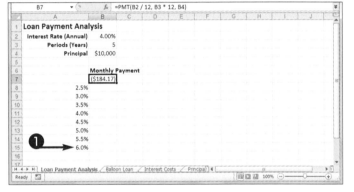

② Select the range that includes the input values and the formula.

③ Click the Data tab.

④ Click What-If Analysis.

⑤ Click Data Table.

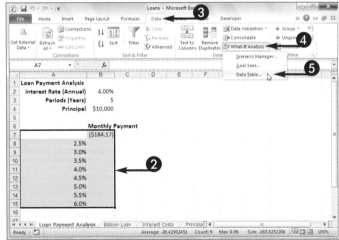

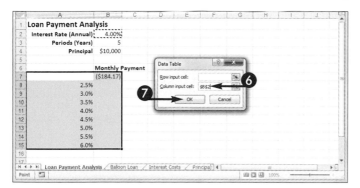

The Data Table dialog box appears.

6 Specify the formula cell you want to use as the data table's input cell.

If the input values are in a column, you can enter the input cell's address in the Column Input Cell text box.

If you entered the input values in a row, you can enter the input cell's address in the Row Input Cell text box.

7 Click OK.

● Excel displays the results.

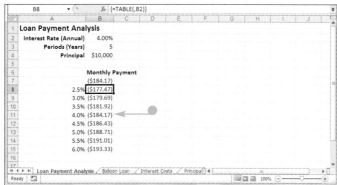

Try This!

The worksheet model shown in this section is an example of a one-input data table, as you are only varying one of the formula's input cells. However, Excel also enables you to set up a two-input data table that varies two formula inputs at the same time. For example, in the loan payment worksheet, you could set up a two-input data table that varies the interest rate and the term.

To set up a two-input data table, you must set up two ranges of input cells. One range must appear in a column directly below the formula, and the other range must appear in a row directly to the right of the formula. Follow steps 2 to 5 to open the Data Table dialog box, specify both the Row Input Cell and the Column Input Cell, and then click OK.

Plug Multiple Input Values into a Formula

You can analyze the result of a formula by creating scenarios that plug multiple input values into the formula.

Many formulas take a number of input values to produce a result. When you are analyzing the formula's results, it helps to manipulate the input values in some systematic way. For example, one set of values might represent a best-case approach, while another might represent a worst-case approach. In Excel, each of these coherent sets of input values — known as *changing cells* — is called a *scenario*.

For example, if you are calculating a monthly mortgage payment, the input values include the initial down payment, the term of the mortgage, and the *paydown* — the amount of money you want to apply directly to the principal each month. The best-case scenario might involve a large down payment, a short term, and a big paydown; a worst-case scenario might involve a small down payment, a long term, and a small paydown.

Excel offers the Scenario Manager tool to help you create and use such scenarios.

Create a Scenario

1 Set up your worksheet model.

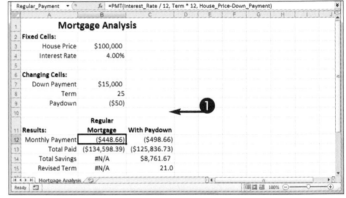

2 Click the Data tab.

3 Click What-If Analysis.

4 Click Scenario Manager.

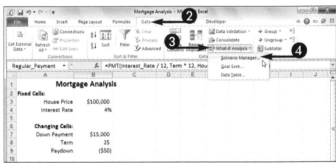

The Scenario Manager dialog box appears.

⑤ Click Add.

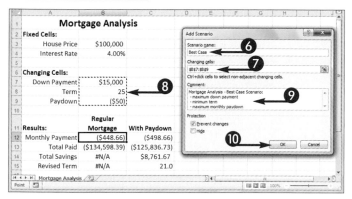

The Add Scenario dialog box appears.

⑥ Type a name for the scenario.

⑦ Click inside the Changing Cells text box.

⑧ Select the cells you want to change in the scenario.

⑨ Type a description for the scenario.

⑩ Click OK.

Important!

When you are building a worksheet model for use with scenarios, there are a couple of techniques you can use to make the model more suited to scenarios. First, it is useful to group all your changing cells in one place and label them. Second, make sure that each changing cell is a constant value. If you use a formula for a changing cell, another cell could change the formula result and throw off your scenarios.

Important!

Once you have one or more scenarios defined, they appear in the Scenario Manager, and for each scenario, you see its changing cells and its description. The description is often very useful, particularly if you have several scenarios defined, so be sure to write a detailed description in step 9 to help you differentiate your scenarios later on.

continued

Excel scenarios are a powerful data analysis tool for a number of reasons. First, Excel enables you to enter up to 32 changing cells in a single scenario, so you can create models that are as elaborate as you need. Second, no matter how many changing cells you have in a scenario, Excel enables you to show a scenario's result with just a few mouse clicks. Third, because the number of scenarios you can define is limited only by the available memory on your computer, you can effectively use as many scenarios as you need to analyze your data model.

The Scenario Values dialog box appears.

⓫ Use the text boxes to specify a value for each changing cell.

● To add more scenarios, you can click Add and then repeat steps 6 to 11.

⓬ Click OK.

The Scenario Manager dialog box appears.

⓭ Click Close.

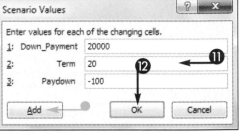

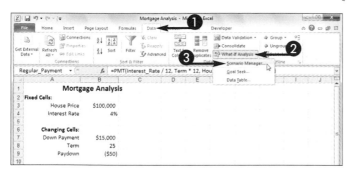

Display Scenarios

❶ Click the Data tab.

❷ Click What-If Analysis.

❸ Click Scenario Manager.

The Scenario Manager dialog box appears.

❹ Click the scenario you want to display.

❺ Click Show.

● Excel enters the scenario values into the changing cells and displays the formula result.

❻ Repeat steps 4 and 5 to display other scenarios.

❼ Click Close.

Change It!

If you need to make changes to a scenario, you can edit the name, the changing cells, the description, and the scenario's input values. Click the Data tab, click the What-If Analysis drop-down arrow, and then click Scenario Manager. In the Scenario Manager dialog box, click the scenario you want to modify, and then click Edit.

Remove It!

If you have a scenario that you no longer need, you should delete it to reduce clutter in the Scenario Manager. Click the Data tab, click the What-If Analysis drop-down arrow, and then click Scenario Manager. Click the scenario you want to delete. Note that Excel does not ask you to confirm the deletion, so double-check that you have selected the correct scenario. Click Delete and then click Close.

Calculate the Break-Even Point

You can use the powerful Goal Seek tool to calculate the break-even point for a worksheet financial model.

In a *break-even analysis,* you determine the number of units you have to sell of a product so that your total profits are zero — that is, the product revenue is equal to the product costs. You might think this would be trivial: create a profit formula that subtracts expenses from revenue, and adjust the units sold until the formula returns zero.

However, in the real world the calculation is usually a bit more complex than that. In particular, there are costs associated with each unit sold, so your model must take those costs into account. This means that the total expenses are to a certain extent dependent on total sales, which makes the break-even analysis more complicated.

Rather than trying to find the break-even point manually, the Goal Seek tool can run the calculation for you in a fraction of the time.

---

① Set up your worksheet model.

● For the number of units, enter any value you like, such as 1.

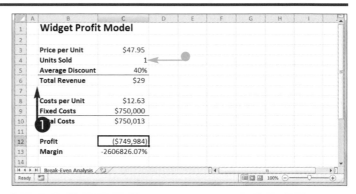

② Click the Data tab.

③ Click What-If Analysis.

④ Click Goal Seek.

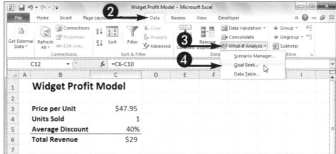

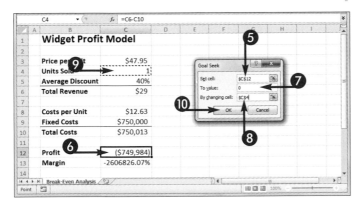

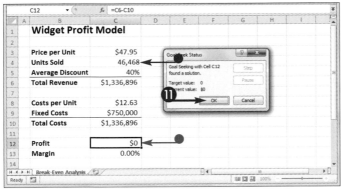

The Goal Seek dialog box appears.

5 Click inside the Set Cell text box.

6 Click the cell that contains the formula you want Goal Seek to work with.

7 Type the value that you want Goal Seek to find.

Note: In a break-even analysis, the set cell is the profit formula, and the value you seek is 0.

8 Click inside the By Changing Cell text box.

9 Click the cell that you want Goal Seek to modify.

10 Click OK.

● Goal Seek adjusts the units sold until it reaches a solution.

● The Profit formula now shows 0.

11 Click OK.

More Options!

In some cases, Goal Seek may not find an exact solution to your model. That can happen if it takes Goal Seek a relatively long time to find a solution, because Goal Seek stops either after 100 iterations or if the current result is within 0.001 of the desired result.

You can get a more accurate solution by increasing the number of iterations that Goal Seek can use, by reducing the value that Goal Seek uses to mark a solution as "close enough," or both. Click the File icon, click Options, and then click Formulas. Increase the value of the Maximum Iterations spin box, decrease the value in the Maximum Change text box, or both, and then click OK.

Consolidate Data from Multiple Worksheets

If you have multiple worksheets with the same or similar data, you can consolidate all of that data into a single worksheet that displays a summary of the data.

It is common to distribute similar worksheets to multiple departments to capture budget numbers, inventory, survey data, and so on. Those worksheets are then usually returned, and all the data must be combined into a summary report showing company-wide totals. This is called *consolidating* the data.

Rather than doing this manually, Excel can consolidate your data automatically. You can

use the Consolidate feature to consolidate the data either by position or by category. In both cases, you specify one or more source ranges (the ranges that contain the data you want to consolidate) and a destination range (the range where the consolidated data will appear).

In the first part of this section, you learn how to consolidate by position, which is the easiest method. To use this method, the sheets you are working with must have the same layout. See the second part of this section to learn how to consolidate by category.

Consolidate By Position

① Create a new worksheet that uses the same layout — including row and column headers — as the sheets you want to consolidate.

② Open the workbooks that contain the worksheets you want to consolidate.

③ Select the upper-left corner of the destination range.

④ Click the Data tab.

⑤ Click Consolidate.

The Consolidate dialog box appears.

⑥ Click the Function drop-down arrow, and then click the summary function you want to use.

⑦ Click inside the Reference text box.

⑧ Select one of the ranges you want to consolidate.

⑨ Click Add.

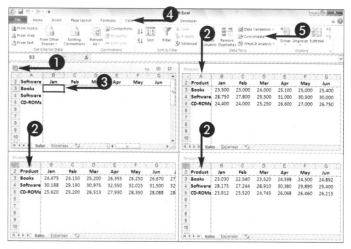

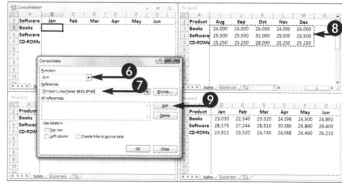

● Excel adds the range to the All References list.

⑩ Repeat steps 7 to 9 to add all of the consolidation ranges.

⑪ Click OK.

● Excel consolidates the data from the source ranges and displays the summary in the destination range.

More Options!

If the source data changes, then you probably want to reflect those changes in the consolidation worksheet. Rather than running the entire consolidation over again, a much easier solution is to select the Create Links to Source Data check box in the Consolidate dialog box. This enables you to update the consolidation worksheet by clicking the Data tab and then clicking Refresh All.

This also means that Excel creates an outline in the consolidation sheet, and you can use that outline to see the detail from each of the source ranges. See the section "Create an Outline Automatically" to learn more about outlines in Excel.

continued

Consolidate Data from Multiple Worksheets *(continued)*

If the worksheets that contain the data you want to summarize do not use the same layout, you can still perform the consolidation. However, in this case you need to tell Excel to consolidate the data *by category*. This method consolidates the data by looking for common row and column labels in each worksheet.

For example, suppose you are consolidating sales, and Division A sells software, books, and videos, Division B sells books and

CD-ROMs, and Division C sells books, software, videos, and CD-ROMs. When you consolidate this data, Excel looks for the common data. For instance, Excel would summarize the software values from Divisions A and C, the CD-ROM values from Divisions B and C, and the book values from all three divisions.

Remember, for this to work, the common data values must use the same row or column labels.

Consolidate By Category

1. Create a new worksheet for the consolidation.

2. Open the workbooks that contain the worksheets you want to consolidate.

3. Select the upper-left corner of the destination range.

4. Click the Data tab.

5. Click Consolidate.

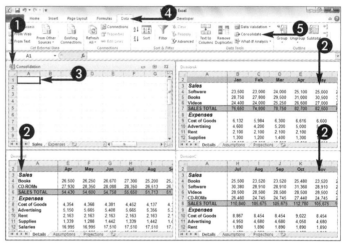

The Consolidate dialog box appears.

6. Click the Function drop-down arrow and then click the summary function you want to use.

7. Click inside the Reference text box.

8. Select one of the ranges you want to consolidate.

Note: *Be sure to include the row and column labels in the range.*

9. Click Add.

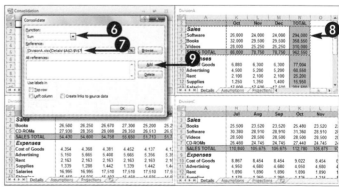

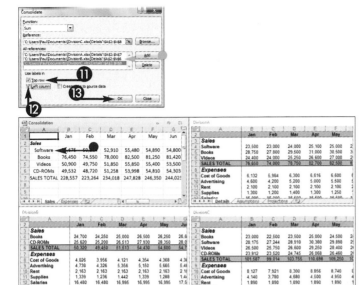

- Excel adds the range to the All References list.

⑩ Repeat steps 7 to 9 to add all of the consolidation ranges.

⑪ If you have labels in the top row of each range, click to select Top Row.

⑫ If you have labels in the left-column row of each range, click to select Left Column.

⑬ Click OK.

- Excel consolidates the data from the source ranges and displays the summary in the destination range.

Remove It!

If the layout of the source data changes, then you will need to run the consolidation again.

If you consolidated by position, then before you can re-run the consolidation, you must first adjust the layout of the consolidation worksheet to match the changes to the source data. (You do not need to do this if you consolidated by category.)

No matter which consolidation method you used, before you run the consolidation again, you must delete the existing source ranges. Click the Data tab and then click Consolidation to display the Consolidate dialog box. For each source range, click the range in the All References list and then click Delete.

Filter Table Data

You can analyze table data most efficiently by filtering the data so that you only view the table records that you want to work with.

Many Excel tables contain hundreds or even thousands of records. These large tables are difficult to work with because it is hard to find the data you need. Sorting the table can sometimes help, but with this technique you still end up working with the entire table. A better method is to define the data that you want to work with and then have Excel display only those records onscreen. This is called

filtering your data and Excel offers a couple of techniques that get the job done.

The first technique uses *filter lists*, and it presents you with a list of check boxes for each unique value in a field. You filter the data by selecting the check boxes for the records you want to see.

The second technique uses *quick filters,* and it enables you to specify criteria for a field, such as only showing those records where the field value is greater than a specified amount.

Filter with a Filter List

① Click inside the table.

② Click the Data tab.

③ Click Filter.

● Excel adds drop-down arrows to each field.

④ Click the drop-down arrow for the field you want to use as the filter.

● Excel displays a list of the unique values in the field.

⑤ Click to select the check box for each value you want to see.

⑥ Click OK.

● Excel filters the table to show only those records that have the field values you selected.

● Excel displays the number of records found.

● The field's drop-down list displays a filter icon.

⑦ To remove the filter, click Clear.

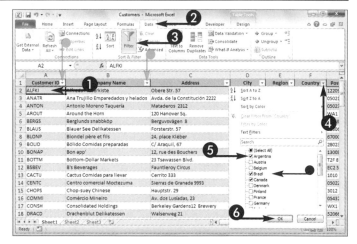

Filter with a Quick Filter

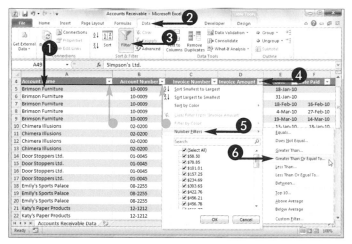

① Click inside the table.

② Click the Data tab.

③ Click Filter.

● Excel adds drop-down arrows to each field.

④ Click the drop-down arrow for the field you want to use as the filter.

⑤ Click Number Filters.

Note: *If the field is a date field, click Date Filters, instead; if the field is a text field, click Text Filters.*

⑥ Click the filter you want to use.

The Custom AutoFilter dialog box appears.

Note: *Some quick filters do not require extra input, so you can skip the next two steps.*

⑦ Type the value you want to use, or use the list box to select a unique value from the field.

⑧ Click OK.

● Excel filters the table to show only those records that have the field values you selected.

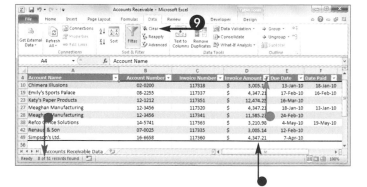

● Excel displays the number of records found.

● The field's drop-down list displays a filter icon.

⑨ To remove the filter, click Clear.

More Options!

You can create custom quick filters that use two different criteria, and you can filter records that match both or at least one of the criteria. Follow steps 1 and 2 under "Filter with a Quick Filter," and then click Custom Filter. In the dialog box, select the operators and values you want to use. To match both criteria, click And; to match at least one criteria, click Or.

Remove Duplicate Values from a Table

You can make your Excel tables more accurate for data analysis by seeking out and removing any duplicate records.

When you need to analyze the data in a table, that analysis might involve filtering the data or creating summary formulas that calculate sums, averages, counts, and so on. For these kinds of analysis to succeed, the data in the table must be accurate. One of the main causes of table inaccuracy is the presence of duplicate records in the table. Duplicate records throw off your calculations by including the same data two or more times.

To prevent this kind of problem, you should delete duplicate records from your table. However, rather than looking for duplicates manually, you can use the Remove Duplicates command, which can quickly find and remove duplicates in even the largest tables.

Before you use the Remove Duplicates command, you must decide what defines a duplicate record in your table. That is, does every field have to be identical, or is it enough that only certain fields are identical?

---

① Click a cell inside the table.

② Click the Design tab.

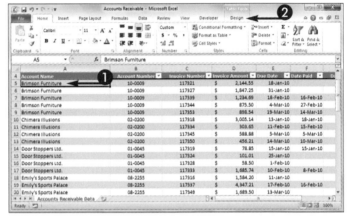

③ Click Remove Duplicates.

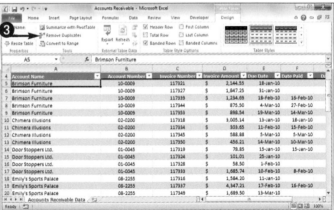

The Remove Duplicates dialog box appears.

④ Select the check box beside each field that you want Excel to check for duplication values.

⑤ Click OK.

Excel deletes any duplicate records that it finds.

● Excel tells you the number of duplicate records that it deleted.

⑥ Click OK.

More Options!

If your table has many fields, you may want Excel to use only one or two of those fields to look for duplicate records. Rather than deactivating all the other check boxes manually, first click Unselect All in the Remove Duplicates dialog box to clear all the check boxes. You can then click to activate just the check boxes you want Excel to use.

Reverse It!

If you run the Remove Duplicates command and then decide you did not want to delete those records after all, immediately press Ctrl+Z, or click the Undo icon in the Quick Access Toolbar.

Create an Outline Automatically

You can control a worksheet range display by creating an outline automatically based on the worksheet formulas and data.

Like Microsoft Word, Excel also offers outlines. In a worksheet outline, you can "collapse" sections of the sheet to display only summary cells (such as quarterly or regional totals) or you can "expand" hidden sections to show the underlying detail.

The easiest way to create an outline is to have Excel do it for you. Before you do this, you need to make sure your worksheet is appropriate for outlining. First, the worksheet

must contain formulas that reference cells or ranges directly adjacent to the formula cell. Worksheets with SUM() functions that subtotal cells above or to the left are particularly good candidates for outlining.

Second, there must be a consistent pattern to the direction of the formula references. For example, a worksheet with formulas that always reference cells above or to the left can be outlined. Excel won't outline a worksheet with, say, SUM() functions that reference ranges above and below a formula cell.

Create the Outline

1 **Display the worksheet you want to outline.**

2 **Click the Data tab.**

3 **Click the Group drop-down arrow.**

4 **Click Auto Outline.**

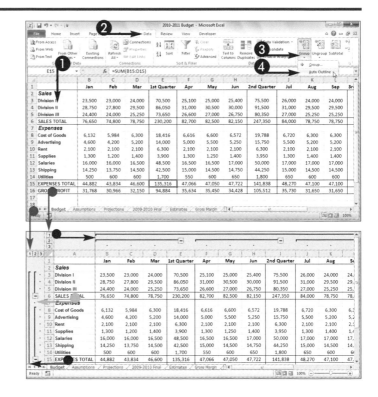

● **Excel outlines the worksheet data.**

● **Excel uses level bars to indicate the grouped ranges.**

● **Excel displays level symbols to indicate the various levels of the detail that are available in the outline.**

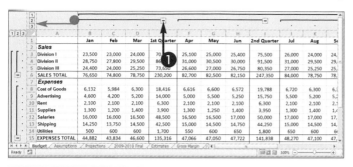

Use the Outline to Control the Range Display

① Click a collapse symbol to hide the range indicated by the level bar.

● You can also collapse multiple ranges that are on the same outline level by clicking the appropriate level symbol.

● Excel collapses the range.

② Click the expand symbol to view the range again.

● You can also show multiple ranges that are on the same outline level by clicking the appropriate level symbol.

Did You Know?

Outlines are most useful for easily hiding and displaying ranges. However, one of the big advantages of outlines is that, once you have hidden some data, you can work with the visible cells as if they were a single range. This means that you can format those cells quickly, print them, create charts, and so on.

Did You Know?

The level symbols that Excel displays for outlined data tell you which level each level bar is on. Click a level symbol to hide or display all the detail data for that level. Somewhat confusingly, Excel has set things up so that lower outline levels have higher level numbers. A good way to keep things straight is to remember that the higher the number, the more detail the level contains.

Enable the Analysis ToolPak Add-In

You can access a number of powerful statistical analysis tools by loading the Analysis ToolPak add-in. The Analysis ToolPak consists of 19 statistical tools, including the following:

Correlation — Returns the correlation coefficient, which is a measure of the relationship between two sets of data.

Covariance — Returns the average of the products of deviations for each data point pair. Covariance is a measure of the relationship between two sets of data.

Descriptive Statistics — Generates a report showing various statistics (such as median, mode, and standard deviation) for a set of data.

Exponential Smoothing — Returns a predicted value based on the forecast for the previous period, adjusted for the error in that period.

Histogram — Calculates individual and cumulative frequencies for a range of data and a set of data bins.

Moving Average — Smoothes a data series by averaging the series values over a specified number of preceding periods.

Random Number Generation — Fills a range with independent random numbers.

Rank and Percentile — Creates a table containing the ordinal and percentage rank of each value in a set.

Regression — Performs a linear regression analysis that fits a line through a set of values using the least squares method.

---

① Click the File tab.

② Click Options.

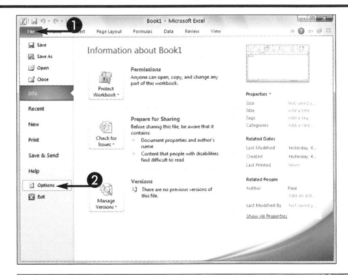

The Excel Options dialog box appears.

③ Click Add-Ins.

④ In the Manage drop-down list, click Excel Add-ins.

⑤ Click Go.

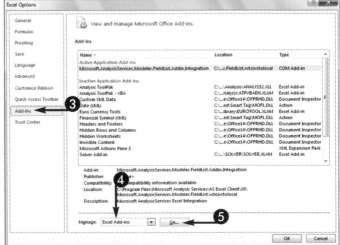

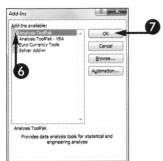

The Add-Ins dialog box appears.

6 Click to select the Analysis ToolPak check box.

7 Click OK.

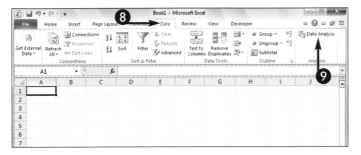

Excel loads the Analysis ToolPak add-in.

8 Click the Data tab.

9 Click Data Analysis to access the Analysis ToolPak tools.

TIPS

Apply It!

To use one of the Analysis ToolPak's statistical tools, click the Data tab and then click Data Analysis. In the Data Analysis dialog box that appears, click the tool you want to use, and then click OK. Excel displays a dialog box for the tool. Use the dialog box to specify the tool settings you want to use (the controls vary from tool to tool), and then click OK.

Remove It!

If you no longer need the Analysis ToolPak, you can disable the add-in to reduce clutter on the Ribbon's Data tab and to save a bit of space on your computer's hard drive. Follow steps 1 to 5 to display the Add-Ins dialog box. Click to deselect the Analysis ToolPak check box, and then click OK.

Analyzing Data with PivotTables

Tables and external databases can contain hundreds or even thousands of records. Analyzing that much data can be a nightmare without the right kinds of tools. To help you, Excel offers a powerful data analysis tool called a *PivotTable*. This tool enables you to summarize hundreds of records in a concise tabular format. You can then manipulate the layout of — or *pivot* — the table to see different views of your data.

A PivotTable is a powerful data analysis tool in part because it automatically groups large amounts of data into smaller, more manageable categories. Excel also displays summary calculations for each group. The default calculation is Sum, which means that for each group, Excel totals all the values in some specified field. A PivotTable also enables you to filter the data to show just a subset of the data.

In this chapter you learn how to create PivotTables, edit them, pivot them, format them, calculate with them, and much more.

Quick Tips

Build a PivotTable from an Excel Table

If the data you want to cross-tabulate exists as an Excel table, you can use the Summarize with PivotTable command to easily build a PivotTable report based on your data. You need only specify the location of your source data and then choose the location of the resulting PivotTable.

Excel creates an empty PivotTable in a new worksheet or in the location you specify. Excel also displays a PivotTable Field List, which contains four areas with the following labels: Report Filter, Column Labels, Row Labels, and Values. To complete the PivotTable, you

must populate some or all of these areas with one or more fields from your data.

When you add a field to the Row Labels, Column Labels, or Report Filter area, Excel extracts the unique values from the field and displays them in the PivotTable in the row, column, or page field, respectively. For example, if you add the Salesperson field to the Row Labels area, Excel updates the PivotTable's row area to display the unique salesperson names as headings that run down the leftmost column of the report.

---

1 Click a cell within the table that you want to use as the source data.

2 Click the Design tab.

3 Click Summarize with PivotTable.

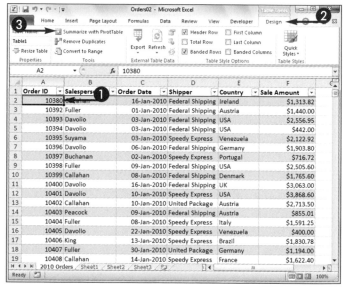

The Create PivotTable dialog box appears.

4 Select the New Worksheet option.

● If you want to place the PivotTable in an existing location, select the Existing Worksheet option and then use the Location box to select the worksheet and cell where you want the PivotTable to appear.

5 Click OK.

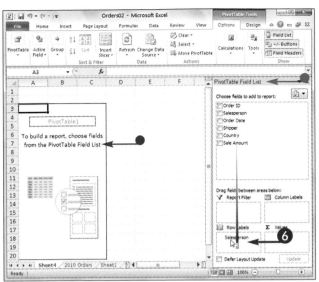

- Excel creates a blank PivotTable.

- Excel displays the PivotTable Field List.

6 Click and drag a field and drop it inside the Row Labels area.

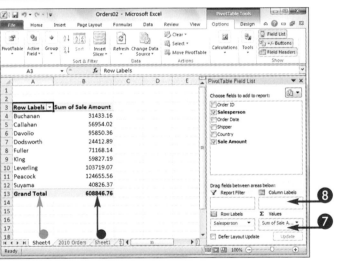

- Excel adds the field's unique values to the PivotTable's row area.

7 Click and drag a numeric field and drop it inside the Values area.

- Excel sums the numeric values based on the row values.

8 If desired, click and drag fields and drop them in the Column Labels area and the Report Filter area.

Each time you drop a field in an area, Excel updates the PivotTable to include the new data.

TIPS

Did You Know?

In the PivotTable Field List, if you click to select a check box for a text or date field, Excel adds the field to the Row Labels area; if you click to select a check box for a numeric field, Excel adds the field to the Values area. You can also right-click a field and then click the area you want to use.

More Options!

Excel usually displays the numbers in the data area of the PivotTable without a numeric format. To fix this, click any cell within the value field range, click the Options tab, click Active Field, and then click Field Settings. In the Value Field Settings dialog box, click Number Format and then use the Format Cells dialog box to choose the format you want to use.

Create a PivotTable from External Data

You can create a PivotTable using an external data source, which enables you to build reports from extremely large datasets and from relational database systems.

Building your PivotTable directly from an Excel table or range is convenient, but it has two major drawbacks. First, Excel offers only simple row-and-column database management. Second, Excel worksheets are limited to 1,048,576 rows, so that is the maximum number of records you can have in a range or list data source.

To overcome these limitations, you need to use a relational database management system (RDBMS) such as Microsoft Access or SQL Server. With these programs, you can set up a table, query, or other object that defines the data you want to work with. In most cases, the data object can be as complex and as large as you need. You can then build your PivotTable based on this external data source.

① Press Alt+D, and then press P.

The PivotTable and PivotChart Wizard - Step 1 of 3 dialog box appears.

② Select the External data source option.

③ Select the PivotTable option.

④ Click Next.

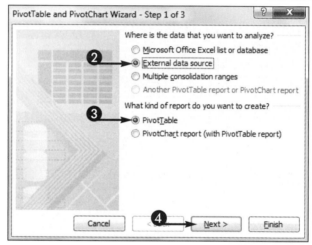

The PivotTable and PivotChart Wizard - Step 2 of 3 dialog box appears.

⑤ Click Get Data.

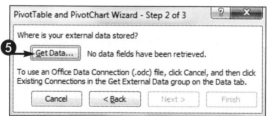

The Choose Data Source dialog box appears.

⑥ Click the data source you want to use.

⑦ Click OK.

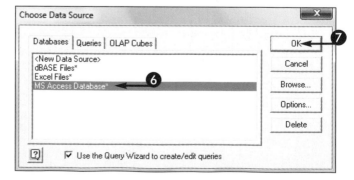

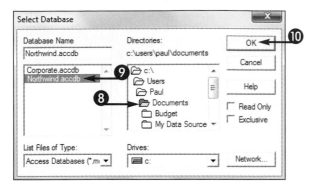

The Select Database dialog box appears.

⑧ Click the folder that contains the database.

⑨ Click the database.

⑩ Click OK.

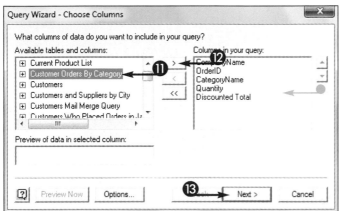

The Query Wizard - Choose Columns dialog box appears.

⑪ Click the table or column you want to use as the source data for your PivotTable.

⑫ Click the > button.

● The table's fields appear in this list.

⑬ Click Next.

Try This!

To create a data source, click the Data tab, click From Other Sources, and then click From Microsoft Query. In the Choose Data Source dialog box, click New Data Source. Click to deselect the Use the Query Wizard to Create/Edit Queries check box, and then click OK. In the Create New Data Source dialog box, type a name for your data source, select the database driver that your data source requires, and then click Connect.

More Options!

You can reduce the size of the new PivotTable by including only those fields that you need to use. In the Query Wizard - Choose Columns dialog box, each table has a plus sign (+). Click a table's plus sign to display a list of that object's fields, or columns, as the Query Wizard calls them. You can then click a field and click the > button to add it to the list of fields to be used with your PivotTable.

continued

The Choose Data Source dialog box and the various Query Wizard dialog boxes are not part of Excel. Instead, they are components of a program called Microsoft Query. You can use this program to work with external data.

This section assumes that you have already defined the appropriate data source, and that you do not want to work with Microsoft Query directly. Note, too, that steps 14 and 15 skip over the Query Wizard dialog boxes that enable you to filter and sort the external data, because this is not usually pertinent for a PivotTable report.

The other assumption made in this section is that you do not want the external data to be imported to Excel. Rather, in this section, the external data resides only in the new PivotTable's pivot cache; you do not see the actual data in your workbook. However, you can still easily refresh and rebuild your PivotTable, just like you can with a report based on a local range or list.

The Query Wizard - Filter Data dialog box appears.

⑭ Click Next.

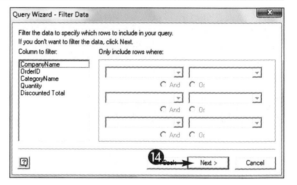

The Query Wizard - Sort Order dialog box appears.

⑮ Click Next.

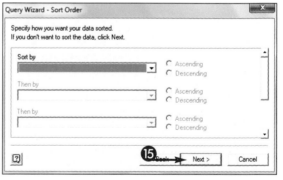

The Query Wizard - Finish dialog box appears.

⑯ Select the Return Data to Microsoft Excel option.

⑰ Click Finish.

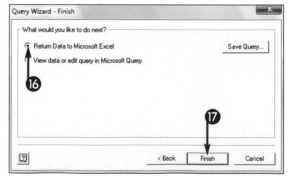

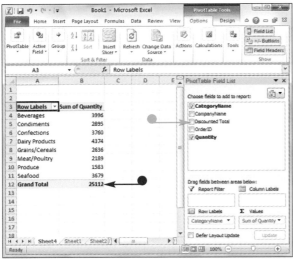

Excel returns you to the PivotTable and PivotChart Wizard - Step 2 of 3 dialog box.

⑱ Click Finish.

Excel creates an empty PivotTable.

● The fields available in the table or query that you chose in step 11 appear in the PivotTable Field List.

⑲ Click and drag fields from the PivotTable Field List and drop them in the PivotTable areas.

● Excel summarizes the external data in the PivotTable.

Important!

The most common drawback to using an external data source is that you often have no control over the actual external file. For example, if you attempt to refresh the PivotTable, Excel may display an error message. If you suspect the problem is a change to the database login data, click OK to display the Login dialog box and find out the new login name and password from the database administrator.

Important!

If you receive an error when you attempt to refresh a PivotTable based on external data, the problem may also be that the database file has been moved or renamed. Click OK in the error message, and then click Database in the Login dialog box. You can then use the Select Database dialog box to find and select the database file.

You can ensure that the data analysis represented by the PivotTable remains up to date by refreshing the PivotTable.

Whether your PivotTable is based on financial results, survey responses, or a database of collectibles such as books or DVDs, the underlying data is probably not static. That is, the data changes over time as new results come in, new surveys are undertaken, and new items are added to the collection. You will need to refresh the PivotTable to ensure that it is current.

Excel offers two methods for refreshing a PivotTable: manual and automatic. A manual refresh is one that you perform yourself, usually when you know that the source data has changed, or if you simply want to be sure that the latest data is reflected in your PivotTable report. An automatic refresh is one that Excel handles for you. For PivotTables based on Excel ranges or tables, you can tell Excel to refresh a PivotTable every time you open the workbook that contains the report.

Refresh Data Manually

① Click any cell inside the PivotTable.

② Click the Options tab.

③ Click Refresh.

You can also press Alt+F5.

● To update every PivotTable in the current workbook, click the Refresh drop-down arrow and then click Refresh All.

You can also update all PivotTables by pressing Ctrl+Alt+F5.

Excel updates the PivotTable data.

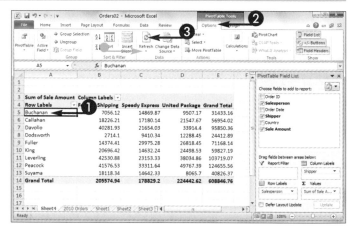

Refresh Data Automatically

① Click any cell inside the PivotTable.

② Click the Options tab.

③ Click PivotTable.

④ Click Options.

Note: You can also right-click any cell in the PivotTable and then click PivotTable Options.

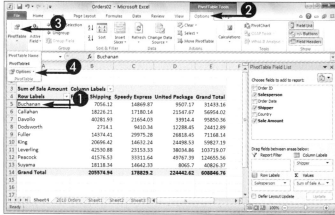

The PivotTable Options dialog box appears.

5 Click the Data tab.

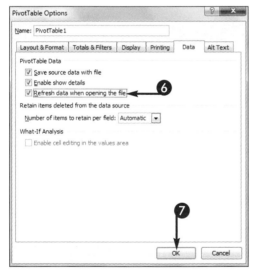

6 Click to select the Refresh Data When Opening the File option.

7 Click OK.

Excel applies the refresh options.

More Options!

If your PivotTable is based on external data, you can set up a schedule that automatically refreshes the PivotTable at a specified interval. Click any cell inside the PivotTable, click the Options tab, click the Refresh drop-down arrow, and then click Connection Properties. Select the Refresh Every check box, and then use the spin box to specify the refresh interval, in minutes.

Caution!

If you set up an automatic refresh, you might prefer not to have the source data updated too frequently. Depending on where the data resides and how much data you are working with, the refresh could take some time, which may slow down the rest of your work.

Add Multiple Fields to the Row or Column Area

Excel enables you to add multiple fields to the PivotTable's row or column area. This is a very powerful technique because it allows you to perform further analysis of your data by viewing the data in an entirely new way.

Adding multiple fields to the row and column areas enables you to break down your data for further analysis. For example, suppose you are analyzing the results of a sales campaign that ran different promotions in several types of advertisements. A basic PivotTable might show you the sales for each Product (the row field)

according to the Advertisement in which the customer reported seeing the campaign (the column field). You might also be interested in seeing, for each product, the breakdown in sales for each promotion. You can do that by adding the Promotion field to the row area, as you see in the example used in this section. You can use either of the techniques in this section to add multiple fields to the row area; you can use the technique on the following page to add multiple fields to the column area.

Add a Field to the Row Area

① Click a cell within the PivotTable.

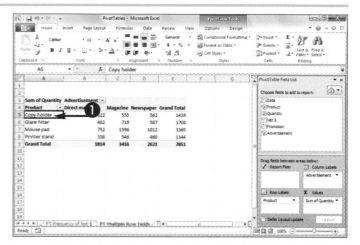

② Select the check box of the text or date field you want to add.

● Excel adds a button for the field to the Row Labels list.

● Excel adds the field to the PivotTable's row area.

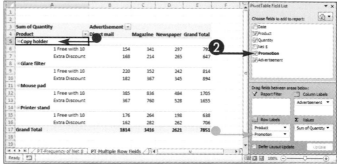

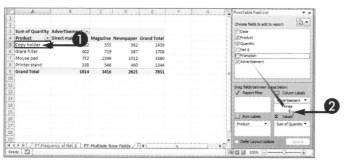

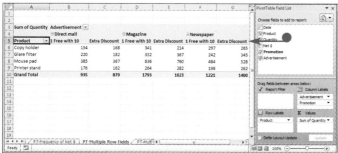

Add a Field to the Row or Column Area

① Click a cell within the PivotTable.

② In the PivotTable Field List, click and drag the field you want to add and drop the field in either the Row Labels section or the Column Labels section.

● Excel adds the field to the PivotTable.

Try This!

After you add a second field to the row or column area, you can change the field positions to change the PivotTable view. In the PivotTable Field List, use the Row Labels or Column Labels list to click and drag the button of the field you want to move and then drop the field above or below an existing field button.

More Options!

Excel does not restrict you to just two fields in the row or column area. Depending on your data analysis requirements, you are free to add three, four, or more fields to the row area or the column area.

Add Multiple Fields to the Data Area

Excel enables you to add multiple fields to the PivotTable's data area, which enhances your analysis by enabling you to see multiple summaries at one time.

For example, suppose you are analyzing the results of a sales campaign that ran different promotions in several types of advertisements. A basic PivotTable might show you the sum of the Quantity sold (the data field) for each Product (the row field) according to the

Advertisement in which the customer reported seeing the campaign (the column field). You might also be interested in seeing, for each product and advertisement, the net dollar amount sold. You can do that by adding the Net $ field to the data area, as you see in the example used in this section. You can use either of the techniques in this section to add multiple fields to the data area.

Add a Field to the Data Area with a Check Box

① Click a cell within the PivotTable.

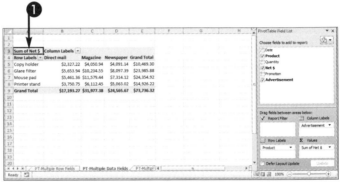

② Select the check box of the field you want to add to the data area.

● Excel adds a button for the field to the Values list.

● Excel adds the field to the PivotTable's data area.

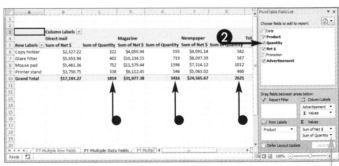

Add a Field to the Data Area by Dragging

1 Click a cell within the PivotTable.

2 In the PivotTable Field List, click and drag the field you want to add and drop the field in the Values section.

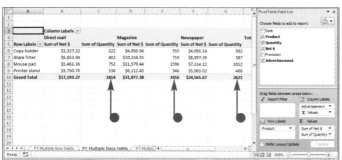

● Excel adds the field to the PivotTable.

Did You Know?

When you add a second field to the data area, Excel moves the labels — for example, Sum of Quantity and Sum of Net $ — into the column area for easier reference. This is also reflected in the addition of a Values button in the Column Labels section of the PivotTable Field List. This enables you to pivot the values within the report. For more information, see the section, "Move a Field to a Different Area."

More Options!

Excel does not restrict you to just two fields in the data area. You are free to add three, four, or more data fields to enhance your analysis of the data.

You can move a PivotTable's fields from one area of the PivotTable to another. This enables you to view your data from different perspectives, which can greatly enhance the analysis of the data.

Moving a field within a PivotTable is called *pivoting* the data. The most common way to pivot the data is to move fields between the row and column areas. If your PivotTable contains just a single non-data field, moving the field between the row and column areas changes the orientation of the PivotTable

between horizontal (column area) and vertical (row area). If your PivotTable contains fields in both the row and column areas, pivoting one of those fields to the other area creates multiple fields in that area.

You can also pivot data by moving a row or column field to the page area, and a page field to the row or column area. This is a useful technique when you want to turn one of your existing row or column fields into a filter. For more information, see the next section, "Apply a Report Filter."

Move a Field between the Row and Column Areas

① Click a cell within the PivotTable.

② Click and drag a column field button and drop it within the Row Labels area.

● Excel displays the field's values within the row area.

You can also drag a field button from the Row Labels area and drop it within the Column Labels area.

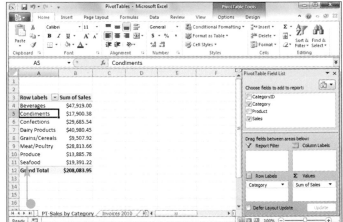

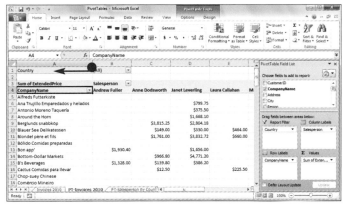

Move a Row or Column Field to the Page Area

❶ Click a cell within the PivotTable.

❷ Click and drag a row field button and drop it within the PivotTable's Report Filter area.

● Excel moves the field to the page area.

You can also drag a field button from the Column Labels area and drop it within the Report Filter area.

Did You Know?

You can also move any row, column, or page area field to the PivotTable's data area. This may seem strange because row, column, and page fields are almost always text values, and the default data area calculation is Sum. How can you sum text values? You cannot, of course. Instead, the default PivotTable summary calculation for text values is Count.

So, for example, if you drag the Category field and drop it inside the data area, Excel creates a second data field named Count of Category. To learn more about working with multiple data area fields, see the section, "Add Multiple Fields to the Data Area."

You can focus in on a specific item from one of the source data fields by taking advantage of the PivotTable's report filter.

By default, each PivotTable report displays a summary for all the records in your source data. This is usually what you want to see. However, there may be situations in which you need to focus more closely on some aspect of the data.

For example, suppose you are dealing with a PivotTable that summarizes data from thousands of customer invoices over some

period of time. A basic PivotTable may tell you the total amount sold for each product that you carry. However, what if you want to see the total amount sold for each product in a specific country? If the Product field is in the PivotTable's row area, then you can add the Country field to the column area. However, there may be dozens of countries, so that is not an efficient solution. Instead, you can add the Country field to the report filter. You can then tell Excel to display the total sold for each product for the specific country that you are interested in.

Filter the PivotTable

① Click the report filter drop-down list box.

Excel displays a list of the report filter items.

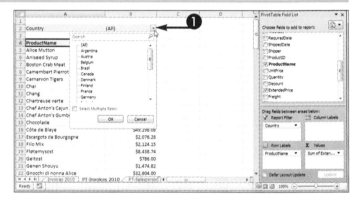

② Click the report filter item you want to view.

● If you want to display data for two or more report filter items, select the Select Multiple Items option and then repeat step 2 to select the other items.

③ Click OK.

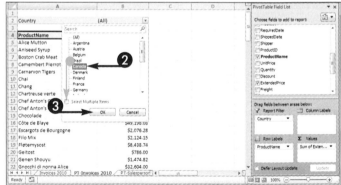

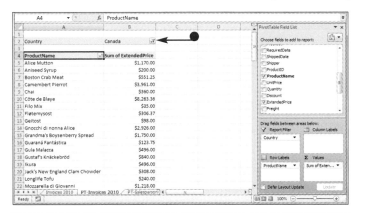

Excel filters the PivotTable to show only the data for the item you selected.

● Excel displays the filter icon to indicate that the PivotTable is filtered.

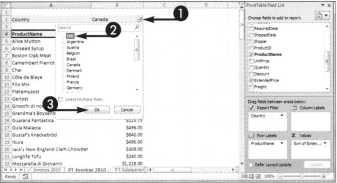

Remove the Report Filter

❶ Click the report filter drop-down list box.

Excel displays a list of the report filter items.

❷ Click All.

❸ Click OK.

Note: You can also click the Options tab, click Clear, and then click Clear Filters.

Excel adjusts the PivotTable to show the data for all the items in the report filter.

More Options!

You can add multiple fields to the report filter by dragging two or more fields to the Report Filter section of the PivotTable Field List. This enables you to apply multiple filters to the data. For example, you could add the Country field and the Salesperson field to the report filter to see each person's sales by country. To do this, you would use the steps shown in this section to choose an item in each report filter list.

Important!

When you filter your PivotTables using multiple fields in the report filter, be aware that not all combinations of items from the fields will produce PivotTable results. For example, a particular salesperson may not have sold any products to customers in a specific country, so combining those filters produces a PivotTable without any data.

You can greatly reduce the time you spend formatting your PivotTables if you apply a Quick Style.

A Quick Style is a collection of formatting options — fonts, borders, and background colors — that Excel defines for different areas of a PivotTable. For example, a Quick Style might use bold, white text on a black background for labels and grand totals, and white text on a dark blue background for items and data. Defining all these formats manually might take a while. But with Quick Styles, you

choose the one you want to use for the whole PivotTable, and Excel applies the individual formatting options automatically.

Excel defines more than 80 Quick Styles, divided into three categories: Light, Medium, and Dark. The Light category includes Pivot Style Light 16, the default formatting applied to PivotTable reports that you create, and None, which removes all formatting from the PivotTable. You can also create your own PivotTable Quick Style format.

① Click any cell within the PivotTable you want to format.

② Click the Design tab.

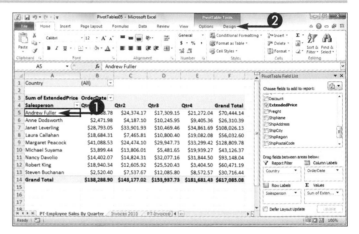

③ In the PivotTable Styles group, click the More button.

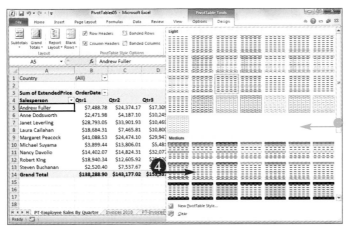

● The Quick Styles gallery appears.

Note: When you hover the mouse pointer over a style, Excel temporarily formats the PivotTable with that style.

④ Click the Quick Style you want to apply.

● Excel applies the Quick Style.

Customize It!

You may find that none of the predefined PivotTable Quick Styles give you the exact look that you want. In that case, you can define that look yourself by creating your own custom PivotTable Quick Style.

There are 25 separate PivotTable elements that you can format. These elements include the entire table, the page field labels and values, the first column, the header row, the Grand Total row, and the Grand Total column.

Click the Design tab, click the drop-down arrow to display the PivotTable Styles gallery, and then click New PivotTable Style. In the New PivotTable Quick Style dialog box, type a name for your custom Quick Style. For each element you want to format, click the element, click Format, use the Format Cells dialog box to select the formatting you want to use, and then click OK.

If your data analysis requires a calculation other than Sum (for numeric data) or Count (for text), you can configure the data field to use any one of the nine other summary calculations that are built into Excel:

- Average — Calculates the mean value in a numeric field.
- Max — Displays the largest value in a numeric field.
- Min — Displays the smallest value in a numeric field.
- Product — Multiplies the values in a numeric field.

- Count Nums — Displays the total number of numeric values in the source field.
- StdDev — Calculates the standard deviation of a population sample, which tells you how much the values in the source field vary with respect to the average.
- StdDevp — Calculates the standard deviation when the values in the data field represent the entire population.
- Var — Calculates the variance of a population sample, which is the square of the standard deviation.
- Varp — Calculates the variance when the values in the data field represent the entire population.

---

① **Click any cell in the data field.**

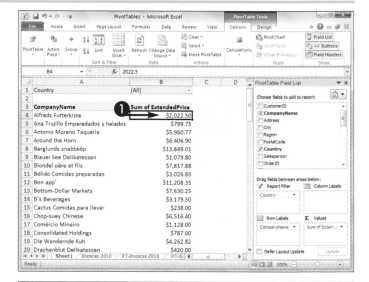

② **Click the Options tab.**

③ **Click Calculations.**

④ **Click Summarize Values By.**

- If you see the calculation you want to use, click it and skip the rest of these steps.

⑤ **Click More Options.**

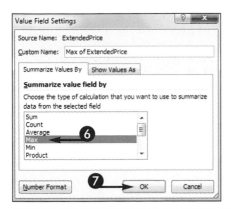

The Value Field Settings dialog box appears with the Summarize Values By tab displayed.

6 Click the summary calculation you want to use.

7 Click OK.

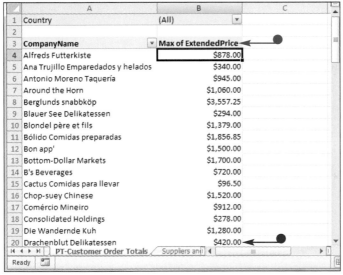

● Excel recalculates the PivotTable results.

● Excel renames the data field label to reflect the new summary calculation.

You can customize the layout of the PivotTable Field List to suit the way you work.

By default, the PivotTable Field List pane is divided into two sections: the Fields Section lists the available fields and appears at the top of the pane, and the Areas Section lists the PivotTable areas and appears at the bottom of the pane.

However, you can customize this layout. For example, you can choose the Field Section and Areas Section Side-By-Side option, which puts the Fields Section on the left and the Areas

Section on the right. This is useful if your source data comes with a large number of fields.

Excel also offers the Fields Section Only option, which is useful if you add fields to the PivotTable by right-clicking the field name and then clicking the area to which you want the field to be added.

Excel also offers two Areas Section Only options, which are useful if you have finished adding fields to the PivotTable and you want to concentrate on moving fields between the areas and filtering the fields.

① Click any cell inside the PivotTable.

② Click here.

● Excel displays the list of PivotTable Field List options.

③ Click the option you want to use.

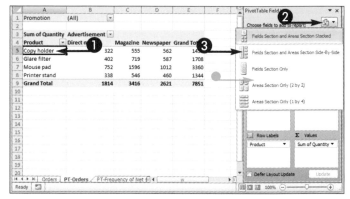

● Excel customizes the PivotTable Field List based on your selection.

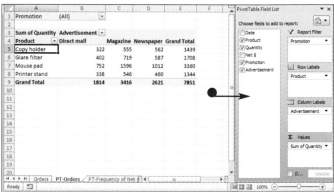

You can create a PivotChart directly from an existing PivotTable. This saves times because you do not have to configure the layout of the PivotChart or any other options.

A *PivotChart* is a graphical representation of the values in a PivotTable report. However, a PivotChart goes far beyond a regular chart because a PivotChart comes with many of the same capabilities as a PivotTable. These capabilities include hiding items, filtering data using the report filter, refreshing the PivotChart to account for changes in the underlying data, and more. Also, if you move fields from one area of the PivotTable to another, the PivotChart changes accordingly. You also have access to most of the regular charting capabilities in Excel, which makes PivotCharts a powerful addition to your data analysis toolkit.

① Click any cell in the PivotTable.

② Press F11.

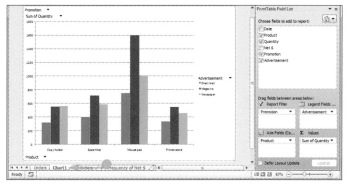

● Excel creates a new chart sheet and displays the PivotChart.

Importing Data into Excel

A vast amount of data exists in the world, and most of it resides in some kind of non-workbook format. Some data exists in simple text files, perhaps as comma-separated lists of items. Other data resides in tables, either in Word documents or, more likely, in Access databases. There is also an increasing amount of data that resides in Web pages and in XML files.

By definition, all this data is not directly available to you in Excel. However, Excel offers a number of tools that enable you to import external data into the program.

Depending on your needs and on the type of data, you can either import the data directly into a PivotTable report, or store the data on a worksheet. In most cases, Excel also enables you to refresh the data so that you are always working with the most up-to-date version of the data.

Excel can access a wide variety of external data types. However, this chapter focuses on the six most common types: data source files, Access tables, Word tables, text files, Web pages, and XML files.

External data is data that resides outside of Excel in a file, database, server, or Web site. You can import external data directly into an Excel PivotTable or worksheet for additional types of data analysis.

Before you learn the specifics of importing external data into your Excel workbooks, you need to understand the various types of external data that you are likely to encounter. For the vast majority of applications, external data comes in one of the following six formats:

data sources, Access tables, Word tables, text files, Web pages, and XML files.

You also need to understand how you access external data. This means understanding where external data resides — such as in a file located on your computer, in a file located on your network, on a network server, on a Web page, or on a Web server — and how you access that data, for example, with a username and password.

Data Source File

In Chapter 8, you learn about Open Database Connectivity (ODBC) data sources, which give you access to data residing in databases such as Access and dBase, or on servers such as SQL Server and Oracle. However, there are many other data-source types that connect to specific objects in a data source. For more information, see the section, "Import Data from a Data Source."

Access Table

Microsoft Access is the Office suite's relational database management system, and so it is often used to store and manage the bulk of the data used by a person, team, department, or company. For more information, see the section, "Import Data from an Access Table."

Word Table

Some simple data is often stored in a table embedded in a Word document. You can only perform so much analysis on that data within Word, and so it is often useful to import the data from the Word table into an Excel worksheet. For more information, see the section, "Import Data from a Word Table."

Text File

Text files often contain useful data. If that data is formatted properly — for example, where each line has the same number of items, all separated by spaces, commas, or tabs — then it is possible to import that data into Excel for further analysis. For more information, see the section, "Import Data from a Text File."

Web Page

People and companies often store useful data on Web pages that reside either on the Internet or on company intranets. This data is often a combination of text and tables, but you cannot analyze Web-based data in any meaningful way in your Web browser. Fortunately, Excel enables you to create a Web query that lets you import text and tables from a Web page. For more information, see the section, "Import Data from a Web Page."

XML

XML — Extensible Markup Language — is redefining how data is stored. This is reflected in the large number of tools that Excel now has for dealing with XML data, particularly tools for importing XML data into Excel. For more information, see the section, "Import Data from an XML File."

Access to External Data

To use external data, you must have access to it. This usually means knowing at least one of the following: the location of the data or the login information required to authorize your use of the data.

Location

To access external data, you must at least know where it is located. Here are the most common possibilities: in a file on your computer; in a file on your network; on a network server, particularly as part of a large, server-based database management system, such as SQL Server or Oracle; on a Web page; and on a Web server.

Login

Knowing where the data is located is probably all that you require if you are dealing with a local file or database or, usually, a Web page. However, after you start accessing data remotely — on a network, database server, or Web server — you will also require authorization to secure that access. See the administrator of the resource to obtain a username or login ID as well as a password.

Import Data from a Data Source

You can quickly import data into just about any format by importing the data from a defined data source file.

In this section, you will learn how to import data from a *data connection file*. This is a data source that connects you to a wide variety of data, including ODBC, SQL Server, SQL Server OLAP Services, Oracle, and Web-based data retrieval services. You can also read the Tip to learn how to create a data connection file.

When you import the data source, you can choose to import the data to an Excel table, directly to a PivotTable, or to both a PivotChart and a PivotTable. You can also import the data to an existing worksheet or to a new worksheet.

---

1 Click the Data tab.

2 Click Get External Data.

3 Click Existing Connections.

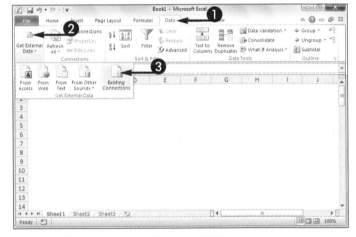

The Existing Connections dialog box appears.

4 Click the data source you want to import.

5 Click Open.

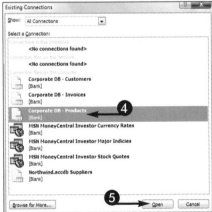

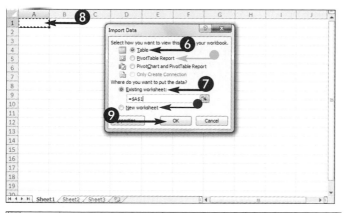

The Import Data dialog box appears.

6 Click to select the Table option.

● If you want to import the data directly into a PivotTable, you can select the PivotTable Report option, instead.

7 Select the Existing Worksheet option.

8 Click the cell where you want the imported data to appear.

● If you want the data to appear in a new sheet, you can select the New Worksheet option, instead.

9 Click OK.

Excel imports the data into the worksheet.

	A	B	C	D	E	F
1	ProductID	ProductName	SupplierID	CategoryID	QuantityPerUnit	UnitPric
2	1	Chai	1	1	10 boxes x 20 bags	
3	2	Chang	1	1	24 - 12 oz bottles	
4	3	Aniseed Syrup	1	2	12 - 550 ml bottles	
5	4	Chef Anton's Cajun Seasoning	2	2	48 - 6 oz jars	
6	5	Chef Anton's Gumbo Mix	2	2	36 boxes	2
7	6	Grandma's Boysenberry Spread	3	2	12 - 8 oz jars	
8	7	Uncle Bob's Organic Dried Pears	3	7	12 - 1 lb pkgs.	
9	8	Northwoods Cranberry Sauce	3	2	12 - 12 oz jars	
10	9	Mishi Kobe Niku	4	6	18 - 500 g pkgs.	
11	10	Ikura	4	8	12 - 200 ml jars	
12	11	Queso Cabrales	5	4	1 kg pkg.	
13	12	Queso Manchego La Pastora	5	4	10 - 500 g pkgs.	
14	13	Konbu	6	8	2 kg box	
15	14	Tofu	6	7	40 - 100 g pkgs.	2
16	15	Genen Shouyu	6	2	24 - 250 ml bottles	
17	16	Pavlova	7	3	32 - 500 g boxes	1
18	17	Alice Mutton	7	6	20 - 1 kg tins	
19	18	Carnarvon Tigers	7	8	16 kg pkg.	

TIP

Try This!

To create your own data connection (.odc) file, click the Data tab, click Get External Data, click From Other Sources, and then click From Data Connection Wizard. Click the data source you want and then click Next.

The next steps depend on the data source. For example, for Microsoft SQL Server or Oracle, you specify the server name or address and your server login data; similarly, for ODBC DSN (Database Source Name), you choose the ODBC data source, specify the location of the file, and select the table or query you want to connect to.

When you get to the Import Data dialog box, click OK to import the data or click Cancel if you just want to create the data source file for now.

Import Data from an Access Table

If you want to use Excel to analyze data from a table within an Access database, you can import the table to an Excel worksheet.

In Chapter 8, you learn how to use Microsoft Query to create a database query to extract records from a database, to filter and sort the records, and then to return the results to Excel. In Chapter 8 you also learn that you can create a database query for any ODBC data source, including an Access database.

However, Excel gives you an easier way to do this: you can import the table directly from the Access database. To make this technique even easier, Excel automatically creates a data connection file for the database and table that you import. Therefore, you can import the same table in the future simply by opening the data connection file.

Note, too, that you can also use the steps in this section to import data from any query that is already defined in the Access database.

① Click the Data tab.

② Click Get External Data.

③ Click From Access.

The Select Data Source dialog box appears.

④ Open the folder that contains the Access database.

⑤ Click the Access database file.

⑥ Click Open.

Note: *If another user has the database open, you may see the Data Link Properties dialog box. If so, make sure the login information is correct and then click Test Connection until you are able to connect successfully. Then click OK.*

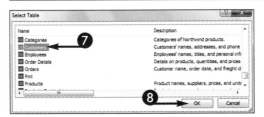

The Select Table dialog box appears.

⑦ Click the table or query you want to import.

⑧ Click OK.

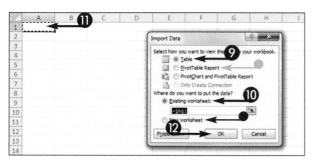

The Import Data dialog box appears.

⑨ Select the Table option.

● If you want to import the data directly into a PivotTable, you can select the PivotTable Report option, instead.

⑩ Select the Existing Worksheet option.

⑪ Click the cell where you want the imported data to appear.

● If you want the data to appear in a new sheet, you can select the New Worksheet option, instead.

⑫ Click OK.

Excel imports the data to the worksheet.

	A	B	C	D
1	CustomerID	CompanyName	ContactName	ContactTitle
2	ALFKI	Alfreds Futterkiste	Maria Anders	Sales Representative
3	ANATR	Ana Trujillo Emparedados y helados	Ana Trujillo	Owner
4	ANTON	Antonio Moreno Taqueria	Antonio Moreno	Owner
5	AROUT	Around the Horn	Thomas Hardy	Sales Representative
6	BERGS	Berglunds snabbköp	Christina Berglund	Order Administrator
7	BLAUS	Blauer See Delikatessen	Hanna Moos	Sales Representative
8	BLONP	Blondel père et fils	Frédérique Citeaux	Marketing Manager
9	BOLID	Bólido Comidas preparadas	Martín Sommer	Owner
10	BONAP	Bon app'	Laurence Lebihan	Owner
11	BOTTM	Bottom-Dollar Markets	Elizabeth Lincoln	Accounting Manager
12	BSBEV	B's Beverages	Victoria Ashworth	Sales Representative
13	CACTU	Cactus Comidas para llevar	Patricio Simpson	Sales Agent
14	CENTC	Centro comercial Moctezuma	Francisco Chang	Marketing Manager
15	CHOPS	Chop-suey Chinese	Yang Wang	Owner
16	COMMI	Comércio Mineiro	Pedro Afonso	Sales Associate
17	CONSH	Consolidated Holdings	Elizabeth Brown	Sales Representative
18	DRACD	Drachenblut Delikatessen	Sven Ottlieb	Order Administrator
19	DUMON	Du monde entier	Janine Labrune	Owner

More Options!

If the Access database requires a login password, you may need to type the password again when you refresh the imported data. To avoid this extra step, tell Excel to save the database password along with the external data. If you have the Import Data dialog box onscreen, click the Properties button; if you have already imported the data, click the Data tab, click the Refresh All drop-down arrow, and then click Connection Properties. In the Connection Properties dialog box, click the Definition tab, click to select the Save Password check box, and then click OK.

Import Data from a Word Table

You can improve your analysis of Word table data by importing the table into an Excel worksheet.

Word tables are collections of rows, columns, and cells, which means they look something like Excel ranges. Moreover, you can insert fields into Word table cells to perform calculations. In fact, Word fields support cell references such as B1 — the cell in the second column and first row of the table — and you can use cell references, built-in functions such

as SUM and AVERAGE, and operators such as addition (+), multiplication (*), and greater than (>), to build formulas that calculate results based on the table data.

However, even the most powerful Word field formula cannot perform the functions that are available to you in Excel, which offers much more sophisticated data analysis tools. Therefore, to analyze your Word table data properly, you should import the table into an Excel worksheet.

① Launch Microsoft Word and open the document that contains the table.

② Click a cell inside the table you want to import.

③ Click the Layout tab.

④ Click Select.

⑤ Click Select Table.

● You can also select the table by clicking the table selection handle.

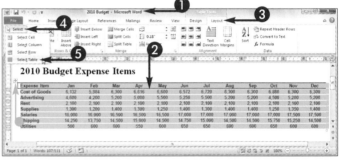

⑥ Click the Home tab.

⑦ Click Copy.

You can also press Ctrl+C.

Word copies the table to the Clipboard.

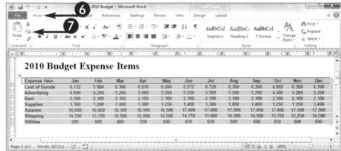

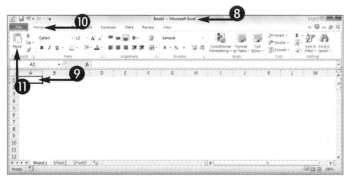

⑧ Switch to the Excel workbook into which you want to import the table.

⑨ Click the cell where you want the table to appear.

⑩ Click the Home tab.

⑪ Click Paste.

You can also press Ctrl+V.

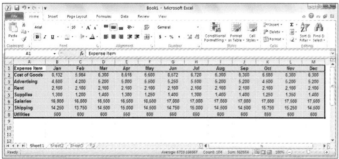

Excel pastes the Word table data.

TIP

Important!

The problem with this copy-and-paste method is that there is no connection between the data in Word and the data in Excel. If you make changes to one set of data, those changes are not automatically reflected in the other set of data.

A better approach is to shift the data's container application from Word to Excel. That is, after you paste the table data into Excel, copy the Excel range, switch to Word, click the Home tab, click the Paste drop-down arrow, and then click Paste Special. In the Paste Special dialog box, click HTML Format in the As list, select the Paste Link option, and then click OK. The resulting table is linked to the Excel data, which means that any changes you make to the data in Excel automatically appear in the Word table. Note, however, that if you change the data in Word, you cannot update the original data in Excel.

Import Data from a Text File

You can analyze the data contained in certain text files by using the Text Import Wizard to import some or all of the data into an Excel worksheet. However, you can only import a text file into Excel if the file uses either a delimited or fixed-width format.

A *delimited* format is a text structure in which each item on a line of text is separated by a character, called a *delimiter*. The most common text delimiter is the comma (,). Excel imports a delimited text file by placing each line of text on a separate row and each item between the delimiter in a separate cell.

A *fixed-width* format is a text structure in which each item on a line of text uses up a set amount of space and these widths are the same on every line of text. For example, the first item on every line might use 5 characters, the second item on every line might use 15 characters, and so on. Excel imports a fixed-width text file by placing each line of text on a separate row and each fixed-width item in a separate cell.

Start the Text Import Wizard

1 Click the cell where you want the imported data to appear.

2 Click the Data tab.

3 Click Get External Data.

4 Click From Text.

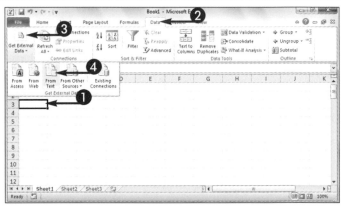

The Import Text File dialog box appears.

5 Open the folder that contains the text file.

6 Click the text file.

7 Click Import.

The Text Import Wizard – Step 1 of 3 dialog box appears.

Note: *For delimited text, continue with Import Delimited Data; for fixed-width text, skip to Import Fixed-Width Data.*

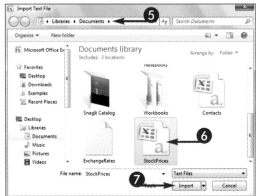

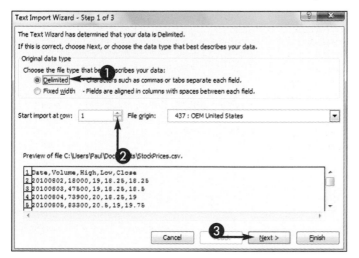

Import Delimited Data

① Select the Delimited option.

② Use the Start Import at Row spin box to set the first row you want to import.

③ Click Next.

The Text Import Wizard – Step 2 of 3 dialog box appears.

④ Click to select the check box beside the delimiter character that your text data uses.

● If you choose the correct delimiter, the data appears in separate columns.

⑤ Click Next.

The Text Import Wizard – Step 3 of 3 dialog box appears.

Note: *To complete this section, follow the steps under "Finish the Text Import Wizard."*

TIP

More Options!

It is common for text files to include a title or one or more lines of explanatory text at the top of the document. In this case, you probably do not want to import this introductory text into Excel. The exception to this would be if the text file has a line of column headings. In that case, you should import the headings so that Excel includes them at the top of the range of imported data.

To skip text at the beginning of the text file, use the Start Import at Row spin box in the Text Import Wizard – Step 1 of 3 dialog box. Set the value of this control to the row number where the data starts. For example, if you have four lines of introductory text that you want to skip over, set the spin box value to 5.

continued

If you are importing data that uses the fixed-width structure, then you need to tell Excel where the separation between each field occurs.

In a fixed-width text file, each column of data is a constant width. The Text Import Wizard is usually quite good at determining the width of each column of data, and in most cases the wizard automatically sets up *column break lines,* which are vertical lines that separate one field from the next. However, titles or introductory text at the beginning of the file can impair the wizard's calculations, so you should check carefully that the proposed break lines are accurate. In the Text Import Wizard – Step 2 of 3 dialog box, you can scroll through all the data to see if any break line is improperly positioned for the data in a particular field. If you find a break line in the wrong position, you can move it to the correct position before importing the text.

Import Fixed-Width Data

Note: *You need to have run through the steps under "Start the Text Import Wizard" earlier in this task before continuing with this section.*

① Select the Fixed Width option.

② Use the Start Import at Row spin box to set the first row you want to import.

③ Click Next.

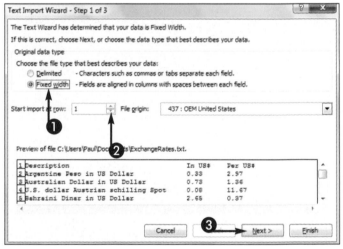

The Text Import Wizard – Step 2 of 3 dialog box appears.

④ Click and drag a break line to set the width of each column.

To create a break line, you can click the ruler at the point where you want the break to appear.

To delete a break line, you can double-click it.

⑤ Click Next.

The Text Import Wizard – Step 3 of 3 dialog box appears.

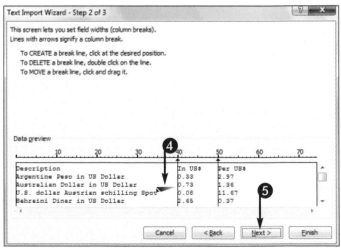

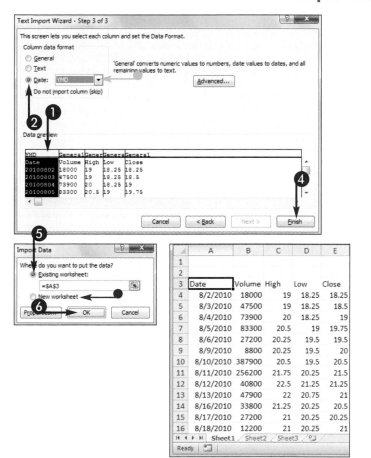

Finish the Text Import Wizard

1 Click a column.

2 Click to select the data format you want Excel to apply to the column.

● If you select the Date option, you can use this drop-down list to select the date format your data uses.

3 Repeat steps 1 and 2 to set the data format for all of the columns.

4 Click Finish.

The Import Data dialog box appears.

5 Select the Existing Worksheet option.

● If you want the data to appear in a new sheet, you can select the New Worksheet option, instead.

6 Click OK.

Excel imports the data to the worksheet.

More Options!

Some text files may contain numbers that use a comma instead of a dot as the decimal separator, or a dot instead of a comma as the thousands separator. To import such data, click the Advanced button in the Text Import Wizard – Step 3 of 3 dialog box to display the Advanced Text Import Settings dialog box. Use the Decimal Separator drop-down list to click the text's decimal separator, and use the Thousands Separator drop-down list to click the text's thousands separator.

Important!

If you make a mistake when importing a text file, you do not need to start the import from scratch. Click any cell in the imported data, click the Data tab, click the Refresh All drop-down arrow, and then click Connection Properties. Click the Definition tab and then click Edit Query. The Import Text File dialog box appears. Click the file you want to import and then click Import. Excel launches the Import Text Wizard to enable you to run through the wizard's options again.

Import Data from a Web Page

You can analyze Web page data by importing it into Excel using a Web query.

To make data more readily available to a wide variety of users, many people are placing data on Web pages that are accessible through the Internet or a corporate network. Although this data is often text, most Web page data comes in one of two formats: a table or preformatted text.

A Web page *table* is a rectangular array of rows and columns, with data values in the cells created by the intersection of the rows and columns. *Preformatted text* is text that has been structured with predefined spacing. In many cases, this spacing is used to organize data into columns with fixed widths.

Both types of data are suitable for import into Excel, which enables you to perform more extensive data analysis using the Excel tools.

① Click the cell where you want the imported data to appear.

② Click the Data tab.

③ Click Get External Data.

④ Click From Web.

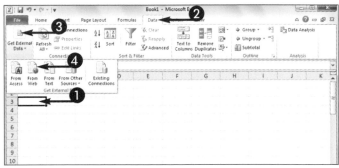

The New Web Query dialog box appears.

⑤ Type the address of the Web page that contains the data you want to import.

⑥ Click Go or press Enter.

● Excel loads the page into the dialog box.

⑦ Click the Select Table icon beside the table that you want to import.

● Excel selects the table.

⑧ If the page has other tables that you want to import, repeat step 7 for each table.

⑨ Click Import.

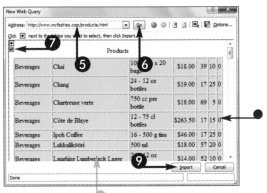

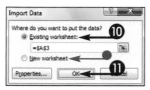

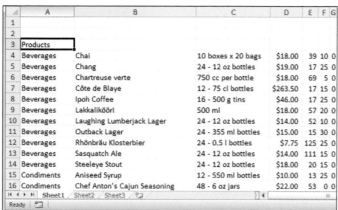

The Import Data dialog box appears.

⑩ Select the Existing Worksheet option.

● If you want the data to appear in a new sheet, you can select the New Worksheet option, instead.

⑪ Click OK.

Excel imports the data to the worksheet.

	A	B	C	D	E	F	G
1							
2							
3	Products						
4	Beverages	Chai	10 boxes x 20 bags	$18.00	39	10	0
5	Beverages	Chang	24 - 12 oz bottles	$19.00	17	25	0
6	Beverages	Chartreuse verte	750 cc per bottle	$18.00	69	5	0
7	Beverages	Côte de Blaye	12 - 75 cl bottles	$263.50	17	15	0
8	Beverages	Ipoh Coffee	16 - 500 g tins	$46.00	17	25	0
9	Beverages	Lakkalikööri	500 ml	$18.00	57	20	0
10	Beverages	Laughing Lumberjack Lager	24 - 12 oz bottles	$14.00	52	10	0
11	Beverages	Outback Lager	24 - 355 ml bottles	$15.00	15	30	0
12	Beverages	Rhönbräu Klosterbier	24 - 0.5 l bottles	$7.75	125	25	0
13	Beverages	Sasquatch Ale	24 - 12 oz bottles	$14.00	111	15	0
14	Beverages	Steeleye Stout	24 - 12 oz bottles	$18.00	20	15	0
15	Condiments	Aniseed Syrup	12 - 550 ml bottles	$10.00	13	25	0
16	Condiments	Chef Anton's Cajun Seasoning	48 - 6 oz jars	$22.00	53	0	0

Sheet1 / Sheet2 / Sheet3

Ready

TIP

More Options!

Besides the steps you learned in this section, Excel gives you two other methods for creating Web queries. Both of these alternative methods assume that you already have the Web page open in Internet Explorer:

● Right-click the page and then click Export to Microsoft Excel.

● Copy the Web page text, switch to Excel, and then paste the text. When the Paste Options smart tag appears, click the smart tag drop-down arrow and then click Refreshable Web Query.

Each of these methods opens the New Web Query dialog box and automatically loads the Web page.

If you want to save the Web query for future use in other workbooks, click the Save Query button in the New Web Query dialog box and then use the Save Workspace dialog box to save the query file.

Import Data from an XML File

You can analyze data that currently resides in XML format by importing that data into Excel and then manipulating and analyzing the resulting XML table.

XML is a standard that enables the management and sharing of structured data using simple text files. These XML files organize data using tags, among other elements, that specify the equivalent of a table name and field names. Here is a simple XML example that constitutes a single record in a table named "Products":

```
<Products>
<ProductName>Chai</ProductName>
```

```
<CompanyName>Liquid Depot</CompanyName>
<ContactName>Sue Sellars</ContactName>
</Products>
```

These XML files are readable by a wide variety of database programs and other applications, including Excel 2010. Excel usually stores imported XML data in an XML table, a range that looks and operates much like a regular Excel table, except that it has a few XML-specific features.

---

① Click the cell where you want the imported data to appear.

② Click the Data tab.

③ Click Get External Data.

④ Click From Other Sources.

⑤ Click From XML Data Import.

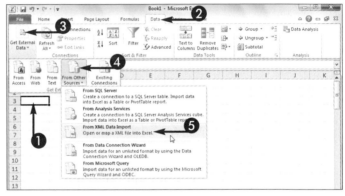

The Select Data Source dialog box appears.

⑥ Select the folder that contains the XML file you want to import.

⑦ Click the XML file.

⑧ Click Open.

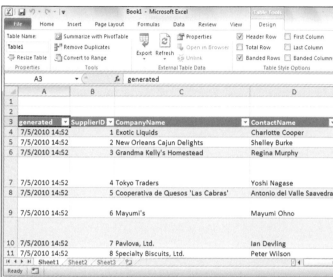

The Import Data dialog box appears.

9 Click to select the XML Table in Existing Worksheet option.

10 Click OK.

Excel imports the data into the worksheet as an XML table.

Customize It!

You can use the XML Source pane to control the fields that display in the XML table, create your own XML maps, and more. The easiest way to display the XML Source pane is to add the XML button to the Quick Access Toolbar. Right-click the Quick Access Toolbar, click Customize Quick Access Toolbar, use the Choose Commands From list to click All Commands, click XML, click Add, and then click OK.

More Options!

If there are fields in the XML list that you do not want to use, you can remove them. First display the XML Source pane by clicking the XML button that you added in the previous Tip. The XML Source pane displays a list of the fields — called *elements* in the XML table. To remove an element, right-click it and then click Remove Element. To add an element back into the XML list, right-click the element and then click Map Element.

Refresh Imported Data

External data often changes; you can ensure that you are working with the most up-to-date version of the information by refreshing the imported data.

Refreshing the imported data means retrieving the most current version of the source data. This is a straightforward operation most of the time. However, it is possible to construct a query that accesses confidential information or destroys some or all of the external data.

Therefore, when you refresh imported data, Excel always lets you know the potential risks and asks if you are sure the query is safe.

Remember, as well, that most external data resides on servers or in remote network locations. Therefore, the refresh may take some time, depending on the amount of data, the load on the server, and the amount of traffic on the network.

Refresh Non-Text Data

① Click any cell inside the imported data.

② Click the Data tab.

③ Click Refresh All.

④ Click Refresh.

Note: *You can also refresh the current data by pressing Alt+F5.*

● To refresh all the imported data in the current workbook, you can click Refresh All, or press Ctrl+Alt+F5.

Excel refreshes the imported data.

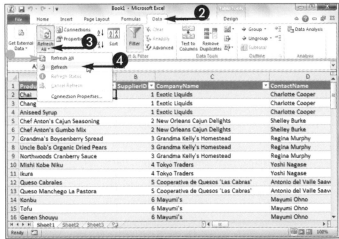

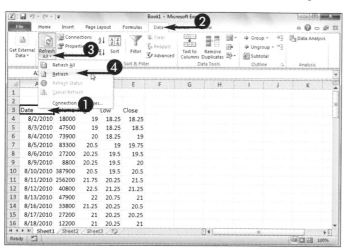

Refresh Text Data

① Click any cell inside the imported text data.

② Click the Data tab.

③ Click Refresh All.

④ Click Refresh.

Note: *You can also refresh the current data by pressing Alt+F5.*

The Import Text File dialog box appears.

⑤ Open the folder that contains the text file.

⑥ Click the text file.

⑦ Click Import.

Excel refreshes the imported text data.

TIPS

More Options!	**More Options!**
For certain types of external data, you can set up a schedule that automatically refreshes the data at a specified interval. This is useful when you know that the source data changes frequently and you do not want to be bothered with constant manual refreshes. Follow steps 1 to 3 under "Refresh Non-Text Data," and then click Connection Properties. Select the Refresh Every option and then use the spin box to specify the refresh interval, in minutes.	The refresh may take a long time. To check the status of the refresh, follow steps 1 to 3 under "Refresh Non-Text Data," and then click Refresh Status to display the External Data Refresh Status dialog box; click Close to continue the refresh. If the refresh is taking too long, follow steps 1 to 3 again, and then click Cancel Refresh to cancel it.

Separate Cell Text into Columns

You can make imported data more useful and easier to analyze by separating the text in each cell into two or more columns of data.

When you import data into Excel, one column of that data may contain multiple items of data. In imported contact data, for example, a column might contain each person's first and last name, separated by a space. This is problematic if you want to sort the contacts by last name, so you need some way of separating

the first and last names into their own columns.

Excel makes this easy by offering the Text to Columns feature, which examines a column of data and then separates it into two or more columns, depending on whether the original data uses a delimited or fixed-width format. For more information about these two formats, see the section, "Import Data from a Text File."

① Insert a column to the right of the column you want to separate.

Note: *If the data will separate into three or more columns, you can insert as many new columns as you need to hold the separated data.*

② Select the data you want to separate.

③ Click the Data tab.

④ Click Text to Columns.

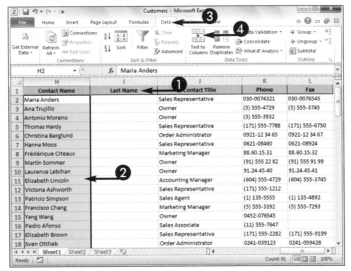

The Convert Text to Columns Wizard – Step 1 of 3 dialog box appears.

⑤ Click to select the Delimited option.

⑥ Click Next.

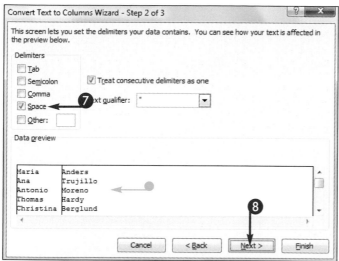

⑦ Click to select the check box beside the delimiter character that your text data uses.

● If you choose the correct delimiter, the data appears in separate columns.

⑧ Click Next.

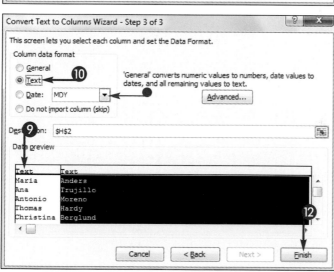

⑨ Click a column.

⑩ Click to select the data format you want Excel to apply to the column.

● If you click the Date option, you can use this list to click the date format your data uses.

⑪ Repeat steps 9 and 10 to set the data format for all the columns.

⑫ Click Finish.

Excel asks if you want to replace the contents of the destination cells.

⑬ Click OK (not shown).

Excel separates the data.

More Options!

If the column contains fixed-width text, follow steps 1 to 4 to start the Convert Text to Columns Wizard. Click to select the Fixed Width option, and then click Next. Click and drag a break line to set the width of each column, and then click Next. Follow steps 9 to 13 to complete the wizard.

Caution!

Before separating data into columns, check the data to see exactly how many columns Excel will create. For example, in a column of contact names, if any of those names use three words, Excel will assume that you want to create two extra columns for all the data, and it may overwrite some of your existing data.

Chapter 8

Querying Data Sources

If you want to build a table or a PivotTable using a sorted, filtered subset of an external data source, you must use Microsoft Query to specify the sorting and filtering options and the subset of the source data that you want to work with.

Databases such as those used in Microsoft Access and SQL Server are often very large and contain a wide variety of data scattered over many different tables. When your data analysis requires a table or PivotTable, you can never use an entire database as the source for the report. Instead, you can

extract a subset of the database: a table or perhaps two or three related tables. You may also require the data to be sorted in a certain way, and you may also need to filter the data so that you only work with certain records.

You can accomplish all three operations — extracting a subset, sorting, and filtering — by creating a database query, as described in this chapter. Remember, however, that for an Access database it is usually easier to import the data directly from the database to Excel; see Chapter 7 for details.

Quick Tips

Understanding Microsoft Query

In Excel, the program that you use to create and run database queries is Microsoft Query. You will learn how to use Microsoft Query in this chapter. This section gets you started by introducing you to various query concepts and how they apply to Microsoft Query.

Microsoft Query is a special program that you can use to perform all the database query tasks mentioned in this section. You can use

Microsoft Query to create data sources, add tables to a query, specify fields, filter records using criteria, and sort records. You can also save your queries as query files so that you can reuse them later. If you start Microsoft Query from within Excel, you can return the query records to Excel and use them in a table or PivotTable.

Data Source

All database queries require two things at the very beginning: access to a database, and an Open Database Connectivity (ODBC) data source for the database installed on your computer. ODBC is a database standard that enables a program to connect to and manipulate a data source. You learn how to create a new data source in the next section, "Define a Data Source."

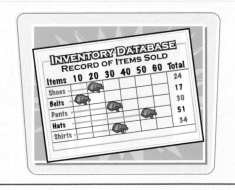

Database Query

Database queries make a large database more manageable by enabling you to perform three tasks: selecting the tables and fields you want to work with; filtering the records so that you only get the records you want; and sorting the data that you are extracting.

Query Criteria

You can specify the filtering portion of a database query by specifying one or more *criteria*. These are usually logical expressions that, when applied to each record in the query's underlying table, return either a true or false result. Every record that returns a true result is included in the query, and every record that returns a false result is filtered out of the query. For example, if you only want to work with records where the Country field is equal to USA, then you can set up criteria to handle this, and the query discards all records where the Country field is not equal to USA.

Criteria Operators

The following table lists the operators you can use to build your criteria expressions:

Excel's Criteria Operators	
Operator	*Value in the Field*
Equals (=)	Is equal to a specified value.
Does not equal (< >)	Is not equal to a specified value.
Is greater than (>)	Is greater than a specified value.
Is greater than or equal to (≥=)	Is greater than or equal to a specified value.
Is less than (<)	Is less than a specified value.
Is less than or equal to (≤=)	Is less than or equal to a specified value.
Is one of	Is included in a group of values.
Is not one of	Is not included in a group of values.
Is between	Is between (and including) one value and another.
Is not between	Is not between (and does not include) one value and another.
Begins with	Begins with the specified characters.
Does not begin with	Does not begin with the specified characters.
Ends with	Ends with the specified characters.
Does not end with	Does not end with the specified characters.
Contains	Contains the specified characters.
Does not contain	Does not contain the specified characters.
Like	Matches a specified pattern.
Not like	Does not match a specified pattern.
Is Null	Is empty.
Is Not Null	Is not empty.

Before you can do any work in Microsoft Query, you must select the data source that you want to use. If you have a particular database that you want to query, you can define a new data source that points to the appropriate file or server.

Most data sources point to database files. For example, the relational database management programs Access and Visual FoxPro use file-based databases. You can also create data sources based on text files and Excel workbooks. However, some data sources point to server-based databases. For example, SQL Server and Oracle run their databases on special servers.

As part of the data source definition, you need to include the software driver that Microsoft Query uses to communicate with the database. For example, an Access database requires an Access driver, a SQL Server database requires a SQL Server driver, and so on.

Finally, you must include in the data source any information that you require to access the database. Most file-based databases do not require a login, but some are protected with a password. For server-based data, you are almost certainly required to provide a username and password.

① Click the Data tab.

② Click Get External Data.

③ Click From Other Sources.

④ Click From Microsoft Query.

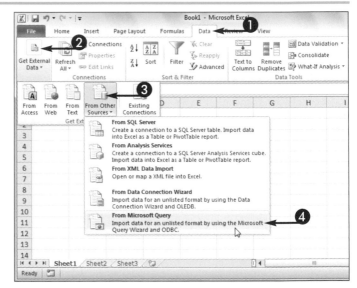

The Choose Data Source dialog box appears.

⑤ Click New Data Source.

⑥ Click to deselect the Use the Query Wizard to Create/Edit Queries check box.

⑦ Click OK.

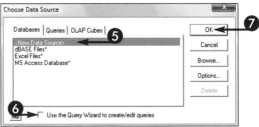

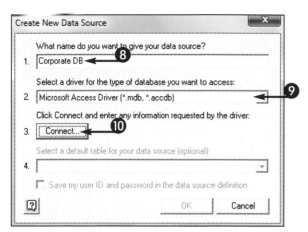

The Create New Data Source dialog box appears.

⑧ Type a name for your data source.

⑨ Use this drop-down list to select the database driver that your data source requires.

⑩ Click Connect.

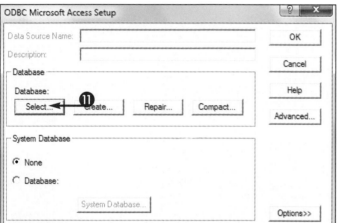

The dialog box for the database driver appears.

Note: The steps that follow show you how to set up a data source for a Microsoft Access database.

⑪ Click Select.

The Select Database dialog box appears.

More Options!

Many medium- and large-sized businesses store their data on the Microsoft SQL Server database system. This is a robust and powerful server-based system that can handle the largest databases and hundreds or thousands of users. If you need to define a data source for a SQL Server installation on your network or some other remote location, first follow steps 1 to 8.

In the drop-down list of database drivers, click SQL Server. Click the Connect button to display the SQL Server Login dialog box. Ask your SQL Server database administrator for the information you require to complete this dialog box.

Type the name or remote address of the SQL Server in the Server text box, type your SQL Server login ID and password, and then click OK. Perform steps 16 and 17 later in this section to complete the SQL Server data source.

Your system probably comes with a few data sources already defined, and you can use these predefined data sources instead of creating new ones.

In the Choose Data Source dialog box, the list in the Databases tab often shows one or more predefined data sources. These data sources are created by programs that you install on your system. When you install Microsoft Office and, in particular, the Microsoft Query component, the installation program creates three default data sources: dBase Files, Excel Files, and MS Access Database. These are incomplete data sources, as they do not point to a specific file. Instead, when you click one of these data sources and then click OK, Microsoft Query prompts you for the name and location of the file. These data sources are useful if you often switch the files that you are using. However, if you want a data source that always points to a specific file, you can follow the steps in this section.

⑫ Open the folder that contains the database.

⑬ Click the database file.

⑭ Click OK.

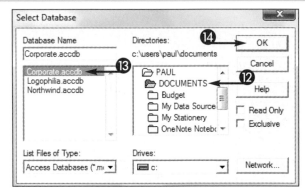

You are returned to the database driver's dialog box.

● If you must provide a login name and password to access the database, click Advanced to display the Set Advanced Options dialog box. Type the login name and password and then click OK.

⑮ Click OK.

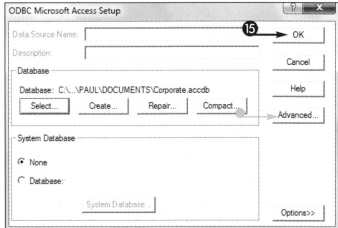

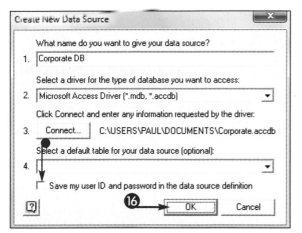

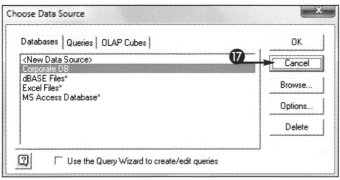

You are returned to the Create New Data Source dialog box.

● If you specified a login name and password as part of the data source, you can click to select this check box to save the login data.

⑯ Click OK.

You are returned to the Choose Data Source dialog box.

⑰ Click Cancel to bypass the steps for importing the data.

Note: *You will learn how to perform these steps in the rest of this chapter.*

You can now use the data source in Microsoft Query.

 TIPS

Change It!

The Choose Data Source dialog box does not enable you to reconfigure a data source. To reconfigure a data source, press Windows Logo+R to open the Run dialog box, type **odbcad32**, and then click OK. In the ODBC Data Source Administrator dialog box that appears, click the File DSN tab. Click the data source you want to work with and then click the Configure button to open the Setup dialog box for the database driver.

Remove It!

If you have a data source that you no longer use, you should delete it to ensure that only usable data sources appear in the Choose Data Source dialog box. Click the Data tab, click the Get External Data drop-down arrow, click From Other Sources, and then click From Microsoft Query to display the Choose Data Source dialog box. Click the data source and then click the Delete button. When Microsoft Query asks you to confirm the deletion, click Yes.

To create a query that defines the fields and records that you want to work with in Excel, you must begin by starting the Microsoft Query program.

Microsoft Query is part of the Office Tools collection that ships with Microsoft Office. If you like, you can start the program on its own by pressing Windows Logo+R to open the Run dialog box, typing the following path, and then clicking OK:

`%programfiles%\microsoftoffice\office14\msqry32.exe`

However, you can almost always start it from within Excel. That way, the data you configure with the query is automatically returned to Excel so that you can immediately begin analyzing the data.

① Click the Data tab.

② Click Get External Data.

③ Click From Other Sources.

④ Click From Microsoft Query.

The Choose Data Source dialog box appears.

⑤ Click the data source you want to work with.

⑥ Click to deselect the Use the Query Wizard to Create/Edit Queries check box.

⑦ Click OK.

The Microsoft Query window and the Add Tables dialog box appear.

Note: *To learn how to use the Add Tables dialog box, see the section, "Add a Table to the Query."*

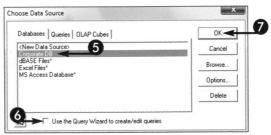

You can get the most out of Microsoft Query if you understand the layout of the screen and what each part of the Microsoft Query window represents.

Although you have not yet created a query using the Microsoft Query program, it is worthwhile to pause now and take a look at the various elements that make up the Microsoft Query window. Do not worry if what you currently see on your screen does not look like the window shown in this section. By the time you finish this chapter, you will have seen and worked with all the elements shown here.

Query Window

This window is where you create and edit, as well as preview, the results. The query window is divided into three panes: the table pane, the criteria pane, and the results pane.

Toolbar

The toolbar contains buttons that give you one-click access to many of the most useful features in Microsoft Query.

Table Pane

This pane displays one list for each table that you add to the query. For more information, see the section, "Add a Table to the Query." Each list shows the fields that are part of the table. Click View and then click Tables to toggle this pane on and off.

Criteria Pane

This pane is where you define the criteria that filter the records you want to return to Excel. For more information, see the section, "Filter the Records with Query Criteria." Click View and then click Criteria to toggle this pane on and off.

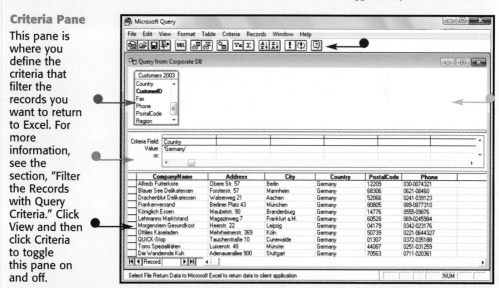

Query Results

This pane gives you a preview of the fields and records that your query will return to Excel. As you add fields to the query, change the query criteria, and sort the query (see the section, "Sort the Query Records"), Microsoft Query automatically updates the results pane (also called the *data grid*) to show you what effect your changes will have.

With your data source running and Microsoft Query started, the next step you must take is to add a table to the query.

In a database, a *table* is a two-dimensional arrangement of rows and columns that contain data. The columns are *fields* that represent distinct categories of data, and the rows are *records* that represent individual sets of field data. In some database management systems, the actual database files are tables. However, in most systems, each database contains a number of tables. Therefore, your first Microsoft Query

task in most cases is to select which table you want to work with.

Note, too, that many database systems also enable you to filter and sort data using their own versions of the querying process. Creating a query in Microsoft Access, for example, is similar to creating one in Microsoft Query. By default, when Microsoft Query shows you a list of the tables in the database, it also includes any queries that are defined in the database, so you can add these objects to your query, if required.

---

① Click Table.

② Click Add Tables.

Note: *When you start Microsoft Query from Excel, the Add Tables dialog box appears automatically, so you can skip steps 1 and 2.*

The Add Tables dialog box appears.

● You can also open this dialog box by clicking the Add Tables toolbar button.

③ Click the table you want to add.

④ Click Add.

● Microsoft Query adds the table to the table pane.

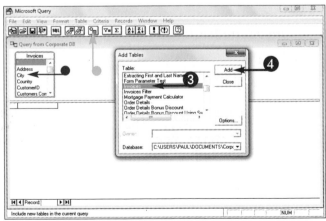

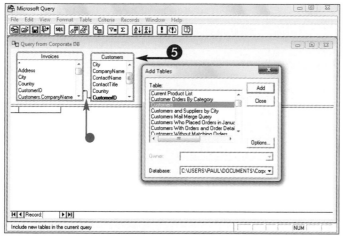

⑤ Repeat steps 3 and 4 if you want to add multiple, related tables to the query.

● If the tables are related, Microsoft Query displays a join line that connects the common fields.

⑥ Click Close.

You are now ready to add fields to the query, as described in the next section.

More Options!

If two tables are related, but no join line appears, you can create the join yourself. After you add the two tables to your query, click Table and then click Joins to display the Joins dialog box. In the Left list, click the common field from one of your tables. In the Right list, click the common field from the other table. In the Operator list, click = (equals). Click the Add button to add the join to the query, and then click Close.

Remove It!

To remove a table from the query, first click the table in the table pane. Click Table and then click Remove Table. Alternatively, click the table and then press Delete. Microsoft Query deletes the table list. If you added fields from the table to the criteria pane or the results pane, Microsoft Query removes those fields as well.

To display records in the query's results pane, you must first add one or more fields to the query.

After you add one or more tables to the query, your next step is to filter the resulting records so that you return to Excel only the data you need. Filtering the records involves two tasks: specifying the fields you want to work with and specifying the criteria you want to apply to records. This section shows you how to add

fields — or *columns,* as Microsoft Query calls them — to the query. See the next section, "Filter the Records with Query Criteria," to learn how to add criteria to the query.

At the top of each table list, you see an asterisk (*) item. The asterisk item represents all the fields in the table. So if you know that you want to include in your query every field from a particular table, you can do this easily by adding the asterisk "field" to the query.

① Click Records.

② Click Add Column.

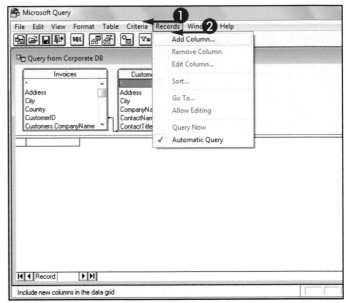

The Add Column dialog box appears.

③ In the Field drop-down list, click the field you want to add.

● If you want to use a different field name, you can use the Column Heading text box to type the new name.

④ Click Add.

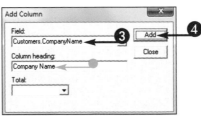

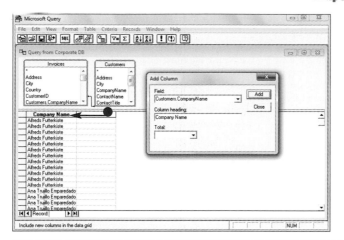

● Microsoft Query adds the field to the results pane.

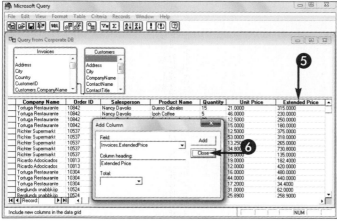

⑤ Repeat steps 3 and 4 until you have added all the fields that you want to appear in the query.

⑥ Click Close.

You can also either double-click a field name in a table list, or click and drag a field name in a table list and drop it inside the results pane.

Note: *To change where a field appears in the data grid, first click the field heading to select the entire field. Then click and drag the field heading to the left or right and drop the field into the new position.*

Change It!
If you want to make changes to a field — that is, you want to change to a different field or edit the name displayed in the field header — click the field heading or click any cell in the field, click Records, and then click Edit Column. (You can also double-click the field heading.) In the Edit Column dialog box that appears, change the field or edit the field heading, and then click OK.

Remove It!
If you no longer need a field in the query, you should delete it from the data grid. Click the field heading or click any cell in the field; note that Microsoft Query does not ask for confirmation when you delete a field, so be sure you click the correct field. Click Records and then click Remove Column (or just press Delete).

To display specific records that you want to return to Excel, you must use criteria to filter the records.

After you add your fields to the data grid, your next step is to specify which records you want to include in the results. You can do this by specifying the conditions that each record must meet to be included in the results. These conditions are called *criteria*, each of which is an expression — an operator and one or more

values — applied to a specific field. Only those records for which the expression returns a true answer are included in the query results.

You can enter just a single criterion or you can enter two or more criteria. If you use multiple criteria, you must decide if you want Microsoft Query to include in the results those records that match *all* the criteria, or those records that match *any one* of the criteria.

① Click the Show/Hide Criteria icon.

● Microsoft Query displays the criteria pane.

② Click Criteria.

③ Click Add Criteria.

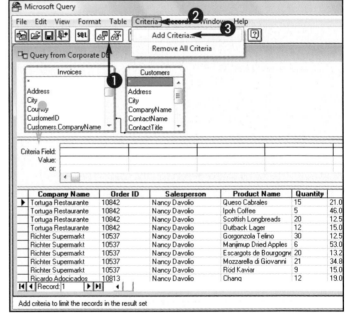

The Add Criteria dialog box appears.

④ Use the Field drop-down list to select the field to which you want the criteria applied.

⑤ Use the Operator drop-down list to select the operator you want to use.

⑥ Type the value or values for the criteria.

● To use a value from the selected field, you can click Values, click the value you want to use, and then click OK.

⑦ Click Add.

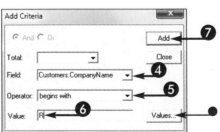

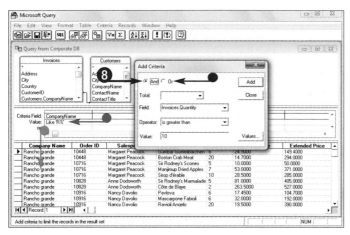

- Microsoft Query adds the criteria to the criteria pane.

- Microsoft Query filters the results to show only those records that satisfy the criteria.

Note: *If you do not want to specify multiple criteria, skip to step 10.*

⑧ Select the And option to add another criterion and to display records that meet all the criteria you specify.

- You can also select the Or option to display records that meet at least one of the criteria that you specify.

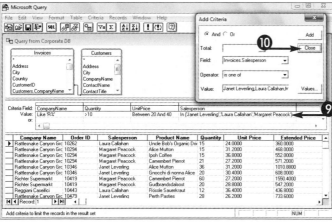

⑨ Repeat steps 3 to 7 until you have added all the criteria that you want to appear in the query.

⑩ Click Close.

Microsoft Query filters the records to show just those that match your criteria.

Change It!

To change the field to which a criteria expression applies, click the field name and then use the drop-down list to click the field you want to use. To change the criteria expression, either edit the expression directly in the criteria pane, or double-click the expression to display the Edit Criteria dialog box. Use the Operator drop-down list and the Value text box to specify a different expression, and then click OK.

Remove It!

If you no longer need a criterion in the query, you should delete it from the criteria grid. Click the bar just above the field name to select the entire criterion; note that Microsoft Query does not ask for confirmation when you delete a criterion, so be sure you click the correct one. Then press Delete. If you want to remove all the criteria and start over, click Criteria and then click Remove All Criteria.

You can sort the query results on one or more fields to get a good look at your data.

You can sort the records either in ascending order (0 to 9, A to Z) or descending order (9 to 0, Z to A). You can also sort the records based on more than one field. In this case, Microsoft Query sorts the records using the first field, and then sorts within those results

on the second field. For example, in the invoice data, suppose you are sorting first on the OrderID field and then on the Quantity field. Microsoft Query first orders the records by OrderID. Then, within each OrderID value, Microsoft Query sorts the Quantity field values.

---

① Click Records.

② Click Sort.

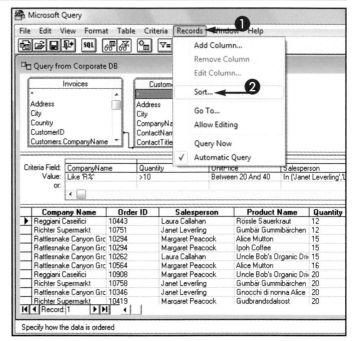

The Sort dialog box appears.

③ In the Column drop-down list, click the field you want to sort.

④ Click the Ascending or Descending option to select a sort order.

⑤ Click Add.

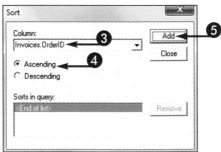

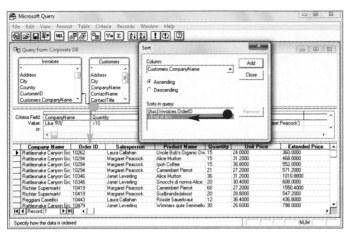

- Microsoft Query sorts the records in the results pane.

- Microsoft Query adds the sort to the Sorts in Query list.

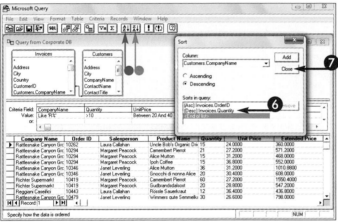

⑥ Repeat steps 3 to 5 until you have added all the sorts that you want to use.

⑦ Click Close.

Microsoft Query sorts the records.

If you only want to sort the query results on a single field, you can click any cell in that field and then click one of the following icons:

- Click the Sort Ascending icon to sort the field in ascending order.

- Click the Sort Descending icon to sort the field in descending order.

More Options!
You can use the toolbar to sort on multiple fields. First, organize the fields in the results pane so that all the fields you want to use in the sort are side by side, in the order you want to apply the sort. Click and drag the mouse pointer from the heading of the first sort field to the heading of the last sort field. You should now have all the sort fields selected. Finally, click either the Sort Ascending or Sort Descending icon.

Remove It!
If you have applied a sort that you no longer want to use, you should remove it from the query. Click Records and then click Sort to display the Sort dialog box. In the Sort in Query list, click the sort that you want to delete, and then click the Remove button.

After you finish adding fields to the query, filtering the data using criteria, and sorting the data, you are ready to return the results to Excel for use in your worksheet.

Microsoft Query is just a helper application, so the data that resides in the query results does not really "exist" anywhere. To manipulate or analyze that data, you must store it in a different application. In your case, you are interested in using the query results as the

source data for an Excel table or PivotTable report. Therefore, you need to return the query results to Excel, and then start a new table or PivotTable based on those results.

If you think you will reuse the query at a later date, you should save the query before returning the results. This section also shows you how to save and open Microsoft Query files.

---

❶ Click File.

● You can combine steps 1 and 2 by clicking the Return Data icon in the toolbar.

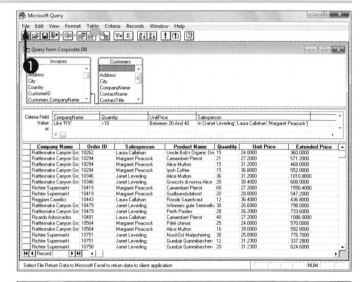

❷ Click Return Data to Microsoft Excel.

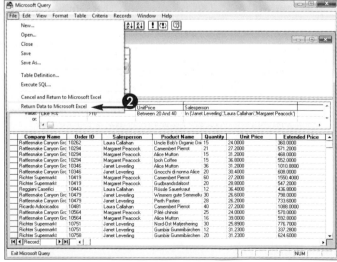

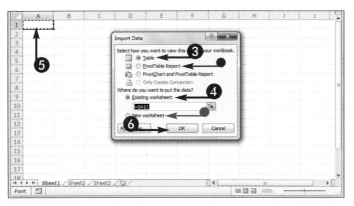

The Import Data dialog box appears.

③ Click to select the Table option.

● If you want to create a PivotTable instead, you can click to select the PivotTable Report option.

④ Click to select the Existing Worksheet option.

⑤ Click the cell where you want the imported data to appear.

● If you want the data to appear in a new sheet, you can select New Worksheet instead.

⑥ Click OK.

● Excel imports the query data into the worksheet.

TIPS

Change It!
If you want to make changes to your query, click any cell in the table (or PivotTable), click the Design tab, click the Refresh drop-down arrow, and then click Connection Properties to open the Connection Properties dialog box. Click the Definition tab and then click the Edit Query button. This starts Microsoft Query and loads the query results. Make your changes and then return the data to Excel.

More Options!
To save a query using Microsoft Query, click File and then click Save to display the Save As dialog box. Click the folder in which you want to store the query file, type a filename, and then click Save. To use the query file, do the following: start Microsoft Query, click File, click Open to display the Open Query dialog box, click the query file, and then click Open.

Protecting Excel Data

Many Excel models are exceedingly complex structures that are the result of many hours of patient and painstaking work. However, even simple Excel worksheets may contain data that is vital and irreplaceable. Whether your Excel data is complex, important, or one-of-a-kind, you want to protect that data to avoid having to recreate your work or to ensure that you do not lose crucial information.

Fortunately, Excel is loaded with useful and powerful tools that enable you to apply multiple layers of protection to your data. As you will see in this chapter, Excel enables you to protect data at four levels: at the workbook level by preventing file changes and ensuring your work is saved; at the worksheet level by protecting sheet data and hiding sheets from others; at the range level by applying range passwords and tracking changes; and even at the cell level by locking cells and hiding formulas.

Quick Tips

You can prevent accidental edits and other workbook changes by opening a read-only version of a file.

Once you have a workbook just the way you want it, you may still have to open the file from time to time to check some data. Each time you open the file, there is some danger that you will accidentally add, edit, or delete data. If you realize your mistake, you can click Undo or close the file without saving your changes.

However, if your goal is to prevent accidental changes to a document, perhaps the easiest solution is to open the document as read-only. You can still make changes to the document, but you cannot save those changes. If you select the Save command for a read-only workbook, Excel displays the Save As dialog box and forces you to save the revised workbook to a different file.

① Click File.

② Click Open.

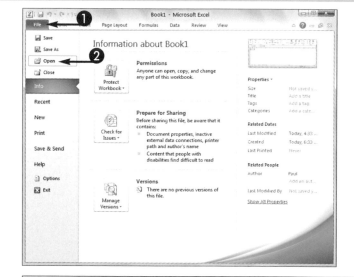

The Open dialog box appears.

③ Open the folder containing the workbook you want to open.

④ Click the workbook.

⑤ Click the Open drop-down arrow.

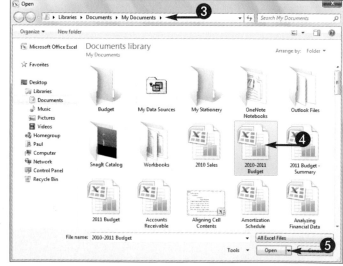

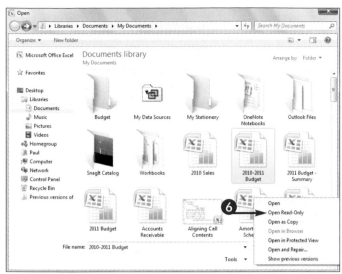

Excel displays a list of options for opening the workbook.

6 Click Open Read-Only.

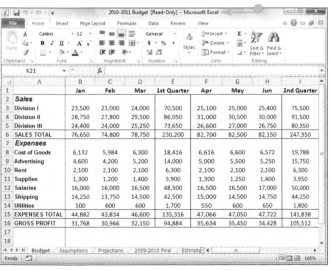

Excel opens a read-only copy of the workbook.

● Read-Only appears in the title bar.

TIP

More Options!

If other people will be opening the workbook, you can add an extra level of safety by telling Excel to recommend that the file be opened as read-only. Click File, and then click Save As to open the Save As dialog box. Click Tools and then click General Options to open the General Options dialog box. Click to select the Read-Only Recommended check box, click OK, click Save, and then click Yes.

Now, each time someone tries to open the workbook, Excel displays a dialog box asking the user whether the file should be opened as read-only. The user then clicks Yes to open the workbook as read-only, or No to open the workbook normally.

You can help ensure that neither you nor anyone else can make accidental changes to a workbook by marking that workbook as final.

When other people will be opening a workbook, the read-only options discussed in the "Open a Read-Only Version of a Workbook" section are less-than-perfect solutions because they rely upon the other user making the choice to open the workbook as read-only. If you want to ensure that a workbook is always opened in read-only mode, Excel offers a more effective technique: marking the workbook as final. This feature puts the workbook in a default read-only state each time it is opened. Users can still elect to edit the file.

① Open the workbook you want to protect.

② Click File.

③ Click Info.

④ Click Mark as Final.

⑤ In the warning dialog box that appears, click OK.

6 In the dialog box that appears, click OK.

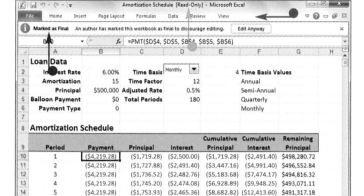

● Excel opens a read-only version of the workbook.

● The Marked as Final message bar appears.

● Excel hides the Ribbon.

More Options!
Although Excel hides the Ribbon when you open a workbook that has been marked as final, some Ribbon commands are still enabled. For example, on the Home tab you can still use the Copy and Find commands. Similarly, most of the commands on the View tab still operate normally.

Reverse It!
If you open a workbook marked as final and decide you want to make changes to the workbook, you can enable editing in a couple of ways. If you see the Mark as Final message bar, click the Edit Anyway button; if you do not see the message bar, click File, click Info, and then click to select the This Workbook is Still Being Edited option.

You can help prevent losing unsaved changes by configuring Excel to use a shorter AutoRecover interval.

To minimize the amount of work lost if your document shuts down without warning (and therefore minimize the amount of time you have to spend redoing that work), you can do two things. First, get into the habit of saving frequently, at least every few minutes; second, use the Excel AutoRecover feature, which tracks changes made to a document, and enables you to recover files that had unsaved changes in the event of a program crash.

AutoRecover is one of those great tools that you hope you never have to use. If AutoRecover has a downside, it is that the default interval for saving the recovery data is every 10 minutes. That might sound quite short, but when you are focused, you can get quite a bit of work done in 10 minutes. To help AutoRecover recover even more of your work, you should shorten the interval.

① Click File.

② Click Options.

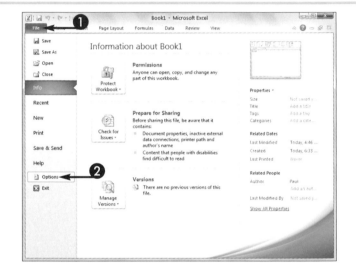

The Excel Options dialog box appears.

③ Click Save.

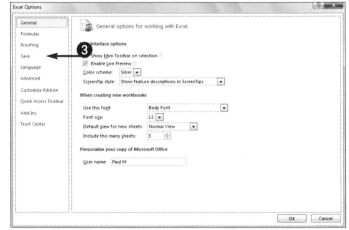

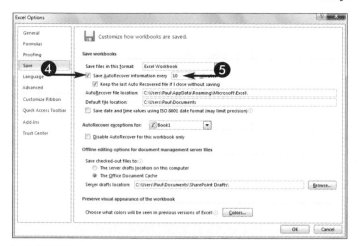

④ Click to select the Save AutoRecover Information Every check box.

⑤ Use the spin box to set the AutoRecover interval, in minutes.

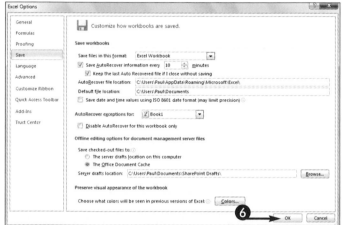

⑥ Click OK.

Excel puts the new AutoRecover interval into effect.

Caution!

For small workbooks, a shorter AutoRecover interval is better. However, for large workbooks, saving the AutoRecover data can take Excel a noticeable amount of time, so a very short interval can slow you down. Try a 4- or 5-minute interval as a compromise.

More Options!

When you close a workbook that contains unsaved changes, Excel prompts you to save those changes. If you click No, you might regret that decision later on. To prevent this, you can configure Excel to automatically preserve a full copy of any file that you close without saving. Follow steps 1 to 4, and then click to select the Keep the Last Auto Recovered File If I Close without Saving check box.

If other people will be entering or editing data in a worksheet, you can ensure that those users do not edit the wrong cells by specifying the cells that they are allowed to edit.

A common Excel scenario is to create a worksheet template or data entry model for other people to use to enter or edit data. In such worksheets, you generally do not want the users to edit, format, or delete the cells that create the worksheet structure — the model's labels, headings, formulas, and instructions. However, it is not practical to protect the entire worksheet because the user must be able to enter or edit data in the appropriate places.

The solution is to configure the data entry cells as *unlocked*. That way, when you turn on protection for the worksheet, users will only be able to edit those unlocked cells. For more information, see the section, "Protect the Data in a Worksheet."

---

① Display the worksheet that contains the cells you want to work with.

② Select the cells you want to unlock.

③ Click the Home tab.

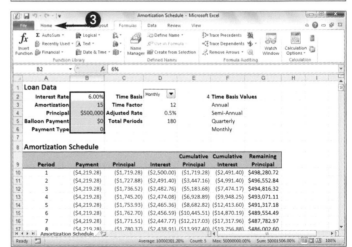

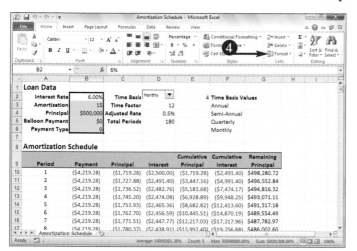

④ Click Format.

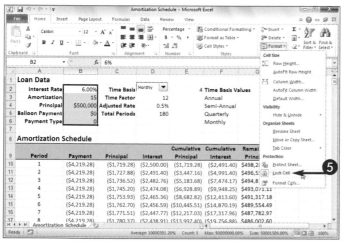

⑤ Click Lock Cell.

Excel unlocks the selected cells.

Note: *Remember that the remaining cells are not locked until you protect the worksheet; for more information, see the section, "Protect the Data in a Worksheet."*

Did You Know?

In some cases, you might prefer to unlock all but a few selected cells. To do this, first press Ctrl+A to select all the cells in the worksheet, and then follow steps 2 to 4 to unlock them. Select the cells you want to be protected and then follow steps 2 to 4 to lock them.

More Options!

If you do not want users to make any changes to a worksheet, you should lock every cell in the sheet. All sheet cells are locked by default, so if you have not unlocked any cells, then you can leave everything as is and turn on the worksheet protection (as described in the section, "Protect the Data in a Worksheet").

You can configure a cell to hide its formula so that other people cannot see it.

If you will be distributing a workbook to other people, there may be elements of the workbook that you do not want them to see. A good example is a formula that is proprietary or that contains private data. If you do not want other users to see that formula, you can configure the formula's cell to hide it.

When you then turn on protection for the worksheet, the hidden formula does not appear in the formula bar when a user selects the cell. If the cell is also locked, then users also cannot edit the cell, which means they cannot view the formula in the cell. For more information, see the sections, "Protect the Data in a Worksheet" and "Specify the Cells that Users Can Edit."

---

① **Display the worksheet that contains the cell you want to work with.**

② **Select the cell that contains the formula you want to hide.**

Note: *You can select multiple cells, if needed.*

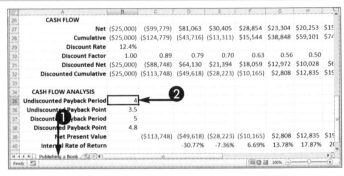

---

③ **Click the Home tab.**

④ **Click Format.**

⑤ **Click Format Cells.**

You can also press Ctrl+1.

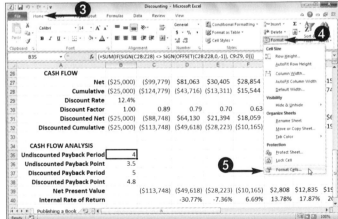

The Format Cells dialog box appears.

6 Click the Protection tab.

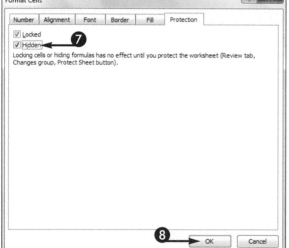

7 Click to select the Hidden check box.

8 Click OK.

Note: *Remember that the formula is not hidden until you protect the worksheet; for more information, see the section, "Protect the Data in a Worksheet."*

TIPS

Try This!

In some cases you might want to hide not only a formula, but also the formula's result. To do this, you need to create a custom numeric format, as described in Chapter 3. Specifically, you need to create an empty custom numeric format, which consists of just three semi-colons (;;;). You then assign this format to the formula's cell.

More Options!

If your workbook contains one or more scenarios (see Chapter 5), you might not want other users to see those scenarios. To hide a scenario, click the Data tab, click What-If Analysis, and then click Scenario Manager. In the Scenario Manager dialog box, click the scenario and then click the Edit button. Click to select the Hide check box, and then click OK.

If you want to prevent unauthorized users from editing within a range, you can set up that range with a password.

If you will be distributing a workbook that contains important data or formulas in a range, you want to ensure that other users do not edit or delete that range. You could lock the range (see the section, "Specify the Cells that Users Can Edit"), but what if you want to edit the range yourself, or what if you want a few trusted users to be able to edit the range? In

this scenario, you can protect the range with a password, and then distribute that password only to the trusted users.

When you then turn on protection for the worksheet, only authorized users who know the password can edit the range. When a user attempts to open any cell in the range for editing, Excel displays a dialog box that prompts the user for the password. For more information, see the section, "Protect the Data in a Worksheet."

① **Select the range you want to protect.**

② **Click the Review tab.**

③ **Click Allow Users to Edit Ranges.**

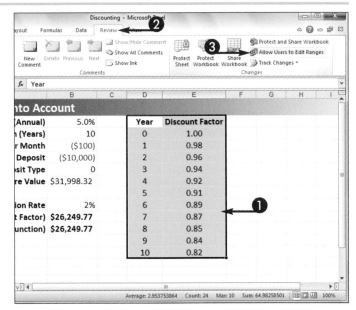

The Allow Users to Edit Ranges dialog box appears.

④ **Click New.**

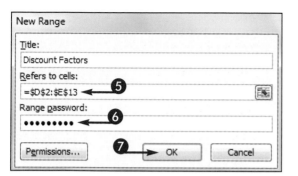

The New Range dialog box appears.

⑤ Type a title for the range.

⑥ Use the Range Password text box to type a password.

⑦ Click OK.

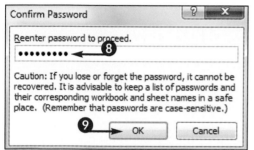

Excel prompts you to reenter the password.

⑧ Type the password.

⑨ Click OK.

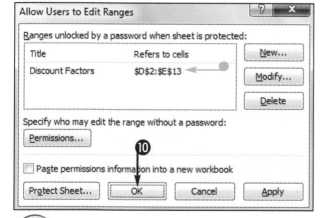

● Excel adds the range to the Allow Users to Edit Ranges dialog box.

⑩ Click OK.

Note: *Remember that the range password does not go into effect until you protect the worksheet; for more information, see the section, "Protect the Data in a Worksheet."*

Change It!

If you want to change the range password, the range title, or the range coordinates, click the Review tab and then click Allow Users to Edit Ranges to open the Allow Users to Edit Ranges dialog box. Click the range, click the Modify button, and then use the Modify Range dialog box to make your changes.

More Options!

To avoid having to enter the range password yourself when the sheet is protected, you can configure the range to allow your Windows user account to edit the range. Click the Review tab and then click Allow Users to Edit Ranges to open the Allow Users to Edit Ranges dialog box. Click the Permissions button, click Add, type your username, click OK, and then click OK again.

You can activate the Excel options for safeguarding worksheet data by activating the sheet's protection feature.

In the previous three sections, you saw three methods you can use to safeguard worksheet data: you can unlock only those cells that users are allowed to edit; you can configure a cell not to show its formula when the cell is selected; and you can configure a range to require a password before it can be edited.

To put some or all of these safety features into effect, you must then activate the protection option for the worksheet. You can also configure the worksheet to require a password to unprotect it. This means that no one can turn off the worksheet's protection without first entering the password.

① **Display the worksheet you want to protect.**

② **Click the Review tab.**

③ **Click Protect Sheet.**

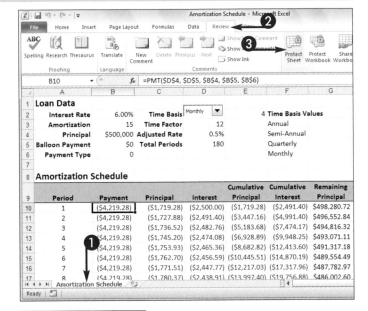

The Protect Sheet dialog box appears.

④ **Make sure the Protect Worksheet and Contents of Locked Cells check box is selected.**

⑤ **Use the Password to Unprotect Sheet text box to type a password.**

6 Click to select the check box beside each action that you want to allow unauthorized users to perform.

7 Click OK.

Excel asks you to confirm the password.

8 Type the password.

9 Click OK.

Excel protects the worksheet data.

More Options!

You can protect the worksheet at the same time as you configure a range with a password. In the "Protect a Range with a Password" section, follow steps 1 to 9 to create the password-protected range. When you return to the Allow Users to Edit Ranges dialog box, click Protect Sheet and then follow steps 4 to 9 in this section.

Reverse It!

If you no longer need to protect a worksheet, you should turn off the sheet protection to make the sheet data easier to work with. Display the worksheet you have protected, click the Review tab, and then click Unprotect Sheet. In the Unprotect Sheet dialog box, type the unprotect password and then click OK.

Protect a Workbook's Windows and Structure

You can prevent unwanted changes to a workbook by activating protection for the workbook's windows and structure.

When you activate protection for windows, Excel takes the following actions:

- It hides the window's Close, Maximize, and Minimize buttons. If the workbook is not maximized, Excel also disables the window borders. This means the window cannot be moved, sized, or closed.

- It disables the View tab's New Window, Split, Freeze Panes, and View Side By Side

commands when the window is active. The Arrange All command remains active, but it has no effect on the protected window. The Hide and Unhide commands remain active.

When you protect a workbook's structure, Excel takes the following actions:

- It disables most sheet-related commands, including Insert Sheet, Delete Sheet, Rename Sheet, Move or Copy Sheet, Tab Color, Hide Sheet, and Unhide Sheet.

- It prevents the Scenario Manager from creating a summary report.

---

① **Display the workbook you want to protect.**

② **Click the Review tab.**

③ **Click Protect Workbook.**

The Protect Structure and Windows dialog box appears.

④ **Click to select the Structure check box to protect the workbook's structure.**

⑤ **Click to select the Windows check box to protect the workbook's windows.**

⑥ **Type a password in the Password text box, if required.**

⑦ **Click OK.**

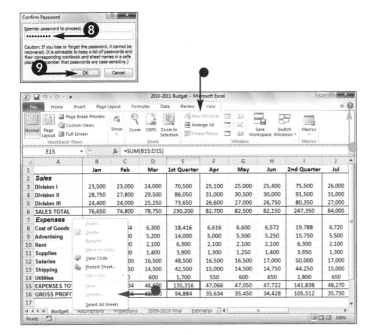

If you specified a password, Excel asks you to confirm it.

8 Type the password.

9 Click OK.

● If you protected the windows, Excel hides the window controls.

● If you protected the windows, Excel disables many window-related commands on the View menu.

● If you protected the structure, Excel disables most sheet-related commands on the sheet shortcut menu.

Reverse It!

If you no longer need to protect a workbook's windows and structure, you should turn off the workbook protection to make the workbook easier to work with. Display the workbook you have protected, click the Review tab, and then click Protect Workbook. In the Unprotect Workbook dialog box, type the unprotect password and then click OK.

More Options!

You can also protect and unprotect a workbook using the File tab. Click the File tab and then click Info to display the Info pane. Click the Protect Workbook button, click Protect Workbook Structure, and then follow steps 4 to 9. To unprotect the workbook, click the File tab, click Info, click the Protect Workbook button, and then click Protect Workbook Structure.

If you improperly edit a workbook, accidentally delete it, or corrupt it through a system crash, you can often restore a previous version of the workbook.

The Excel AutoRecover feature protects your data by automatically saving your work at a specified interval. (For more information, see the section, "Protect Workbooks by Shortening the AutoRecover Interval.") In Excel 2010, each time the AutoRecover interval comes up, the program checks to see if the current workbook has unsaved changes. If it does, Excel takes a "snapshot" of the workbook's current contents and saves that state of the workbook as a previous version of the file.

This gives Excel the capability to reverse the changes you have made to a file by reverting to the version of the file that existed when Excel took its AutoRecover snapshot.

① **Open the workbook you want to work with.**

② **Click the File tab.**

③ **Click Info.**

● Excel displays the previous versions of the workbook.

④ **Click the version you want to restore.**

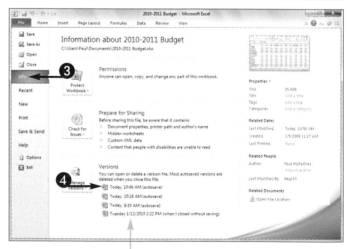

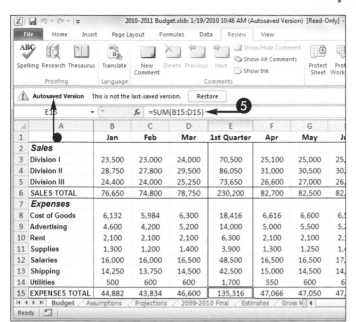

- The Autosaved Version message bar appears.

5 Click Restore.

Excel warns you that you will overwrite the most recently saved version of the workbook.

6 Click OK.

Excel restores the previous version of the workbook.

Did You Know?

Why would you want to revert to a previous version of a workbook? One reason is that you might improperly edit the file by deleting or changing important data. In some cases, you may be able to restore that data by going back to a previous version of the file. Another reason is that the file might become corrupted if the program or Windows crashes. You can get a working version of the file back by restoring a previous version.

More Options!

What happens if you never saved a new workbook and you lost your work either by closing the file without saving or because of a program or system crash? Excel 2010 maintains draft versions of new and unsaved workbooks. Click File, click Info, and then click the Manage Versions button. Click Recover Draft Versions to open the Unsaved Files folder, click the draft version you want to recover, and then click Open.

You can hide a worksheet so that it no longer appears in the workbook. This is useful if you need to show the workbook to other people, but the workbook contains a worksheet with sensitive data that you do not want them to see.

Another common reason to hide a worksheet is to avoid having other people edit, add to, or delete data on the worksheet. Although it is

relatively easy for someone to unhide a worksheet, most people do not look for hidden worksheets, so hiding the worksheet is a quick and simple data protection measure.

If you want to ensure that another person cannot unhide the worksheet, then you must protect the workbook's structure. For more information, see the section, "Protect a Workbook's Windows and Structure."

Hide a Worksheet

① Click the tab of the worksheet you want to hide.

② Click the Home tab.

③ Click Format.

④ Click Hide & Unhide.

⑤ Click Hide Sheet.

● You can also right-click the worksheet tab and then click Hide Sheet.

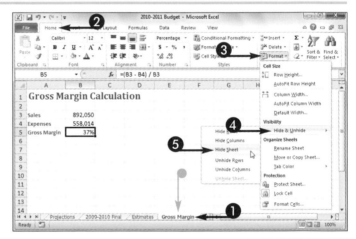

● Excel temporarily removes the worksheet from the workbook.

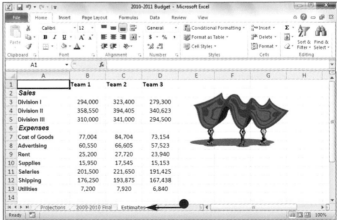

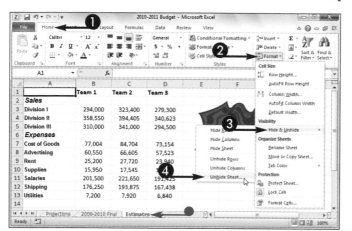

Unhide a Worksheet

① Click the Home tab.

② Click Format.

③ Click Hide & Unhide.

④ Click Unhide Sheet.

● You can also right-click any worksheet tab and then click Unhide Sheet.

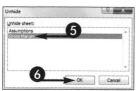

The Unhide dialog box appears.

⑤ Click the worksheet you want to restore.

⑥ Click OK.

● Excel returns the worksheet to the workbook.

(TIP)

More Options!

If you have several worksheets that you need to hide, you do not have to hide them individually. Instead, you can select all the sheets you want to work with and then hide them. To select multiple worksheets, click the tab of one of the worksheets, hold down the Ctrl key, and then click the tabs of the other worksheets.

If your workbook has many worksheets and you want to hide most of them, an easy way to select the sheets is to right-click any worksheet tab and then click Select All Sheets. Hold down the Ctrl key, and then click the tabs of the worksheets that you do not want to hide.

After you have selected your worksheets, follow steps 2 to 5 in the "Hide a Worksheet" section to hide all the selected worksheets at once.

Whether you are a company employee, a consultant, or a freelancer, you will almost certainly work with other people in one capacity or another. Most of the time, your work with others will be informal and consist of ideas exchanged during meetings, phone calls, or e-mail messages. However, you may often be called upon to work with others more closely by collaborating with them on a document.

One way to do this is to ask another person to make changes to a workbook. This method can save you a lot of time and effort, but it can also

lead to problems if you do not know what parts of the document the user edited. For example, if you do not know what the user changed, you have no way of checking the changes for errors.

When you turn on the Excel Track Changes feature, the program monitors the activity of each reviewer and stores their cell edits, row and column additions and deletions, range moves, worksheet insertions, and worksheet renames. You can also filter the changes by date, reviewer, or worksheet location.

① Open the workbook you want to use for the collaboration.

② Click the Review tab.

③ Click Track Changes.

④ Click Highlight Changes.

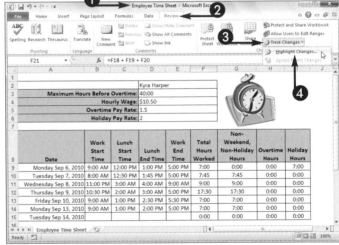

The Highlight Changes dialog box appears.

⑤ Click to select the Track Changes while Editing check box.

● To filter the displayed changes by time, click to select the When check box and then use the drop-down list to specify the time interval.

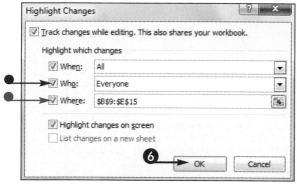

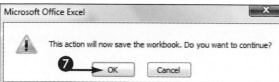

- To filter the displayed changes by reviewer, click to select the Who check box and then use the drop-down list to select users.

  The Who list contains Everyone and Everyone but Me. Later, when other users have made changes, the list includes the name of each reviewer.

- To specify the tracked range, click to select the Where check box, click the range box, and then select the range.

⑥ Click OK.

  Excel displays a dialog box letting you know that it will save your workbook.

⑦ Click OK.

Caution!

When you activate Track Changes, Excel does not track formatting changes. Excel also prevents users from performing a number of operations, including the following: inserting and deleting ranges (although you can insert and delete entire rows and columns); inserting charts, symbols, pictures, diagrams, objects, and hyperlinks; deleting or moving worksheets; applying conditional formatting; working with scenarios; subtotaling, validating, grouping, and outlining data; merging cells; and checking for formula errors.

More Options!

By default, Excel keeps track of changes made for the past 30 days. To change the number of days of history that Excel tracks, click the Review tab and then click the Share Workbook button to open the Share Workbook dialog box. Click the Advanced tab. Use the Keep Change History for *X* Days spin box to set the number of days you want to save, and then click OK.

Maximizing Excel Security and Privacy

Excel security and privacy are multi-faceted topics that encompass a number of different concerns. For example, much of Excel security is concerned with external threats to your documents and even to your computer. The most common concern here is the threat of malicious code embedded in workbooks and Visual Basic for Applications (VBA) macros, so Excel offers a number of techniques you can use to block malicious programs.

Also, there is the important concept of Excel privacy, which mostly deals with preventing the inadvertent leak of private data, from personal information to corporate knowledge such as payroll data or trade secrets. Excel offers a number of methods you can apply to ensure data privacy for your Excel workbooks.

This chapter takes you through various Excel tips and techniques that cover different aspects of Excel security and privacy.

Quick Tips

Open a Workbook in Protected View

You can ensure that a potentially unsafe workbook does no harm to your documents or to your system by opening that workbook in Protected View.

You probably know that VBA macros may contain unsafe code that can harm your system. However, malicious programmers have also figured out how to hack some Excel file types so that when you open a compromised workbook, the malicious code runs automatically.

To help you protect yourself from such files, Excel 2010 offers Protected View, a new file opening option that not only puts a workbook into read-only mode, but also ensures that any malicious code in the workbook cannot harm your system. Excel 2010 automatically opens workbooks in Protected View when you open a file from the Internet or from an e-mail attachment. However, it is also possible to open any workbook in Protected View.

---

① Click File.

② Click Open.

The Open dialog box appears.

③ Open the folder containing the workbook you want to open.

④ Click the workbook.

⑤ Click the Open drop-down arrow.

Excel displays a list of options for opening the workbook.

6 Click Open in Protected View.

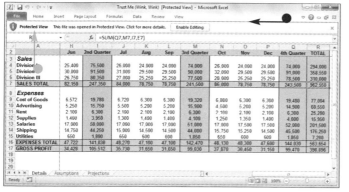

Excel opens the workbook in Protected View.

● The Protected View message bar appears.

● Excel hides the Ribbon.

TIP

More Options!

Excel 2010 opens a workbook in Protected View not only when you open a file from the Internet or from an e-mail attachment, but also if you open a workbook from a potentially unsafe folder, such as the Temporary Internet Files folder, which is where Internet Explorer stores its cache. Excel 2010 also scans each file it opens to validate the file's structure, and if a workbook fails this validation, Excel opens it using Protected View.

These are sensible precautions, but you can disable one or more of them if you find Protected View to be inconvenient in some situations. Click the File tab, and then click Options to open the Excel Options dialog box. Click the Trust Center tab and then click the Trust Center Settings button to open the Trust Center dialog box. Click the Protected View tab. In the Protected View section, click to select the check box beside the scenario you want to disable, and then click OK.

You can configure Excel to block potentially dangerous file types that may contain macro viruses and other malicious code.

When you open a workbook in Protected View, Excel gives you the option of making changes to the workbook by clicking the Enable Editing button in the Protected View message bar. However, there may be some Excel file types that you never want to allow to be opened outside of Protected View. These

might include old Excel file formats such as Excel 95 workbooks, or Excel 2007 macro-enabled files. For more information, see the section, "Open a Workbook in Protected View."

You can use the Excel File Block settings to configure the program to always open certain file types in Protected View, as well as to disable the Enable Editing button.

---

① Click **File**.

② Click **Options**.

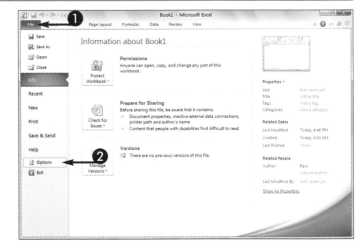

The Excel Options dialog box appears.

③ Click the **Trust Center** tab.

④ Click **Trust Center Settings**.

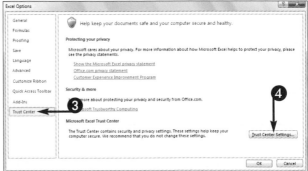

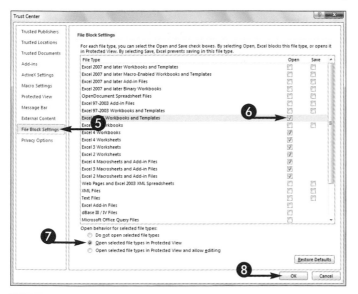

The Trust Center dialog box appears.

⑤ Click the File Block Settings tab.

⑥ For each file format you want to block, click to select the Open check box.

⑦ Click to select the Open Selected File Types in Protected View option.

⑧ Click OK.

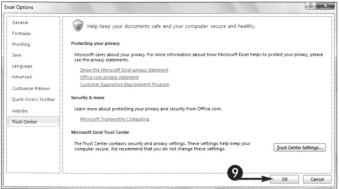

⑨ Click OK.

Excel puts the new File Block settings into effect.

More Options!

For maximum safety, you can configure Excel to not open potentially dangerous file types. Follow steps 1 to 5 to display the File Block Settings tab. Click to select the Do Not Open Selected File Types option, and then click OK.

Remove It!

If you find that you occasionally need to open one or more of the file types that you have blocked, you can restore the Excel 2010 default settings. Follow steps 1 to 5 to display the File Block Settings tab, and then click the Restore Defaults button. When Excel asks you to confirm your selection, click the Restore Defaults button, and then click OK.

Set the Macro Security Level

You can gain more control over how Excel treats macros by setting the macro security level.

VBA is a powerful programming language that can make your life easier and more efficient. Unfortunately, VBA's power is all too often used for nefarious ends — such as viruses that can destroy entire systems — so Excel comes with VBA macros disabled as a security precaution. The exception is macros stored in the Excel Personal Macro Workbook, which you can always run.

You can adjust the Excel macro security setting to one of the following values:

- Disable All Macros without Notification — Excel disables all macros and does not give you a way to enable then. This gives you total macro safety, but it is more than what most people require.

- Disable All Macros with Notification — Excel warns you when a document you are about to open contains macros. It disables the macros but gives you the option of enabling them.

- Disable All Macros Except Digitally Signed Macros — Excel only enables macros if they come from a source that has digitally signed the VBA project.

- Enable All Macros — Excel runs all macros without prompting.

---

① Click File.

② Click Options.

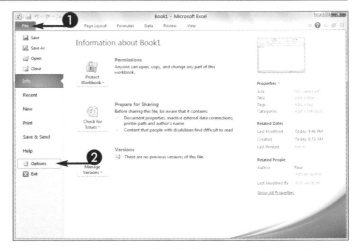

The Excel Options dialog box appears.

③ Click Trust Center.

④ Click Trust Center Settings.

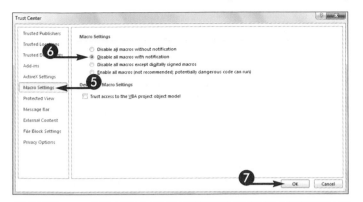

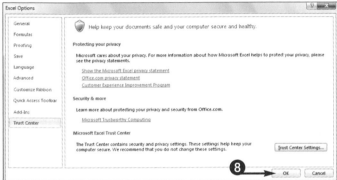

The Trust Center dialog box appears.

If you have the Developer tab displayed, a quicker way to open the Trust Center is to click the Developer tab and then click the Macro Security icon (🔺).

⑤ Click Macro Settings.

⑥ Click to select the security level you want to use.

⑦ Click OK.

⑧ Click OK.

Excel puts the new macro security level into effect.

Important!
If you are not sure which macro setting to use, consider the Disable All Macros Except Digitally Signed Macros option. With this setting, Excel only enables macros if the VBA project has been digitally signed using a trusted code-signing certificate. Macros from any other source are automatically disabled. This gives you almost total macro safety. However, you need to self-sign your own macros, as described in the section, "Digitally Sign Your Excel Macros."

Caution!
If you do not have a virus scanner installed, use the Enable All Macros level if you only run your own macros and you never open documents created by a third party. If you do have a virus scanner, this level is probably safe if you only open third-party documents from people or sources you know.

Digitally Sign Your Excel Macros

You can make it easier and more convenient to run your own macros if you digitally sign your VBA projects.

If you set Excel macro security to disable all macros without notification, you immediately run into a problem: Excel does not allow you to run any of your own macros that reside outside the Personal Macro Workbook. This makes sense because Excel has no way to tell whether you are the author of such macros. By definition, macros in the Personal Macro Workbook are yours, but code in any other file could have come from a third party, which makes that code a potential security risk.

However, it is possible to "prove" that you are the author of your own macros. You can do that by *self-certifying*, which creates a trust certificate that applies only to your own work and to using that work on your own computer.

After you run the SelfCert.exe program to create your personal digital certificate as described in this section, the next step is to assign that certificate to a VBA project. Note that you need to assign the certificate to each project that contains macros you want to run.

---

① Press Alt+F11.

● Excel opens the Visual Basic for Applications Editor.

② Click the project to which you want to assign the certificate.

③ Click Tools.

④ Click Digital Signature.

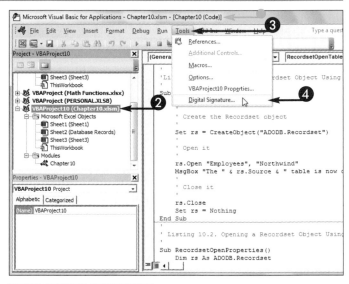

The Digital Signature dialog box appears.

⑤ Click Choose.

The Windows Security – Confirm Certificate dialog box appears.

● Windows displays your digital certificate.

Note: *Remember that you only see this digital certificate after you have run the SelfCert.exe program, as described in this section.*

❻ Click OK.

● The certificate appears in the Digital Signature dialog box.

❼ Click OK.

❽ Switch to Excel, save the workbook that you just signed, and then close the workbook (not shown).

❾ Reopen the signed workbook (not shown).

If you have macros disabled, the Microsoft Excel Security Notice dialog box appears.

❿ Click Trust All from Publisher.

Excel opens the workbook with macros enabled.

Excel no longer displays the Security Notice dialog box for workbooks signed with your digital signature.

Important!
Before you can digitally sign a VBA project, you must create a digital certificate for signing your macros. Press Windows Logo+R to open the Run dialog box, type the following address in the Open text box, and then click OK:

```
%ProgramFiles%\MicrosoftOffice\Office14\SelfCert.exe
```

In the Create Digital Certificate dialog box, type your name in the Your Certificate's Name text box, and then click OK. Excel creates a digital certificate in your name and displays a dialog box when it is done. Click OK. You can now use the digital certificate to sign your VBA code, as described in this section.

Create a Trusted Location for Opening Files

You can make it easier to use macro-enabled workbooks by creating a trusted location to store those files.

For macros to work in Excel 2010, the workbook must come with a digital signature that is both valid and current, and the macro developer must be set up on your computer as a trusted publisher.

If you just want to run your own macros, you need to sign your own projects, and then set yourself up as a trusted publisher (see the section, "Digitally Sign Your Excel Macros").

If you do not want to sign your own VBA projects, and you do not want to enable all macros, Excel gives you a third choice: to store your macro-enabled documents in a trusted location. A *trusted location* is a folder that Excel assumes contains only trustworthy documents, so it automatically enables any macros contained in those documents.

By default, Excel comes with several trusted locations, but none of them are particularly convenient for file storage. However, it is possible to set up a more suitable folder as a trusted location. For more information on enabling macros, see the section, "Set the Macro Security Level."

---

① Click File.

② Click Options.

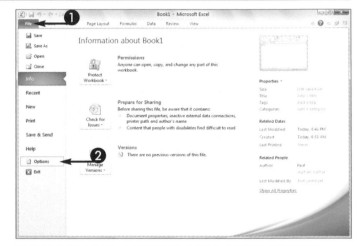

The Excel Options dialog box appears.

③ Click Trust Center.

④ Click Trust Center Settings.

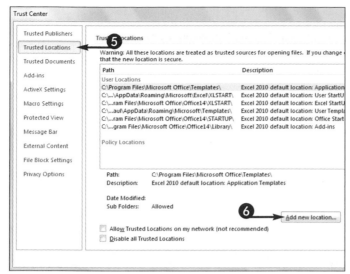

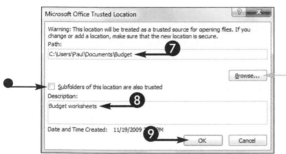

If you have the Developer tab displayed, a quicker way to open the Trust Center is to click the Developer tab and then click Macro Security (⚠).

⑤ Click Trusted Locations.

⑥ Click Add New Location.

⑦ Type the full path of the folder you want to set up as a trusted location.

● You can also click Browse and then use the Browse dialog box to select the folder.

● If you also want subfolders to be trusted, click to select the Subfolders of this Location Are Also Trusted check box.

⑧ Type a description for the folder.

⑨ Click OK.

⑩ Click OK in the bottom right-hand corner of the Trust Center dialog box (not shown).

⑪ Click OK in the Excel Options dialog box (not shown).

More Options!

By default, Excel does not allow you to specify a network path as a trusted location. If you routinely open macro-enabled workbooks from a network location, you can configure Excel to allow network shares as trusted locations. Follow steps 1 to 5 to display the Trusted Locations tab, and then click to select the Allow Trusted Location on My Network check box.

Remove It!

If you no longer use a trusted location for macro-enabled workbooks, you should remove the folder from the Trusted Locations list as a security precaution. Follow steps 1 to 5 to display the Trusted Locations tab, click the trusted location you no longer require, and then click the Remove button.

Inspect a Workbook for Private Data

If you will be distributing a workbook to other users, you can use the Document Inspector to remove personal information from the workbook.

Excel workbooks are often riddled with data that can disclose information about you, other people who have used the document, file locations, e-mail addresses, and much more. This type of information is known as *metadata*, and if you are concerned about maintaining your privacy, you should take steps to minimize or remove metadata from your workbooks.

Much metadata is generated by collaboration techniques such as tracked changes, comments, and annotations, which generate metadata about the reviewers. This is useful in a collaborative environment, but after the document is finished, all that metadata is no longer required. If you will be publishing the document, the metadata is a serious privacy concern, as well.

To help you eliminate metadata and other private content, Excel offers the Document Inspector, which you can use to automate the removal of the private workbook data.

---

① Open the workbook that you want to inspect.

② Click Save to save the workbook.

③ Click File.

④ Click Info.

⑤ Click Check for Issues.

⑥ Click Inspect Document.

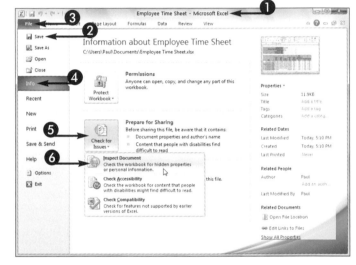

The Document Inspector dialog box appears.

⑦ For each content type that you do not want inspected, click to deselect its check box in order to deactivate it.

⑧ Click Inspect.

- The Document Inspector checks each type of content and then displays the results.

9 To remove a content type from the workbook, click that type's Remove All button.

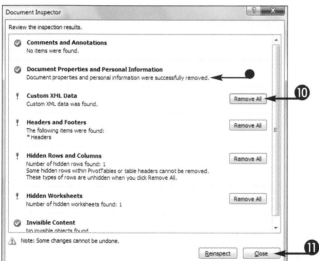

- Excel displays the results of the removal.

10 Repeat step 9 to remove other content types from the workbook, as needed.

11 Click Close.

Did You Know?

You do not need to run the Document Inspector to know whether your workbook has metadata and other private content. Click the File tab and then click Info to display the workbook's Information pane.

If the workbook contains any private data, Excel displays a bulleted list of the data types in the Prepare for Sharing section. This section also tells you whether the workbook has accessibility issues (see Chapter 1) or compatibility issues (see Chapter 2).

If you do not see any private data types listed in this section, then you do not need to run the Document Inspector.

Assign a Password to a Workbook

You can ensure that only authorized users can open an Excel workbook by assigning a password to the workbook.

If you have a workbook that contains private, confidential, or sensitive data, then there are two situations where you want to prevent unauthorized users from opening the workbook.

The first situation is when an unauthorized user gains physical access to your computer, particularly if you are already logged in. In this scenario, the person can open the workbook directly and inspect its contents.

The second situation is when you have shared the workbook with another person who is

authorized to open the workbook, for example through e-mail or by placing a copy on your network. In this scenario, you no longer have any control over the workbook copy, so you cannot be certain of whether an unauthorized user will gain access to the file.

To ensure that only authorized users can open the workbook, Excel enables you to assign a password to the workbook. If users do not have this password, they cannot even open the document. Assigning a password also encrypts the workbook, so even users who can access the file directly on the hard disk cannot view the file's contents.

---

① Open the workbook you want to protect with a password.

② Click File.

③ Click Save As.

The Save As dialog box appears.

④ Click Tools.

⑤ Click General Options.

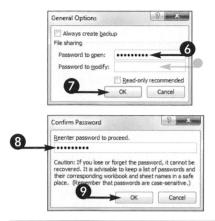

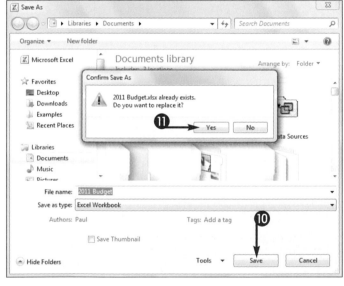

The General Options dialog box appears.

⑥ Type the password in the Password to Open text box.

● For extra protection, you can also type a password in the Password to Modify text box. This password is required to edit the document's contents. If users do not have this password, they can open the document, but cannot change it in any way.

⑦ Click OK.

The Confirm Password dialog box appears.

⑧ Retype the password.

⑨ Click OK.

⑩ Click Save.

Excel asks if you want to replace the existing file.

⑪ Click Yes.

Excel saves the workbook with the password.

Important!
The password you use should be a minimum of eight characters (longer is better) and should be a mix of uppercase and lowercase letters and numbers. Note, too, that Excel differentiates between uppercase and lowercase letters, so remember the capitalization that you use.

Caution!
If you forget your password, there is no way to retrieve it, and you will never be able to access your document. As a precaution, you might want to write down your password and store the piece of paper in a safe and secure place.

If you have children who use Excel, you can turn on the Parental Control feature to make sure that they are not exposed to offensive content in the Research task pane.

The Research task pane enables you to look up data in reference works such as a dictionary, a thesaurus, and a translator. However, the Research task pane also enables lookups through the Bing search engine and other Internet-based reference sites.

These reference tools make the Research task pane a useful feature, particularly for children working on school assignments. However, most of the reference tools have some offensive content that is not suitable for young children. To ensure that your children do not see this content, you can turn on the Excel Parental Control feature, which blocks such content.

---

1 Start Excel using the Windows Administrator account (not shown).

Note: *For information on how to launch Excel under the Administrator account, see the Tips section.*

2 Click the Review tab.

3 Click Research.

● Excel displays the Research task pane.

4 Click Research Options.

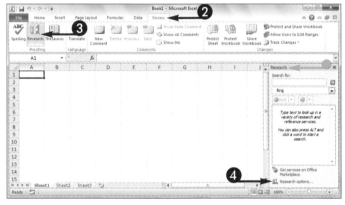

The Research Options dialog box appears.

5 Click Parental Control.

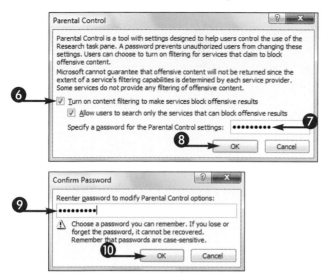

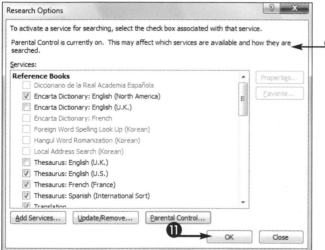

The Parental Control dialog box appears.

⑥ Click to select the Turn On Content Filtering to Make Services Block Offensive Results check box.

⑦ Type a password in the Specify a Password for the Parental Control Settings text box.

⑧ Click OK.

The Confirm Password dialog box appears.

⑨ Retype the password.

⑩ Click OK.

● The Research Options dialog box indicates that Parental Control is turned on.

⑪ Click OK.

Excel now filters offensive content from Research task pane results.

Important!
To run Excel under the Administrator account, press Windows Logo+R to open the Run dialog box, use the Open text box to type **"%progamfiles%\Microsoft Office\ Office14"** (including the quotation marks), and click OK. In the folder window, right-click the EXCEL file, click Run as Administrator, and then enter your User Account Control credentials.

You can enhance your or another user's Excel privacy and security by disabling external workbook content such as data connections and links to other workbooks.

A *data connection* is a communications channel between Excel and an external data source, such as a database file or server. Most data connections are benign, but malicious hackers can use data connections to gather information about your system or trick you into running malicious code.

A *workbook link* is a formula reference to a cell, range, or macro in another workbook. Workbook links are often very useful, but a nefarious user might link to a macro that runs malicious code.

By default, Excel temporarily disables a workbook's data connections and links. If you trust the source, you can click the Enable Content button in the message bar to use the connections or links. To protect yourself or another user from potentially malicious external content, you can disable data connections and workbook links permanently.

① Click File.

② Click Options.

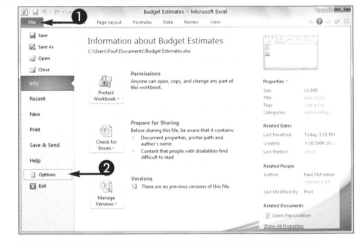

The Excel Options dialog box appears.

③ Click Trust Center.

④ Click Trust Center Settings.

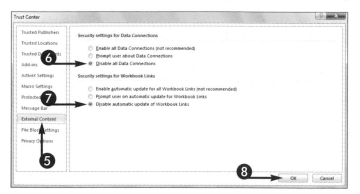

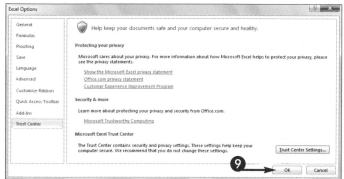

The Trust Center dialog box appears.

If you have the Developer tab displayed, a quicker way to open the Trust Center is to click the Developer tab and then click Macro Security (⚠️).

⑤ Click External Content.

⑥ To turn off external data connections, click to select the Disable All Data Connections option.

⑦ To turn off link updating, click to select the Disable Automatic Update of Workbook Links option.

⑧ Click OK.

⑨ Click OK.

Excel puts the new external content settings into effect.

More Options!

If you only deal with workbooks that you have created yourself and that you never distribute to other users, then you might prefer to take the opposite approach and enable external data connections and workbook links. This can save you time compared to the Excel default settings of prompting you about external content because you no longer have to enable the content manually using the message bar.

Follow steps 1 to 5 to display the External Content tab. To turn on external data connections, click to select the Enable All Data Connections option. To turn on link updating, click to select the Enable Automatic Update for All Workbook Links option.

Apply a Digital Signature to a Workbook

When you send a workbook to another user, you can verify to that person that you are the author of the workbook by applying your digital signature to the file.

If you send someone a document, how does that person know it came from you? The only certain way to authenticate yourself as the originator of a document is to sign it with a digital signature that you have obtained from a certified trust authority. The other person can then inspect the signature to ensure that it came from a trusted publisher and that the document has not since been tampered with, which would invalidate the signature.

This section also includes information about how to obtain a digital signature to use with your Excel workbooks.

---

① Open the workbook that you want to sign.

② Click File.

③ Click Info.

④ Click Protect Workbook.

⑤ Click Add a Digital Signature.

A dialog box appears, explaining how digital signatures are used in Microsoft Office.

⑥ Click OK.

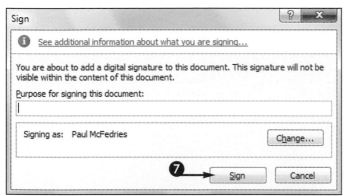

The Sign dialog box appears.

⑦ Click Sign.

The Signature Confirmation dialog box appears.

⑧ Click OK.

Excel applies the digital signature to the workbook.

Note: Excel also marks the workbook as final. If you click the Edit Anyway button in the message bar, Excel removes the digital signature from the workbook.

Important!
To digitally sign an Excel workbook, you must have a digital ID from a registered signing authority, and that digital ID must be usable for securing Microsoft Office documents. Follow steps 1 to 5, and then click the Signature Services from the Office Marketplace button. This opens the Available Digital IDs Web page, which offers descriptions of and links to several trusted signing authorities.

Remove It!
To remove your digital signature from one of your workbooks, open the workbook, click the File tab, click Info, and then click the View Signatures button to display the Signatures pane. Click the signature, click the signature's drop-down arrow, and then click Remove Signature. When Excel asks you to confirm the removal, click Yes and then click OK.

Learning
VBA Basics

This book's approach to Excel 2010 consists mostly of examining the features and settings found in some of the relatively obscure and hard-to-find sections of the Excel interface. However, there are things you can make Excel do that are *not* available through the program's interface. How? By programming them using the Visual Basic for Applications (VBA) programming language that comes with Excel. You use VBA to build small sets of instructions called *macros*. With these instructions, you can make Excel perform multiple tasks in a single operation or perform tasks that you cannot access through the interface.

VBA is a large and complex topic, so in this chapter, you will not learn how to program in VBA. (If you are interested in learning VBA, see the Wiley book *VBA for Dummies*.) Instead, you will learn how to record your own macros and work with macros that you have obtained from other sources, such as the VBA macro examples used throughout this book. For these kinds of macros you will learn how to add a macro to a module using the VBA Editor, and you will learn various ways to run a macro.

Quick Tips

Record a Macro

You can save time and make the process of creating a macro easier by recording some or all of the actions you want your macro to perform.

VBA is a powerful language that can perform a wide variety of tasks, but its main purpose is to operate on the application in which it is running. With Excel VBA, for example, you can create macros that add text and formulas to cells, format ranges, insert or delete worksheets, and much more.

To build a macro that manipulates Excel in some way, VBA gives you a method that is faster and easier than writing the macro

yourself: the macro recorder. After you activate this tool, you use Excel to perform the action or actions that you want in the macro. All the text or formulas you insert in cells, all the formatting you apply, and all the commands and buttons that you click, are recorded, translated into the equivalent VBA statements, and then stored as a macro for later use.

You can store your recorded macros in any workbook, but Excel provides a special workbook for this purpose: the Personal Macro Workbook.

---

① Click the View tab.

② Click the Macros drop-down arrow.

③ Click Record Macro.

● If you have the Developer tab displayed, you can also click the Macro Recording icon in the status bar.

The Record Macro dialog box appears.

④ Type a name for the macro.

⑤ Click the Store Macro In drop-down arrow to select the name of the workbook you want to use to store the macro.

Note: *For most macros, it is best to store the code in the Excel Personal Macro Workbook.*

⑥ (Optional) Type a description of the macro.

⑦ Click OK.

Excel starts the macro recorder.

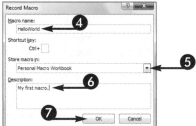

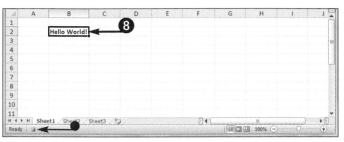

● The Recording icon appears in the status bar.

❽ Perform the Excel steps you want to record.

❾ Click the Recording icon.

Excel stops the macro recorder and saves the macro in the workbook that you selected in step 5.

TIPS

Did You Know?

When you specify the macro name in step 4, keep in mind that there are a few restrictions you must observe. For example, the name must be no longer than 255 characters; the name must begin with either a letter or an underscore (_); the name cannot contain a space or a period; and the name cannot be the same as an existing Excel function.

More Options!

You can also start a recorded macro using the Ribbon's Developer tab, which is not displayed by default. To display it, right-click the Ribbon, click Customize the Ribbon, click to select the Developer check box, and then click OK. To start a macro recording, click the Developer tab and then click Record Macro. You can also use the Developer tab to open the VBA Editor, as described in the section, "Open the VBA Editor."

If you want to view or make changes to your recorded macro, or if you want to create macros from scratch, you need to open the VBA Editor.

After you finish recording your actions, Excel translates them into VBA statements. Excel then saves the macro in a *module,* a special window in which you can view, edit, and run macros. If you are satisfied that your recording is accurate and properly executed, then you may not need to view the module in which it was stored. You can run the macro from Excel any time you want; for more information, see the section, "Run a Macro."

However, if you make mistakes during the recording, or if you want to augment the recorded macro with other VBA statements, then you need to view the module to work with the macro. Similarly, you also require access to the module if you want to paste macros from other sources or create new macros from scratch.

In both cases, you can access the module using the VBA Editor, a program that enables you to view, create, edit, and run VBA macros.

---

① Click the Developer tab.

② Click Visual Basic.

Note: *See the section "Record a Macro" to learn how to display the Developer tab.*

You can also press Alt+F11.

The Microsoft Visual Basic for Applications window appears.

③ Click the plus sign to open the workbook that contains the recorded macro.

● PERSONAL.XLSB is the Personal Macro Workbook.

If you do not see the Project pane, click View and then click Project Explorer, or press Ctrl+R.

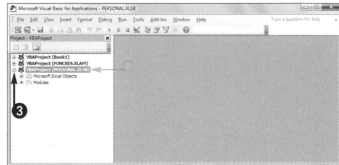

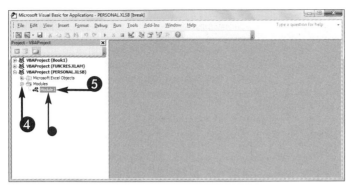

④ Click the plus sign beside the Modules branch.

● Excel displays the workbook's modules.

⑤ Double-click the module you want to open.

The module window opens.

● The VBA Editor opens the module in a new window.

● If you recorded a macro and are working with the workbook that you used to store that macro, the recorded code appears in the module window.

Important!

You should store all your macros in the Personal Macro Workbook. Excel keeps this workbook open all the time, so the macros you store in it are always available to you. Note, however, that Excel keeps the Personal Macro Workbook hidden, which is why you do not see it when you are working in Excel. To see the Personal Macro Workbook, you must unhide it. Switch to Excel, click View, click Unhide Window, click Personal, and then click OK.

Important!

If the Unhide command is disabled, or if you do not see the Personal Macro Workbook in the Unhide dialog box, then it is likely that the Personal Macro Workbook does not exist. In most cases, Excel only creates this workbook after you use it to store a recorded macro for the first time. Follow the steps in the section, "Record a Macro," and be sure to select Personal Macro Workbook from the Store Macro In drop-down list in the Record Macro dialog box.

Explore the Excel Object Model

To program Excel with VBA, you need to understand the Excel object model.

In the programming lexicon, an *object model* is a complete summary of the objects associated with a particular program or feature, the hierarchy used by those objects, and the properties and methods supported by each object. Here an *object* is a distinct, manipulable item such as a worksheet or range; a *property* is a programmable characteristic of an object

such as a worksheet's name or whether a range is formatted with bold text; and a *method* is an action you can perform on an object, such as creating a new worksheet or clearing the formatting from a range.

This section shows you a few properties and methods for the three main objects in the Excel model: the workbook, the worksheet, and the range.

Workbook Object

You can use VBA to create new workbooks, open, save, and close workbooks, and more. You can reference a specific workbook either by using the ActiveWorkbook object, which represents the workbook that currently has the focus, or by using the Workbooks collection, which represents all the workbooks currently open in Excel. Here are some examples:

```
Workbooks(1)
Workbooks("Budget.xlsx")
```

Workbook Properties

Property	Description
Name	Returns the filename of the workbook.
Path	Returns the location of the workbook.
FullName	Returns the location and filename of the workbook.
Saved	Returns False if the workbook has unsaved changes.

Workbook Methods

Method	Description
Add	Creates a new workbook.
Open	Opens an existing workbook.
Save	Saves a workbook.
Close	Closes a workbook.

Worksheet Object

You can use VBA to create new worksheets, copy, move, and delete worksheets, and more. You can reference a specific worksheet either by using the ActiveSheet object, which represents the worksheet that currently has the focus, or by using the Worksheets collection, which represents all the worksheets currently open in Excel. Here are some examples:

```
Worksheets(1)
Worksheets("Sheet1")
```

Worksheet Properties	
Property	**Description**
Name	Returns the name of the worksheet.
StandardHeight	Returns or sets the standard row height.
StandardWidth	Returns or sets the standard column width.
Visible	Hides or displays a worksheet.
Worksheet Methods	
Method	**Description**
Add	Creates a new worksheet.
Copy	Copies a worksheet.
Move	Moves a worksheet.
Delete	Deletes a worksheet.

Range Object

You can use VBA to select a range, add data to a range, format a range, and more. You can reference a specific cell by using the ActiveCell object, which represents the worksheet cell that currently has the focus. You can also use the WorkSheet object's Range method to specify a range using a reference or a defined name. Here are some examples:

```
Worksheets(1).Range("A1:B10")
ActiveSheet.Range("Expenses")
```

Range Properties	
Property	**Description**
Address	Returns the address of the range.
Count	Returns the number of cells in the range.
Value	Returns or sets the data or formula for the range.
Range Methods	
Method	**Description**
Cut	Cuts a range to the Clipboard.
Copy	Copies a range to the Clipboard.
Clear	Clears all data and formatting from a range.

If you have a macro that you want to create or copy, you need to add the VBA code for the macro to a module in the VBA Editor.

As you become familiar with manipulating Excel using VBA, you will likely come up with many ways to simplify complex tasks and automate routine and repetitive chores using macros. To implement these macros, you need

to type your code into an existing module in the VBA Editor.

Similarly, you may run across a macro that you want to use for your own work, either as it is or by modifying the code to suit your needs. You can either transcribe these macros into a module on your system, or better yet, copy the macros and then paste them into a module.

---

1 Start the VBA Editor.

Note: *For more information, see the section, "Open the VBA Editor."*

2 Double-click the module into which you want to add the macro.

If you prefer to add your code to a new module, you can click Insert and then click Module, instead.

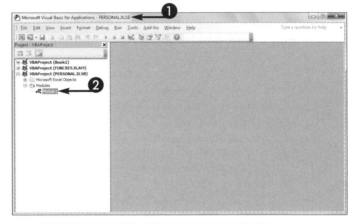

Excel opens the module window.

3 Position the cursor where you want to start the new macro.

Note: *You must add the new macro either before or after an existing macro.*

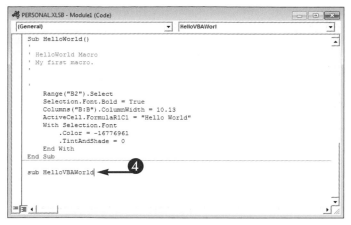

④ Type **Sub**, a space, and then the name of the new macro.

Note: *Make sure the name you use is not the same as any existing macro name in the module.*

⑤ Press Enter.

The VBA Editor adds the line `End Sub` to denote the end of the macro.

If you copied the macro code from another source, click Home and then click Paste, instead.

⑥ Type the macro statements between the Sub and `End Sub` lines.

● As you type a VBA function, object, property, or method, the VBA Editor displays the syntax in a pop-up box.

Important!

If you want to begin your macro with a few comments — notes that describe what the macro does — type an apostrophe (') at the beginning of each comment line. Also, to make your code easier to read, indent each statement by pressing the Tab key at the beginning of the line — you do not need to do this for the Sub and End Sub lines. VBA preserves the indentation on subsequent lines, so you only have to indent the first line.

Did You Know?

After you enter a statement, VBA converts keywords to their proper case. For example, if you type **msgbox**, VBA converts it to MsgBox when you press Enter. By always entering VBA keywords in lowercase letters, you can catch typing errors by looking for those keywords that VBA does not recognize — in other words, the ones that remain in lowercase.

You can run a macro from any open workbook. You have the option of running the macro from the VBA Editor or from Excel.

Excel maintains a list of the macros that are stored in each open workbook. When you want to run a macro, you can either open the module that contains the macro or display the list of available Excel macros. Either way, to run a macro, you must first open the workbook in which the macro is stored.

After you open a workbook, you have two ways to run one of its macros: from the VBA Editor or from Excel. It is best to use the VBA Editor if you are testing the macro, because although VBA switches to Excel to execute the code, it returns you to the VBA Editor when it is done. Therefore, you can run the code, see whether it works properly, and then adjust the code as necessary. When your code is working properly, you can run it from Excel without having to load the VBA Editor.

Run a Macro from the VBA Editor

1 Open the module that contains the macro.

2 Click any statement within the macro you want to run.

● The macro name appears in the list of macros.

3 Click Run.

4 Click Run Sub/UserForm.

● You can also click the Run icon (or press F5).

The VBA Editor runs the macro.

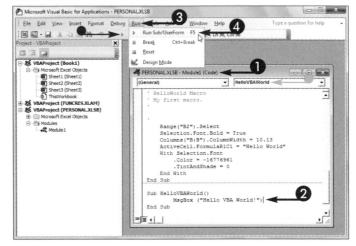

Run a Macro from Excel

1 Open the workbook that contains the macro.

You can skip step 1 if the macro is stored in the Personal Macro Workbook.

2 Click the View tab.

3 Click Macros.

If you have the Developer tab displayed, you can also click the Developer tab and then click Macros.

You can also press Alt+F8.

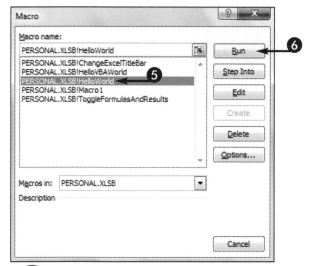

The Macro dialog box appears.

④ Click the Macros In drop-down arrow and select the workbook that contains the macro you want to run.

If you are not sure which workbook contains the macro, select All Open Workbooks, instead.

● Excel displays a list of macros in the workbook.

⑤ Click the macro you want to run.

⑥ Click Run.

If you assigned a shortcut key to the macro, you can avoid steps 2 to 6 by pressing the shortcut key.

Excel runs the macro.

Important!
The default macro security settings in Excel may prevent you from running any macros stored outside the Personal Macro Workbook. If you cannot perform the steps in this section — particularly after you create one or more macros and then close and restart Excel — then you either need to lower the macro security settings in Excel or "self-sign" your own macros. See Chapter 10 to learn how to digitally sign your own macros.

More Options!
You can also use the Macro dialog box as an easy method for displaying a macro in the VBA Editor. Follow steps 1 to 3 to open the Macro dialog box and select the macro you want to work with. Click the Edit button. Excel launches the VBA Editor, opens the module that contains the macro, and then displays the macro code.

Assign a Shortcut Key to a Macro

If you have a VBA macro that you use fairly often, you can quickly access the code by setting up a shortcut key that runs the macro.

Macros are meant to be timesavers, so it is not unusual to have a macro that you run several times each day, or even several times in a row. In such situations, those mouse clicks can start to add up and you may begin to wonder whether the macro is really saving you time.

To work around this problem, you can assign a shortcut key to a macro. In the section, "Record a Macro," you learn that you can assign a shortcut key when you record an Excel

macro. Fortunately, it is also possible to assign a shortcut key to a macro later on, either after you have recorded the macro or after you have added a macro to a module using the VBA Editor. In either case, as long as the workbook containing the macro is currently open, you can press the shortcut key within Excel to run the macro.

To ensure that your macro shortcut keys do not interfere with Excel's built-in shortcut keys (see the Tips later in this section), access Excel's Help system and locate the Help article titled "Keyboard shortcuts in Excel 2010."

---

① **Open the workbook that contains the macro.**

You can skip step 1 if the macro is stored in the Personal Macro Workbook.

② **Click the View tab.**

③ **Click Macros.**

If you have the Developer tab displayed, you can also click the Developer tab and then click Macros.

You can also press Alt+F8.

The Macro dialog box appears.

④ **Click the Macros In drop-down arrow and select the workbook that contains the macro you want to run.**

If you are not sure which workbook contains the macro, select All Open Workbooks, instead.

● Excel displays a list of macros in the workbook.

⑤ **Click the macro you want to work with.**

⑥ **Click Options.**

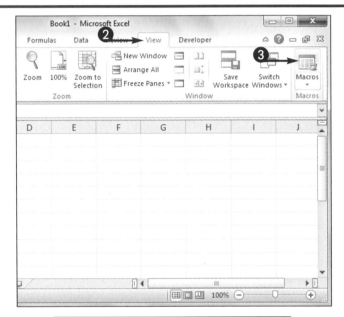

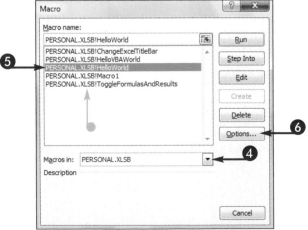

The Macro Options dialog box appears.

⑦ Type the character you want to use as part of the shortcut key.

⑧ Click OK.

Excel assigns the shortcut key to the macro.

⑨ Click Cancel.

You can now run the macro by pressing the shortcut key.

Caution!

Do not specify a shortcut key that conflicts with the built-in Excel shortcuts — such as Ctrl+B for bold formatting or Ctrl+C for copying text. If you use a key that clashes with an Excel shortcut, Excel overrides its own shortcut and runs your macro instead, provided that the macro workbook is open. Remember, too, that your macro shortcut keys apply only to your copy of Excel. If you share the workbook with another user, that person does not have access to your shortcut keys.

Did You Know?

Only five letters are not assigned to Excel commands that you can use with your macros: e, j, m, q, and t. You can create extra shortcut keys by using uppercase letters. For example, if you type **e** into the Ctrl+ text box of the Macro Options dialog box, you press Ctrl+E to run the macro. However, if you type **E** into the Ctrl+ text box, you press Ctrl+Shift+E to run the macro. Note that Excel uses four built-in Ctrl+Shift shortcuts: A, F, O, and P.

Assign a Macro to the Quick Access Toolbar

If you have a VBA macro that you use frequently, you can give yourself one-click access to the code by assigning that macro to a button on the Excel Quick Access Toolbar. The Quick Access Toolbar is the row of buttons that appears, by default, on the left side of the title bar.

The more macros you have, the longer it can take to run the macro you want because you have to scroll through a long list of macros. Assigning a shortcut key can help — as described in the section, "Assign a Shortcut

Key to a Macro" — but Excel only has a limited number of macro shortcut keys available.

A better solution is to create a new Quick Access Toolbar button and assign the macro to that button. As long as you leave open the workbook in which the macro is stored, you have one-click access to the macro. Because you must have the macro's workbook open, it is a good idea to only create toolbar buttons for macros in your Personal Macro Workbook, which is always open.

---

① Click the Customize Quick Access Toolbar icon.

② Click More Commands.

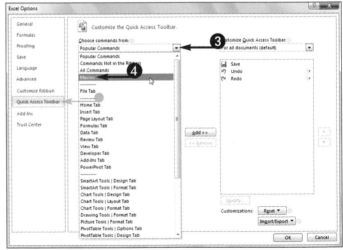

The Excel Options dialog box appears.

● Excel automatically displays the Quick Access Toolbar tab.

③ Click the Choose Commands From drop-down arrow.

④ Click Macros.

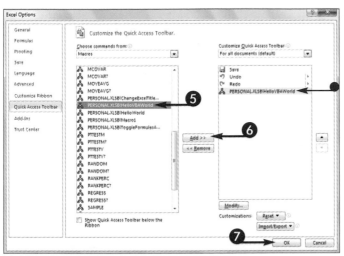

⑤ Click the macro you want to add to the Quick Access Toolbar.

⑥ Click Add.

● The macro appears in the list of Quick Access Toolbar buttons.

⑦ Click OK.

● Excel adds a button for the macro to the Quick Access Toolbar.

More Options!

Unfortunately, Excel applies the same icon image for every macro that you assign to a Quick Access Toolbar button. To help distinguish one macro button from another, you can customize each button with a suitable icon image. Follow steps 1 and 2 to open the Quick Access Toolbar tab. Click the macro you want to customize and then click the Modify button. In the Modify Button dialog box, click the icon you want to use and then click OK.

More Options!

If you want to add a number of macros to the Quick Access Toolbar, you may find that you soon run out of space in the toolbar's default location on the left side of the title bar. You can give yourself much more space to add macros by moving the Quick Access Toolbar below the ribbon. The easiest way to do this is to click the Customize Quick Access Toolbar icon and then click Show Below the Ribbon.

Assign a Macro to the Ribbon

You can improve your Excel productivity by customizing the Ribbon with buttons that run the macros you use frequently.

If you are looking for a quick way to run a frequently used macro, you can assign a shortcut key to the macro, or you can assign a Quick Access Toolbar button to the macro, as described in the section, "Assign a Macro to the Quick Access Toolbar."

However, neither of these methods enables you to organize your macros in any way. For

example, you might have a set of macros related to formatting, another set related to file management, and so on. To organize these and other related macros, you can add them to the Excel Ribbon.

To add a new command to the Ribbon, you must first create a new tab or a new group within an existing tab, and then add the command to the new tab or group.

Display the Customize Ribbon Tab

❶ Right-click any part of the Ribbon.

❷ Click Customize the Ribbon.

Add a New Tab or Group

The Excel Options dialog box appears.

● Excel automatically displays the Customize Ribbon tab.

❶ Click the tab you want to customize.

● You can also click New Tab to create a custom tab.

❷ Click New Group.

● Excel adds the group.

❸ Click Rename.

❹ In the Rename dialog box, type a name for the group.

❺ Click OK.

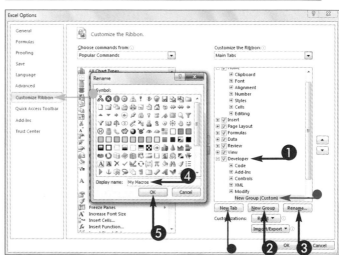

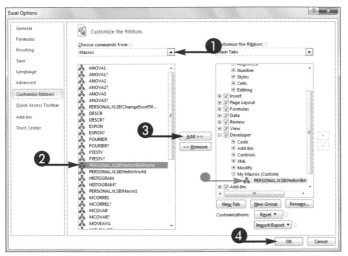

Add a Command

1 Click the Choose Commands From drop-down arrow, and select Macros.

2 Click the macro you want to add to the Ribbon.

3 Click Add.

● Excel adds the macro to the tab.

4 Click OK.

● Excel adds the new group and command to the Ribbon.

TIPS

More Options!

When it assigns a name to a Ribbon macro button, Excel uses the general form *Workbook!Macro*, where *Workbook* is the name of the workbook that contains the macro, and *Macro* is the name of the macro. To use a shorter name, right-click any part of the Ribbon and click Customize the Ribbon to display the Customize Ribbon tab. Click the macro button, click the Rename button, type a new name, and then click OK.

Reverse It!

Right-click any part of the Ribbon and then click Customize the Ribbon to display the Excel Options dialog box with the Customize Ribbon tab displayed. To restore a tab, click the tab, click Reset, and then click Reset Only Selected Ribbon Tab. To remove all customizations, click Reset and then click Reset All Customizations.

Index

Index

Index

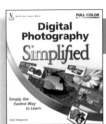

![Visual logo] **Read Less–Learn More®**

There's a Visual book for every learning level...

Simplified®

The place to start if you're new to computers. Full color.

- Computers
- Creating Web Pages
- Digital Photography
- Internet
- Mac OS
- Office
- Windows

Teach Yourself VISUALLY™

Get beginning to intermediate-level training in a variety of topics. Full color.

- Access
- Bridge
- Chess
- Computers
- Crocheting
- Digital Photography
- Dog training
- Dreamweaver
- Excel
- Flash
- Golf
- Guitar
- Handspinning
- HTML
- iLife
- iPhoto
- Jewelry Making & Beading
- Knitting
- Mac OS
- Office
- Photoshop
- Photoshop Elements
- Piano
- Poker
- PowerPoint
- Quilting
- Scrapbooking
- Sewing
- Windows
- Wireless Networking
- Word

Top 100 Simplified® Tips & Tricks

Tips and techniques to take your skills beyond the basics. Full color.

- Digital Photography
- eBay
- Excel
- Google
- Internet
- Mac OS
- Office
- Photoshop
- Photoshop Elements
- PowerPoint
- Windows

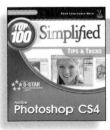

...all designed for visual learners—just like you!

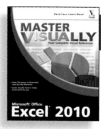

Master VISUALLY

Your complete visual reference. Two-color interior.

- 3ds Max
- Creating Web Pages
- Dreamweaver and Flash
- Excel
- Excel VBA Programming
- iPod and iTunes
- Mac OS
- Office
- Optimizing PC Performance
- Photoshop Elements
- QuickBooks
- Quicken
- Windows
- Windows Mobile
- Windows Server

Visual Blueprint™

Where to go for professional-level programming instruction. Two-color interior.

- Ajax
- ASP.NET 2.0
- Excel Data Analysis
- Excel Pivot Tables
- Excel Programming
- HTML
- JavaScript
- Mambo
- PHP & MySQL
- SEO
- Ubuntu Linux
- Vista Sidebar
- Visual Basic
- XML

Visual Encyclopedia™

Your A to Z reference of tools and techniques. Full color.

- Dreamweaver
- Excel
- Mac OS
- Photoshop
- Windows

Visual Quick Tips

Shortcuts, tricks, and techniques for getting more done in less time. Full color.

- Crochet
- Digital Photography
- Excel
- Internet
- iPod & iTunes
- Knitting
- Mac OS
- MySpace
- Office
- PowerPoint
- Windows
- Wireless Networking

For a complete listing of Visual books, go to wiley.com/go/visual